Jewish Agricultural Colonies in New Jersey, 1882–1920

Utopianism and Communitarianism

Lyman Tower Sargent and Gregory Claeys, *Series Editors*

Jewish Agricultural Colonies in New Jersey, 1882–1920

Ellen Eisenberg

Syracuse University Press

First Edition 1995
95 96 97 98 99 00   6 5 4 3 2 1

The author gratefully acknowledges permission to quote from *The Transformation of the Jews,* by
Calvin Goldscheider and Alan Zuckerman. © 1984 by The University of Chicago Press.

The paper used in this publication meets the minimum requirements of American National Standard for Information Sciences—Permanence of Paper for Printed Library Materials, ANSI
Z39.48-1984. ∞™

Library of Congress Cataloging-in-Publication Data
Eisenberg, Ellen.
    Jewish agricultural colonies in New Jersey, 1882–1920 / Ellen
Eisenberg.
        p.   cm. — (Utopianism and communitarianism)
    Includes bibliographical references and index.
    ISBN 0-8156-2652-5 (cloth). — ISBN 0-8156-2663-0 (pbk.)
        1. Jews—New Jersey—History.   2. Jews, East European—New Jersey—
History.   3. Jews—Colonization—New Jersey—History.   4. Jews—
Europe, Eastern—Migrations.   5. Farmers, Jewish—New Jersey—
History.   6. Immigrants—New Jersey—History.   7. New Jersey—
Emigration and immigration.   8. Europe, Eastern—Emigration and
immigration.   I. Title.   II. Series.
    F145.J5E38   1995
    974.9′004924—dc20   94-40258

For Ami and Alex

Ellen Eisenberg is an associate professor of history at Willamette University in Salem, Oregon. She completed her doctorate in history at the University of Pennsylvania in 1990 and is currently conducting research on the Jewish agricultural colonies of Argentina.

Contents

Illustrations

Tables

Acknowledgments

T HIS BOOK began as my dissertation. While writing it and revising it for publication as a book, I have accumulated a number of debts to persons who helped and inspired me. Without them, it would have been impossible to complete this task.

My research took me to a number of archives, and at all of them I received invaluable help from archivists and research librarians. Those at the Van Pelt library of the University of Pennsylvania, the American Jewish Archives, the Salem County Court House, the National Museum of American Jewish History, and the suburban Philadelphia branch of the Family History Center of the Church of Jesus Christ of Latter-day Saints, were particularly helpful.

Although the sources that I found at libraries, archives, and courthouses helped me piece together the histories of the settlements, the descendants of the settlers brought the colonies to life for me. Bluma Bayuk Rappaport Purmell, who was 101 years old at the time of our interview, recalled events dating as far back as the 1890s, and provided an insider's view of life in Alliance, as well as serving as a key source on the life of her father, Moses Bayuk, one of the Alliance colony leaders. Geraldine Schneeberg, Doris and Sanford Rosenman, and Faith Klein supplied me not only with their memories of their grandparents and of life on the farm but also with substantial genealogical research going back to the time of their great-grandparents' migration. The Rosenmans, Faith Klein, and Mrs. James Gay provided photographs for this book. Jay Greenblatt of the Alliance Colony Foundation not only gave me information on his family but also allowed me to use documents that he collected for the 100th reunion celebration and the Alliance Colony Museum. Mr. Greenblatt also supplied me with his mailing list, including more than seven hundred people, which enabled me to survey colony descendants. Many colony descendants spoke with me in person or by phone, took the time to complete my questionnaire, or sent me letters, memoirs, and other historical documents that their families had preserved.

In many cases where key persons had died before my project began, interviews conducted by earlier researchers allowed me to benefit from their insights. Richard Brotman, great-grandson of the founder of Brotmanville, allowed me to view the twenty hours of videotape that he shot when producing his documentary on the colonies. I also listened to taped interviews conducted in 1979 in preparation for the National Museum of American Jewish History exhibit, "Living on the Land." Mrs. I. Harry Levin permitted me to look through documents preserved by her late husband.

This project was completed in a reasonable time because my research assistantship and fellowship during my final two years of graduate study allowed me to devote nearly all my time to it. I would like to thank Michael Katz for employing me as his research assistant in 1988–89 and thereby providing me with a job that was both fascinating and not overly time-consuming. I am also very grateful for the support I received during the 1989–90 academic year as a Mellon Dissertation Fellow. The New Jersey Historical Commission helped pay for my research expenses, and helped support me as I concluded the writing of the dissertation. Willamette University supported the revision of the dissertation with an Atkinson Summer Research Grant.

Michael Katz and Ewa Morawska, my dissertation advisers, have been great sources of support and inspiration over the past eight years. Their work has been the principal force shaping my ideas about social history and immigration history. They have always been available to discuss my work and have supported me enthusiastically throughout my graduate and postgraduate career. Their achievements as scholars and teachers will continue to inspire me in years to come.

I managed to maintain my sanity throughout this project with the help of my friends and family. Alan Christy and his family kept me housed and entertained during my evenings in Boston after long hours at the American Jewish Historical Society. My fellow graduate students and other friends in Philadelphia provided encouragement and much needed diversions during the writing of the dissertation. Over the past three years at Willamette University and in Salem, Oregon, new friends and colleagues have supported and encouraged my work. My parents, who sparked my interest in Jewish history, have been tremendously supportive, both financially and emotionally, during my lengthy career as a student and since. Their help and encouragement was indispensable.

My greatest debt is to my husband, Ami Korsunsky. His family's experience in Jewish agricultural colonies in Argentina was the initial inspiration for this project. His comments about their origins in the South Pale first suggested to me that it was important to look at immigrant origins. His cooking kept me healthy, his humor kept me sane, and his encouragement kept me going. He provided a world away from my studies and thereby helped me create a balance in my life that many graduate students miss. He has been a wonderful partner and now he is a wonderful father to our son, Alex. In many ways Ami sacrificed much more than I for my graduate studies, and for this project, I hope that, now that I am gainfully employed, he can stop putting his goals aside and begin to follow his dreams.

Introduction

THE COLONIES are quiet now. Farms once owned and worked by the Jewish colonists have passed into different hands. Those few still held by colony descendants are leased to others to farm. Where factories once employed Jewish workers, there are only open fields. Most of the synagogues are gone; one has been converted into a Baptist church. Most passers-by probably never realize that the southern New Jersey communities of Alliance, Brotmanville, Norma, Carmel, and Rosenhayn were once active Jewish colonies, the longest lasting and largest of the settlement experiments undertaken by Russian-Jewish immigrants in America during the late nineteenth century.

If the visitor looks closely, signs of the former colonies are evident. The first clues are the street names, which read like a who's who of New York Jewish society from the 1880s: Schiff Avenue, Isaacs Avenue, Henry Avenue, Eppinger Avenue. Then, set back from the road, the Tiphereth Israel synagogue still stands, and is used by a small congregation annually on the High Holidays. In the small Chevrah Kadisha (burial society) building, there is a modest exhibit depicting colony life, open on occasional weekends. The most vivid evidence of the existence of this once vital community is the large Jewish cemetery, still used and well maintained, and dedicated to "the first colonists who migrated from Russia to the woodlands of South Jersey and on May 9, 1882, founded Alliance, the first Jewish farm colony in the United States."

Despite this tangible evidence, many find it difficult to imagine Jewish agricultural colonies. The idea of a Jewish farm colony seems, at first, an anomaly. Locked into nonagricultural economic roles in Europe for the centuries preceding emancipation, Jews emerged from the ghetto just as the occupations linked to modern capitalist economies began to expand. Jews in eastern Europe, and those who migrated to the United States, were mostly industrial and craft workers, or small-scale merchants.[1] In America, when second-generation Jews expanded the group's occupational profile, they entered the profes-

xvii

sions and civil service—not agriculture, an economic sector that was shrinking rapidly by the turn of the twentieth century in the United States.

Yet enough eastern European Jewish migrants turned to agricultural pursuits to have an impact on the profile of developing Jewish communities in several immigrant-receiving nations. The migration of Jews to Palestine, beginning in the 1880s, included a contingent of aspiring agriculturalists who established the kibbutz movement and, in doing so, played a critical role in the formation of the Yishuv and, eventually, the State of Israel. Similarly, in Argentina, Jewish immigrants founded agricultural colonies that served as a channel through which more than one-quarter of the Argentine-Jewish population entered Argentine society.[2]

In the United States, although many Jews settled independently as farmers, small groups of Jewish immigrants, like their counterparts in Palestine and Argentina, settled on the land in organized groups, or colonies. These immigrants created significant agricultural colonies, although less extensive than those in Argentina and Israel. The most successful attempts at Jewish colonization in the United States, indeed the only colonies to persist for more than one decade, were those in southern New Jersey. Established with an initial population of about 43 families in 1882, Alliance, which within one decade expanded to form Norma and Brotmanville as well, included 187 families and a population of nearly 1,000 by 1908. Similarly, Carmel colony grew from only 17 families when it was established in 1882 to 144 families and a population of 795 by 1908; and Rosenhayn increased from 6 or 7 families at its inception to 98 families and 475 souls by 1908.[3] Although these colonies soon became dependent on industrial as well as agricultural employment, they continued intact into the 1920s, disintegrating as distinct colonies and merging into the nearby Vineland Jewish community in the 1930s and 1940s.

The existence of Jewish agricultural colonies in the United States, Palestine, and Argentina, the three most popular destinations for Jews during the period of mass migration, indicates the importance of understanding the colony movement. What led Jewish immigrants to choose an option so different from the urban existence regarded as the Jewish norm? Did migrants to Jewish colonies in Argentina, Palestine, and the United States share qualities or characteristics with one another? Were those who went to these colonies fundamentally different from urban-bound, industrial Jewish migrants? If so, how did these differences affect the Jewish communities that developed in each nation?

Several narrative accounts have described the Jewish agricultural colonization movement and life in the colonies,[4] but the occupational, geographic, and educational backgrounds of those who settled there have remained clouded. This imprecision about the identity of Jewish immigrants is not unique to the study of the colonies. Although studies of nineteenth-century Jewish communities in eastern Europe, and of nineteenth- and twentieth-century American Jewry are plentiful, the *process* of migration that shifted the center of Jewish population from eastern Europe to the United States has not been thoroughly explored by scholars. Understanding this migration process—the factors that led individuals and groups to move along a particular path and settle in a particular place—is essential for understanding both the subsequent development of immigrant communities and the contrasts among them.

The lack of attention to immigrant origins by historians of Jewish immigration was, until recently, symptomatic of the study of American immigration history. Immigration has most frequently been seen by American historians as the movement of individuals; the classic works of immigration history have focused on the alienation of the immigrant, stressing individual desires and experiences after migration.[5]

During the past decade, however, American historians have paid increasing attention to the premigration origins of immigrants and have begun to overcome the tendency to view the immigrant as an alienated person. This new approach emphasizes analysis of how groups of immigrants used the cultures and kinship networks that they brought with them to adapt to their new society. Such studies stress the collective experience and the importance of premigration origins by focusing on group strategies, chain migrations, and kinship networks.[6] This emphasis on the various premigration networks, cultures, and experiences and their effect on migrants indicates the importance of studying not only the encounter of the newcomer with the host country but also the circumstances of life in the country of origin and the process of migration that disproportionately affects certain regions, ethnic groups, occupational sectors, and economic classes within the home country.

This approach to immigration history is particularly important for comparative studies. For example, recent research on Italian migration to the United States and Argentina has revealed differences in migration streams that linked migrants from particular regions and socioeconomic backgrounds within Italy to the country of destination. This attention to premigration origins has allowed historians to examine the roots of dissimilarities between Italian communities in the United States and Argentina.[7]

Such studies have far-reaching implications for the study of Jewish migration. Exploration of the patterns of Jewish migrations and of variations among migrant pools within eastern Europe could further understanding of the development of Jewish communities in immigrant-receiving countries.[8] Yet many historians of Jewish immigration have failed to specifically examine the backgrounds of immigrants or have assumed that the East European Jews who migrated to the West were essentially of uniform origin. For example, Morton

Winsberg, a historian of the Baron Hirsch colony in Argentina, argues that "those Jews who arrived in Argentina differed little from their brethren who went elsewhere."[9] Judith Elkin, a historian of Latin American Jewry, concurs: "The contrast between the [American and Argentine] . . . communities points up differences that stem not from the immigrants (*for they were similar in their origins and part of the same migratory waves*) [emphasis added]."[10] Similarly, comparative studies of Jewish migrants to the United States and Palestine emphasize the "unity of Russian Jews' experience," arguing that the "motivations, aspirations, and social composition of those who left Russia were basically similar."[11]

Despite such assertions of uniformity in the background of East European Jewish migrants, neither the demographic, political, and economic pressures that spurred migration, nor the responses of Jews to those pressures, were uniform throughout the Jewish Pale of Settlement in Russia ("the Pale"). Historians have demonstrated that the cultural, demographic, and economic configurations of Jewish communities in regions within the Pale led to variations in responses to such pressures among communities and individuals.[12] For example, the particularly desperate situation for Jewish artisans and mechanics in the Northwest Pale led to a disproportionately high representation of such Jews in the total Jewish migration to the United States,[13] despite the fact that the notorious pogroms centered in the South Pale. Similarly, pulls from potential regions or countries of immigration and how opportunities in those countries were perceived by potential migrants influenced the direction of migration streams.[14]

Besides these push and pull factors, external forces, most notably the western Jewish philanthropic organizations, shaped the migration stream by aiding, and sometimes recruiting, certain types of migrants, and encouraging migrations to specific destinations, while discouraging others. This type of organized migration was particularly noteworthy in the post-1880 East European Jewish migration, which included many projects sponsored by western Jewish philanthropists, who attempted to direct and regulate the flow of migrants to the West. In addition, there were also attempts by the migrants themselves to organize, particularly in movements aiming to establish agricultural colonies, in an effort to turn their physical relocation into a more meaningful movement. These organized migration projects provide a unique opportunity to study both the functioning of a migration stream and adaptation as a group experience.

All these factors—variations among communities in the country of origin, pulls from particular sectors within the receiving country, and external forces such as sponsored migration—had an impact both on the intensity of migration and on the characteristics of migrant streams. That different immigrant communities might have been drawn from disparate migrant pools suggests that tracing the origin of an immigrant community might help account for its cultural, social, and economic characteristics.

My study tested the hypothesis that Jewish migrants to American agricultural colonies differed in their premigration origins from the mass of Jewish migrants by examining one cluster of organized migration and settlement projects in southern New Jersey. These colonies, Alliance, Norma, and Brotmanville in Salem County and Rosenhayn and Carmel in Cumberland County, were the only immigrant-led American-Jewish colonies that survived for a substantial time.[15] These colonies grew directly out of the same "back to the land" sentiment that led the parallel, early Zionist BILU movement to establish the first modern Jewish agricultural settlements in Palestine. The New Jersey colonies brought together Russian-Jewish intellectuals espousing socialist and agrarian ideals, and western capitalists and philanthropists as colony sponsors. In addition, the colonies brought self-organized settlers together with migrants recruited by the sponsors, and with individuals migrating independently. The organized nature of these communities and their long relationship with sponsoring organizations make the New Jersey colonies an ideal window through which migration and adaptation can be studied, with attention to the actions and desires of both colonists and sponsors.

In analyzing the influence of the settlers on colony development, it is essential to determine the background and worldview of succeeding waves of settlers, and how they differed from other East European Jewish immigrants of the period. This information about settler origins and views can then be used to explain the development of the immigrant community in the colonies, which differed considerably from other American-Jewish communities. Here I give attention to the regional origin of the colonists and demonstrate that migrants from the South Pale were overrepresented among the early colonists, and that their distinctive background helped shape the early development of the colonies. The changes in the migration stream over time led newcomers with different backgrounds to the colonies in later years. I argue that this change in the origin of new settlers is one important factor explaining the transformation of the settlements from agrarian colonies to mixed agricultural-industrial settlements based on ownership of private property.

The role of philanthropists is examined as a second factor shaping migration and colony development. The survival of the colonies would have been impossible without the financial assistance of the sponsors, yet these sponsors, who had their own goals and worldviews, shaped the colonies' population according to their own objectives. The goals and policies of the sponsors were critical to colony development. Decisions made by the sponsoring organizations in selecting types of recruits, in funneling to the colonies immigrants arriving independently to the United States, in establishing policies on mortgage eligibility, and in allocating aid to the colonies' agricultural and industrial sectors played a key role in shaping colony development.

Migration patterns, sponsor policies, and settler desires and actions combined to shape the adaptation that took place within the colonies. In this study, the adjustment to American life is studied as a group process, with an emphasis on how the settlers drew on their backgrounds and cultural resources to shape their experience.[16] Here the information obtained concerning regional origin and premigration occupational, educational, and religious experience is central. Using this data in conjunction with personal accounts, memoirs, and descriptions of the colonies by outsiders, how the colonists used their experiences to define and come to terms with their new world is explored.

The role of the sponsors' cultural policies are also examined as an important factor shaping the colonists' adaptation to American life. Here attention is paid to the differing (and often conflicting) goals and expectations of colonists and philanthropists. These goals and expectations are studied in the light of the differing values and backgrounds of the American-born, German-Jewish, Reform, assimilated and capitalist philanthropists, and the Russian-Jewish, sometimes socialist, and often religious, colonists. The clash between colonists and sponsors is evident both in routine conflicts over mortgage payments and in overt conflicts, such as strikes and riots launched by colonists to protest sponsor policies.

The analysis is divided into six chapters. The first sets the migration in the East European context and explores differences within the Jewish community that led to the emergence of the agricultural colonization movement in the South Pale. Chapter 2 focuses on the Am Olam movement, which provided the ideology and initial settlers for the New Jersey colonies. The backgrounds of Am Olam members, their philosophies, and their early attempts to actualize their plans are explored. In chapter 3, the aims and backgrounds of the sponsors are discussed, providing context for their actions regarding the colonies. The Am Olam idealists and the sponsors come together in chapter 4, which explores the first decade of colonization in New Jersey and the beginning of the transformation of the colonies into mixed agricultural-industrial communities with economies based on private ownership. This transformation is traced through the peak years of the settlements in chapter 5, and brought to a close with the dissolution of the colonies in chapter 6.

The history of Jewish agricultural colonization in America is relatively unknown. The novelty of Jewish farmers in turn-of-the-century America might, in itself, make their story worth telling, but the history of the New Jersey colonies is more than a novelty. By understanding the process that led

Jewish migrants to follow such a distinct path of migration, we can begin to learn about how migrants and sponsors interacted to shape the process. This understanding may prove a first step to building a comparative history of Jewish agricultural colonization worldwide, and, in turn, help historians understand the forces that shaped the migration and adaptation of Jewish migrants in general.

In many ways, the story of the New Jersey colonies is one of poor timing and incompatible goals. Sponsors and colonists, coming from drastically different backgrounds, shared little in their visions for the colonies. The one goal they did share—"normalizing," or integrating the Jew with the mainstream through the colony experience—placed the immigrants in rural colonies just as such rural life was ceasing to be the norm in America. Given the conflicting goals of the involved parties and the context of urbanization in America, it is not surprising that the colonies were transformed from their early agrarian, communal design into communities with mixed agricultural-industrial economies, based on private ownership, and that the colony idea was ultimately abandoned. Yet ironically, by abandoning colony for city, and farming for professional office, store, or factory, the settlers' descendants were achieving the one goal shared by sponsors and colonists alike—they were joining mainstream American society.

Ellen Eisenberg

Salem, Oregon
January 1994

Jewish Agricultural Colonies in New Jersey, 1882–1920

1

The East European Background

In the year of our Lord [1882] some time in May, I remember late at night I lay in a big wagon all covered up. There were many more people with me but I do not remember anyone saying a word, nor do I know how long we rode. Next I remember we were in a valley near a large ocean. I remember looking up and I thought if I could go up that big hill I could almost touch the sky. There were many people kissing each other and crying. . . . I understand it must have been a port and they were bidding goodbye to each other probably thinking they would never live to see each other again.

—Kate Herder
Arkansas and Carmel colony settler
and daughter of Am Olam founder Moses Herder[1]

IN 1882, THE MASS MIGRATION of Jews from Russia to the United States began. Among the migrants were several hundred young idealists, dedicated to the Am Olam plan of building a new life through the establishment of agricultural colonies. They, and the other millions of Jews who left Russia during the period of mass migration (1882 to 1914), tore themselves away from their homes, friends, and relatives and set out for a foreign land and an uncertain future.

Yet these migrants did not make a complete break with their pasts. Although historians once characterized migration as a completely alienating experience, in which the migrant is ripped away from all that is familiar, recent histories have increasingly stressed the theme of continuity between home society and immigrant community, arguing that immigrants' beliefs, values, rituals, and economic experiences guide their actions in their new country. Thus where immigration histories once began as the newcomers stepped off the boat in America, historians are now paying increasing attention to immigrant origins as a central factor shaping their postmigration experience.

With this new emphasis on immigrant origins has come a recognition of the profound impact of premigration cultures and conditions on the development of immigrant communities. First recognized by labor historians, such as Herbert Gutman, who focused on the impact of a rather generic peasant outlook on the immigrants' adaptation to industrial society, recent works have gone beyond such generalities and have attempted to rigorously probe the background of specific groups of immigrants. For example, historians of Italian migration have focused on specific premigration origins in recent years, and have discovered that contrasting regional origins help explain social, economic, and cultural variations among Italian immigrant communities.[2] In her work on the East-Central European immigrant community in Johnstown, Pennsylvania, Ewa Morawska emphasizes the need to go beyond generalization about the "traditional" worldview of immigrants, and instead offers an analysis that recognizes the complexities inherent in the views of people living in a society undergoing transition. Thus she explores "new combinations and multiform blends, often ill fitting and inconsistent with older traditional values and approaches,"[3] which migrants form and which, in turn, shape their experience in their new country.

Historians of East European Jewish migration have been slower to employ such analysis. Differences between regions or populations within the Jewish Pale of Settlement in Russia are rarely mentioned by historians of American-Jewish immigration. The discussion of premigration origins is often confined to a chapter reviewing the hardships suffered by Jews in the Pale as a whole.[4] A more complete understanding of the development of Jewish immigrant communities and of the roots of differences among such communities is facilitated by an analysis of origins that emphasizes the complexity of the premigration experience and the different ways in which various populations of Jews were affected by and responded to developments in the period preceding migration.

To understand the impact of premigration experiences on immigrant communities, such as the New Jersey colonies, it is necessary to first understand migration in general, and migration to agricultural colonies in particular, as one of several responses by Jews to conditions in Russia in the final decades of the nineteenth century. The ideological roots of the American Jewish agricultural colonies can be traced to the Am Olam, an organization that, by advocating communal agrarian settlements by Jews in the United States, combined elements of the three major autoemancipatory responses emerging in this period: migration, revolutionism, and Jewish territorialism.[5] In examining these responses, this chapter analyzes both the ideological currents in Jewish thought and the material factors of Jewish life in which they were rooted.

The 1880s, and the years 1881 and 1882 in particular, have received much attention as a turning point in the history of East European Jewry. Jonathan Frankel describes these years as "analogous to revolution," characterizing the period as one in which there was a revolt against the old, religious authority by a new leadership "pursuing totally alien ideological strategic, and tactical goals." Similarly, Irving Howe argues that this period was a "plastic hour," a "critical moment when—suddenly, and perhaps unexpectedly—the mounds of historical inertia melt away and a path is cleared for possibilities." The result of this energy, this "passion for transformation," was the emergence of "auto-emancipatory" movements aimed at achieving for East European Jews, through their own efforts, the emancipation that had already been gained by western Jewry.[6]

Although many Jews had hoped in the early and middle nineteenth century that Russia would eventually follow the path of the western European nations and emancipate the Jews, faith in such western-style liberalism began to ebb during the final decades of the century. As Frankel argues, "the assumption that the steady acculturation of the Jew *qua* individual would naturally bring with it the grant of equal rights and security faced a major challenge."[7] Rather than waiting for a benevolent government to grant their rights, many Jews chose to relocate, to work within Russia for a new society, or to create a new Jewish society based on liberal principles elsewhere. Migration, Jewish revolutionism, and territorialism were the three major responses that sprouted in eastern Europe, demonstrating the attempt of many Jews to solve their own "Jewish problem." Yet though these responses departed from earlier strategies, they were firmly rooted in the experiences of their East European Jewish proponents, and, as such, they drew on the past, rather than breaking with it.

Although the growth of these autoemancipatory responses clearly justifies historians' focus on radical change in the 1880s, this focus has often led to an overemphasis of factors in that decade to account for the origins of these movements, and to a neglect of the continuities of these responses with the historical experience of Jews in the Pale. Thus because the early 1880s are usually seen as the beginning of mass migration, this migration is usually linked directly to the notorious pogroms that broke out after the assassination of Tsar Alexander II in 1881, and to the harsh May Laws that followed. Many histories focus on these pogroms as a primary factor in the mass exodus. For example, Arthur Ruppin claims that "the impelling force behind [the mass emigration] was pogroms and the increasingly hostile attitude of the Russian government."[8] Similarly, Mark Wischnitzer begins his chapter on the 1881 to 1890 migration with an account of the pogroms.[9] Although these historians both describe other factors that contributed to the migrations, the focus on persecutions and on the mass nature of the movement tends to blur the economic, geographic, and demographic factors that were equally, if not more, important. Only by examining these factors with regard to specific groups of migrants can the motives, background, and expectations of such groups be understood.

To understand the rootedness of the autoemancipatory responses in the experience of Russian Jewry, it is necessary to review the historical transformations that the Jewish community in the Pale underwent in the nineteenth century. After this discussion, the ways in which different constituencies drew on their experiences to construct the three responses are examined.

✳✳✳

Until the partitions of Poland in 1772, 1793, and 1795, few Jews lived in Russia. With the incorporation of large parts of Poland, the Russian tsars were faced with a Jewish problem for the first time. To isolate the Jews from the Russian people, the tsarina Catherine developed a policy, which Alexander I refined, in which the Jews remained confined primarily to the locations where they already resided, which collectively became known as the Pale of Settlement.[10] Besides this geographic confinement, Jews also faced various social and economic restrictions, such as occupational barriers and limits on communal authority.[11]

Although in popular memory nineteenth-century Russian policy toward Jews is considered unrelentingly hostile, there was little consistency in these policies. For example, Nicholas I's harsh conscription policy, which drafted Jewish males for more than twenty-five years of service in an effort to convert them, contrasts with the more liberal policies of his successor, Alexander II. Even within Alexander II's reign, the early, more liberal phase contrasts with the harsher period that followed the Polish insurrection of 1863. Indeed, tsarist policies fluctuated between efforts to isolate Jews and prevent them from "tainting" Russian populations, as expressed in the confinement of Jews to the Pale, and efforts to convert and assimilate, seen in conscription and educational policies designed to indoctrinate.[12] Although some of these contradictions can be attributed to a clash between practical necessity and policy goals, it is clear that many were rooted in administrative confusion and indecision, both concerning the Jewish problem itself and concerning the larger issue of modernization. As Hans Rogger argues in his analysis of tsarist policy toward the Jews,

> For all its rigor, tsarism's Jewish policy was, until the very end, characterized by inconsistency and inconsistency was the fruit of uncertainty about consequences. Committees, commissions and ministers talked endlessly of the pressing need to solve the Jewish question, yet no attempt at solution, whether in the direction of greater stringency or liberality, was ever more

than partial, temporary ["until revision of existing laws on the Jews"], or went beyond the stage of discussion.[13]

This inconsistency and indecision reflects, according to Rogger, a fear of "far-sighted and far-reaching measures of which the outcome was uncertain and which, in the short run, might make matters irreparably worse," and was rooted in "ambiguities and conflicts over the very nature of state, economy and society."[14]

The impact of restrictive and oppressive policies on Jewish society in Russia was profound. Residency restrictions led to both severe crowding and economic overcompetition within the Pale. This problem was compounded by rapid Jewish population growth in the nineteenth century. Between 1820 and 1880, the Jewish population in Russia increased by 150 percent, from 1.6 million to 4 million.[15] Because this increase took place largely within the confines of the Pale, and there largely in the cities, it worsened the crowding and poverty. Crowding was most severe in the cities of the Northwest Pale, where most of the Jewish population resided.[16] By the late nineteenth century, the Jewish population, which made up 14.7 percent of the total in Lithuania and 13.6 percent in Belorussia, accounted for 50 percent of Lithuania's and 55.2 percent of Belorussia's urban populations. Even in the less crowded South and Southwest, Jews concentrated increasingly in the urban sector: although the Jewish population accounted for 9 percent and 9.7 percent of the South and Southwest, Jews made up 28.2 of the South's and 35.9 percent of the Southwest's urban populations. Similarly, Jews in Russian Poland made up 37.7 percent of the urban population, although their percentage in the total population of the region was only 14.1.[17]

Evidence for increasing pauperization among Jews can be found both in contemporary descriptions of Jewish living conditions and in telling statistics: in 1849 only 3 percent of Jews possessed *any* capital at all. Among Jews in the Ukraine, where crowding was less severe than in the Northwest, the situation was somewhat better, although even there "most Jews were even poorer than the peasants; in view of the extreme poverty of the Ukrainian peasantry, that was saying a great deal."[18]

The poverty caused by overpopulation and residential restrictions was compounded by economic restrictions, discriminatory employment policies, and the freeing of the serfs. Jews, largely excluded from working the land, had traditionally been confined to commerce and crafts. The emancipation of Russian serfs in 1861 led not only to increased competition for nonagricultural work but also to the elimination of several traditional Jewish occupations. For example, Jews' positions as agents of landowners rapidly became obsolete, as did their roles as creditors and innkeepers serving peasant populations. With

the beginnings of industrialization in Russia, the Jews' economic position was
further hindered by the elimination of traditional Jewish occupations through
modernization, as when railroads destroyed Jewish activity as coachmen and
innkeepers who earned their living from coach travel.[19]

Although these processes led to widespread poverty in the Jewish community, the impact was particularly severe among craftsmen concentrated in
the densely populated Northwest.[20] Northwestern Jewish craftsmen experienced the most severe hardships because increasing numbers of Jews were
crowding into this sector at precisely the same time that craftsmen began to
face competition from factories. Jewish craftsmen were severely hurt both by
competition from the new factories and by the refusal of most factory owners
to hire Jewish workers.[21] The increased number of craftsmen in the Northwest
was linked to the dramatic population growth in that region, particularly in
the cities. As Jewish population density grew in the Northwestern cities, the
preferred sector, trade became saturated. Jews accounted for about 90 percent
of the commercial class in the Northwest, and tradesmen crowded out of the
field moved increasingly into craft and manufacturing occupations, which usually represented a step down. Jewish craft and manufacturing workers, largely
excluded from the more modern factories, experienced a tremendous degree
of proletarianization, working primarily in the least mechanized shops, with
the most primitive conditions, at a poverty wage. In the densely populated
Northwest Pale, between 42 and 45 percent of Jews worked in manufacturing
and mechanical occupations and only 23 to 28 percent in commerce; in the
South and Southwest, where Jewish population was less dense, these figures
were nearly reversed, 34 to 36 percent in manufacturing and 35 to 38 percent
in commerce, demonstrating the preference for commerce when lower population density permitted individual choice. In fact, the greater relative opportunities for the merchant in the South led to a migration from the Northwest
to the South in the late nineteenth century.[22]

Population pressures, economic and residential restrictions, and increasing
impoverishment resulted in stresses on community life. The traditional communal authority, the *kahal,* was an all-encompassing communal organization
that had religious, fiscal, and judicial responsibilities. Under Russian rule, the
kahal was gradually restricted, until it was officially abolished in 1844, although
its authority continued in practice throughout the next half century.[23] Both
governmental restrictions and internal strains disrupted communal harmony.
Because the Jewish community was responsible for providing for its own poor,
severe poverty and unemployment created a heavy burden for communal social welfare agencies,[24] as well as making the payment of communal debt and
taxes increasingly difficult. Governmental tax policies, which held the entire
community responsible for the total tax levied on the Jews of that locality,

forced communal leaders to act as tax agents, causing resentment. In addition, Russian law favored certain classes, which compounded such resentments:

> While the community still remained responsible for the total taxes imposed upon the Jews of each district, its wealthiest members, belonging to the first guild, were exempt from the head taxes and certain other imposts. To be sure, it appears that few of them completely shirked their communal responsibilities. Whether voluntarily or under the pressure of public opinion and possible reprisals, they mostly assumed their share in the communal burdens. But such voluntary cooperation always injected an element of uncertainty and frequently lent the voices of such "volunteers" an undue weight in the determination of communal affairs.[25]

Nicholas I's severe conscription policy also contributed to internal strife because it required communal leaders to select the conscripts. Such a policy often led to the overrepresentation of the poor among conscripts, for they lacked the influence on the leadership that the wealthy possessed. The resentment and bitterness produced by this situation is apparent in accounts of violence by poor Jews against *kahal* leaders and in appeals by poor Jews to the government, protesting discrimination by communal authorities. In some cases, groups of Jews, such as the artisans in the town of Belaia Tserkov, withdrew from the community and appealed to the government to be recognized separately as a guild.[26] Evidence of class strife within the community can be found in the literature of the period. For example, in Mordechai Spector's story, "A Meal for the Poor," the poor revolt by refusing to play their role at a wedding feast. Spector's account of their revolt expresses the bitterness of the underlying class issue: "All their lives they had been condemned to silence, forced to swallow with their spittle every insult anyone cared to offer them, anyone who had given them a kopeck or thrown them a crust of dry bread or a gnawed bone. Now for the first time they were tasting the same pleasure as the well-to-do. For the first time these beggars felt that the well-fed people needed them, and they were determined to gain their point."[27]

Yet it was not only the restrictions, harsh taxation, and conscription policies that led to communal disharmony during the nineteenth century. Liberal policies, most notably those during the early reign of Tsar Alexander II, were also divisive for the Jewish community. Although policies such as juvenile conscription under Tsar Nicholas I employed harsh means to achieve integrationist ends, other integrationist policies were more benevolent in their methods. Cases in which residential restrictions were loosened exemplify such relatively liberal policies. Thus, when Catherine and Alexander I developed the policy of restricting Jews to the Pale of Settlement at the turn of the nineteenth century, they included in the Pale the sparsely populated regions of the South. These lands were opened to Jewish settlement as part of a plan to develop the area. Incentives, such as exemptions from taxes and military service, were established for Jews and others who would move into these areas and adopt "useful" occupations, such as farming. These policies led to the establishment of Jewish agricultural colonies in the southern Russian provinces of Kherson, Taurida, and Ekaterinoslav, as well as to a Jewish presence in the cities of these provinces, particularly Odessa.[28]

The most notable of the liberal policies, however, were enacted during the early part of the reign of Tsar Alexander II. On his coronation day in 1859, Alexander II abolished Nicholas's juvenile conscription law. This move, received with tremendous enthusiasm by the Jewish community, was followed by a series of laws reducing restrictions on Jews. Residential restrictions were liberalized in laws that opened western border districts to Jewish settlement, granted Jewish merchants of the first guild and foreign Jews the right to reside and trade inside Russia proper, granted Jewish graduates of higher institutions of learning the right to be employed in government service and to trade throughout Russia, opened cities within the Pale that were previously closed to Jews, and, in 1865, abolished the Pale for Jewish artisans and their families.[29]

Another liberalization was in educational policy. Schools were made more democratic and missionary efforts within them were eliminated as religious instruction became voluntary. The desire, expressed in these policies, to achieve integration through the removal of restrictions is evident in various government documents. For example, in 1856 the Jewish Committee reported to the Tsar that "the aim of the government . . . to bring about the union of the Jewish with the general population, is hampered by the temporarily established restrictions which contradict the general legislation and create confusion."[30] Yet rather than being universally welcomed by the Russian Jews, these liberal policies increased tensions within the Jewish community. Some welcomed them as the dawn of the long-awaited emancipation; others viewed them with suspicion as a threat to the integrity of the Jewish community.

The new policies, particularly the educational reforms, were acclaimed by proponents of the Haskalah (Jewish enlightenment), who, believing in western-style liberalism, advocated secular studies as the path to emancipation and acceptance in the modern world.[31] Even before the ascension of Alexander II to the throne, *maskilim* (advocates of Haskalah) had hoped to institute their educational programs of transforming the traditional *hederim* and *yeshivot* into modern Jewish schools that would "productivize" the Jewish population and lead to emancipation.

The popularity of the ideas of the Haskalah, and the responses to the liberal policies, varied greatly from region to region. In the new southern city of Odessa, enlightenment thought was particularly vital in the early nineteenth century. There, Haskalah ideals were not obscure or impractical as they were in much of the Pale, because, in Odessa, Russian society did seem to be opening to Jewish participation. *Maskilim* had seized control of the *kahal* and Jewish institutions by the 1830s and their establishment of modern Jewish schools and German-style synagogues echoed the experience of western Jews. Thus, "while elsewhere the debates over official rabbis in the 1860s were waged between self-avowed traditionalists and the 'enlightened', in Odessa all claimed to be enlightened."[32] Yet in most of the Pale such ideas remained impractical under Alexander I and Nicholas. Nicholas's plan to integrate Jews through education never gained the trust of Jews, who rightly suspected that the government's aim was to use these schools to convert the Jews.[33]

Under Alexander II, *maskilim* recognized the opportunity presented them by the new liberal policies. Propaganda for secular education was abundant and the response was "widespread, wholehearted, and enthusiastic." Some *maskilim* even began to replace the German enlightenment model with a reverence for Russian language and culture: "'Our fatherland,' declared *Razsvet* [a Jewish, Russian-language newspaper in Odessa], 'is Russia. And just as her air is ours, so too, must her language be ours.'" The number of Jewish students in Russian gymnasiums increased from 159 (1.25 percent of the total) in 1853, to 552 (3.2 percent of the total) in 1863, and 2,362 (13.2 percent of the total) in 1873.[34]

Yet the enthusiasm with which *maskilim* greeted secular education and other liberal reforms was not shared by all sectors of the community. Traditional communities and groups resisted reforms by *maskilim* and liberal government policies as forcefully as they had earlier resisted oppressive, restrictive policies: "The program of the *maskilim* sought to effect a radical change in the traditional system of education and thus appeared to the orthodox masses of Jewry as an attempt to undermine the very foundation of the Jewish faith."[35] By accepting modern ideas and secular education, *maskilim* were rejecting the traditional life-style. Their critique of religious traditionalism was an explicit part of their program. According to historian Salo Baron, "Some became regular muckrakers, particularly with respect to *Hasidism,* to whose mystic and emotional beauties they were completely blind but whose institutional degeneration they described in all its lurid detail."[36] Some degree of alienation from the traditional community was common among *maskilim* and among the products of modern Jewish schools and Russian general schools.[37] In Odessa, where 70 percent of the Jewish students were in Russian schools by the mid-1870s, assimilation among Jewish youth was considered a major problem, even by *maskilim:*

These youths, an Odessa *maskilic* correspondent to the *Jewish Chronicle* wrote in 1860, have only "a smattering of knowledge, principally of foreign languages, just enough to enable them to read the lesser works of French literature and to scoff at all that is venerated and held sacred. Had the Bible been written by Dumas, they would no doubt deem it worthy of perusal. But as it is only the word of an ancient Hebrew, it is a most insipid, worthless composition."[38]

The variety of responses to enlightenment thought and to the more liberal forms of Tsarist policy can be understood using the framework presented by sociologists Calvin Goldscheider and Alan Zuckerman, who argue that modernization is dependent on the degree and persistence of traditional sources of cohesion in a community. Factors determining the tenacity of traditional ties include the size and age of the community and the thickness of occupational and residential ties within the community. Thus they argue that in newer communities "the institutions of the Jewish community were weakest and the power of the windstorm strongest. In the old areas, the well-established *yeshivot* and synagogues, associations and guilds, *parnassim,* and assorted organizations resisted the powers of change."[39]

Strongholds of enlightenment thought could be found in areas that were changing rapidly, were exposed to the outside (and particularly the western) world, and had large population turnovers. These factors explain why Odessa provided particularly fertile ground for enlightenment thought. A new city, Odessa was an international community, a center of trade known for its commercial opportunities and liberal atmosphere.[40] In such a city, in a new area of settlement, a frontier mentality worked against the maintenance of traditional observance, not only because the institutional and traditional sanctions were absent but also because, in general, the most traditional Jews were least likely to uproot themselves and migrate to the isolated South Pale in the first place.[41] For Jews, Odessa offered "not only . . . unprecedented economic opportunities and freedom to pursue their own cultural interests, but its liberal atmosphere allowed some participation in political affairs—a rare prerogative in tsarist Russia."[42] Because of the opportunity to participate both economically and politically, the incentive to establish segregated economic and political institutions was reduced. The opportunities available in Odessa led to a situation in which "traditional Jewish life was weak and the attractions of the non-Jewish world were powerful."[43]

Similarly, Brody, just over the border in eastern Galicia, became a center of the Galician Haskalah. On the border, and designated a free city, Brody became an important trade center during the nineteenth century. Brody's Jews, who made up almost all of the city's population and represented the largest

Jewish community in Galicia, were led by big businessmen and professionals (bookkeepers, clerks, tax collectors, and so on), whose numbers grew as the economy expanded. These leaders, stressing the secular education needed in their occupations, led the Galician Haskalah movement, attacking the fanaticism of Hasidism and proclaiming their acceptance of Austria as fatherland. Looking to the western model of emancipation, these Galician *maskilim* believed that the Jews must modernize themselves to be granted full equality.[44]

In contrast to areas like Odessa and Brody, where the modern ideas of the Haskalah found relatively strong followings, areas more isolated from international borders, from internal migration, and from economic transformations, or that were strongly established traditional centers, were less likely to become seats of enlightenment thought. As Goldscheider and Zuckerman argue, the changes that *maskilim* and other modernizers began to institute under the relatively liberal policies of 1859–65 "varied by the institutional strength of the local Jewish communities. The older and more established the Jewish community, the lower the proportion of Jewish students in general [secular] schools." Thus Jews in rural communities or in well-established urban communities continued to send their children to traditional *hederim* and *yeshivot,* rather than to the new secular Jewish or government schools. Goldscheider and Zuckerman report that

> in Warsaw in 1879–80, there were 450 *hederim* and 494 government schools. All but 860 of the Jewish children attended the traditional Jewish schools. The proportion of Jews in government schools was considerably below their proportion of the school-age population. In 1881, Jews in Vilna, another example of an established Jewish community, were 27 percent of the gymnasium and pre-gymnasium students and 40 percent of the city's residents. In contrast, Odessa, with a very new Jewish community had the same proportion of Jews in the schools as in the population, 35 percent in 1881. Similarly, in Petersburg, Moscow, Kiev, and Kharkow, all new cities of Jewish immigration, the percentage of Jews in the gymnasia equalled or exceeded their percentage in the population.

Goldscheider and Zuckerman conclude, "Within the Jewish community, the rate of modernization varied enormously. So much attention has been lavished on change that the millions of Jews who remained in traditional statuses are frequently overlooked."[45]

Understanding the development of the Russian Jewish community in the nineteenth century helps set the stage for the events leading to post-1880 developments. All the factors explored above—increasing demographic pressure, economic hardship, geographic variations, communal tensions, fluctuations in official Jewish policy, and the development of an enlightened intelligentsia—

played a role in determining the variety of responses to events during the second half of Alexander II's reign and after his assassination.

That the liberal promise seen in Alexander II was illusory became clear when his Jewish policies became increasingly harsh and restrictive in the mid-1860s. Although this change in policy is usually linked to official resentment of Jewish sympathy and support for the 1863 Polish insurrection, many historians argue that Alexander II's liberalism in earlier years has been greatly exaggerated and that acceptance of Jewish equality was never a part of his program. For example, Salo Baron claims, "The only difference from Nicholas' approach was that instead of emphasizing the harm accruing to Russian society from the unproductive or 'useless' Jews, the stress was now [in the early years of Alexander II's reign] laid on enlarging the rights of the 'useful' Jewish citizens."[46] Similarly, historian Louis Greenberg argues that Alexander II's liberal policies "did not reflect his political convictions," but were instead "a concession on his part to the growing demands for social and political change, for the Tsar feared that complete resistance to the currents of the time might bring about the disruption of his empire."[47]

The late 1860s and 1870s saw a renewed attack on Jews through both official policy and public opinion. The popular criticism that the government-sponsored Jewish school system furthered Jewish unity and separatism resulted in the closing in 1873 of all such schools in areas where there were general Russian schools. The rationale for this measure evoked Nicholas's strategy of forced assimilation: "They believed that in the general educational institutions, where from childhood on Jews came into close contact with Christians and were subjected to the influence of Christian teachers, a thorough eradication of deep-rooted Jewish prejudices could be effected."[48] Other restrictions came as proposed quotas to limit the Jewish presence in Russian gymnasiums and universities, and discriminatory legislation relating to local representation, jury duty, and army service. Such policies were justified with claims of Jewish conspiracy and separateness published in newspapers and essays.[49] In Odessa, where economic competition between ethnic groups led to a pogrom that raged for three days in 1871, the formerly sympathetic Russian newspapers joined in the chorus that claimed "that the Jews themselves were to blame for the uprising."

> Even as the pogrom was raging, the city's non-Jewish intellectuals openly maintained that the Jews themselves were to blame for the uprising, since the Jewish community had created the oppressive economic atmosphere in which such action was the only avenue for self-defense (gymnasium teachers had even told this to their classes). The upper classes proved indifferent, and often openly hostile, to the plight of the Jews: one well-dressed woman was seen riding in a carriage in the midst of the pogromists, pointing out to the mob

the houses of wealthy Jews. Friendships and business partnerships between Jews and non-Jews dissolved: one Jew, for instance, who had planned to hide his valuables in the apartment of a non-Jewish business associate during the pogrom was greeted by his acquaintance with violent curses and abuse.[50]

The trend toward harsh restrictive policies continued after Alexander II's assassination in 1881, when "all pretenses at liberalism were . . . dropped."[51] The assassination spurred rumors that the Jews were leading the revolutionary forces, triggering mass violence against Jews. Whether governmental officials instigated the pogroms that swept through the Ukraine, as historians such as Baron claim, or merely tolerated them, as others argue, the psychological and material damage was great.[52] As in the 1871 Odessa pogrom, government officials and Russian newspapers blamed the uprisings on the Jews themselves, and the government responded by placing further restrictions on the Jews.[53] The May Laws of 1882, which remained in effect until 1917, barred Jews from villages and townlets in the Pale, forbade Jewish ownership or management of real estate or farms outside the cities of the Pale, and prevented Jews from conducting business on the Christian Sabbath or holidays. Other restrictions enacted during this period included severe quotas on Jewish enrollment in gymnasiums and universities, restrictions on entering certain professions, and the 1893 banishment of Jews from Moscow.[54]

The Jews who had believed in Alexander II's liberalism were those most disillusioned by the return to restrictive policies and brutality from the 1860s on. In Odessa, the Russian-language Jewish newspaper, *Raszvet,* collapsed in 1871 after the Odessa pogrom, as did the Odessa branch of the St. Petersburg Society for the Promotion of Enlightenment among Jews (ORPME). Both organizations expressed doubt regarding the relevance of their liberal assumptions to the Russian environment. As the ORPME explained, the violence "convinced them that all attempts to establish a rapprochement between Jews and Russians will remain unrealized as long as the Russians stagnate in ignorance and civic backwardness." Although departures from tradition continued among Odessan Jews in the 1870s, the intelligentsia "became increasingly suspicious of the benefits of Russification."[55] This disillusionment spread further throughout the Russian Jewish community after the more widespread pogroms of the early 1880s. The fact that the pogroms were centered in the relatively modern and integrated South and the fact that Jews in "productive" occupations, such as farming and other forms of labor, suffered most made the experience "particularly shattering from an ideological point of view."[56] As Jonathan Frankel argues, "in essence what the crisis of 1881–82 did was to deal a heavy blow to the hitherto prevailing faith in the onward march of liberalism as the natural solution to the Jewish question."[57]

For *maskilim* and other nontraditional Jews, principally products of the secular Jewish and general school systems and the universities, the resumption of harsh policies was not only problematic from an ideological standpoint but also for practical reasons. For Jews with secular educations, there were few careers open. Such persons were "unable to become securely attached to the Russian bourgeoisie."[58] Lack of career opportunities for university graduates in a society where the liberal professions had not developed and capital investment was low, combined with exposure to radical and liberal political ideologies in the university environment, led to a high degree of radicalism among students in general. Jewish students, whose prospects for achieving middle-class status in Russian society were particularly low, and whose proportion in Russia's universities and gymnasiums was high, were drawn to radicalism. Increasing official anti-Semitism increased the attractiveness of revolutionary ideologies.[59]

A common response for many secularly oriented Jewish students and intellectuals was involvement in Russian revolutionary movements. As members of the Jewish community who were furthest from traditional Jewish life and educated in Russian language and culture, these revolutionaries became active as *Russians*. For example, when the students "went to the people" in the 1873–74 *narodnik* movement, the proportion of Jews in the movement was about the same as the proportion of Jews in the university student population. These Jews "placed themselves squarely within the general movement. They identified with the Russian—not the Jewish masses."[60]

The failure of the peasants to accept the revolutionaries, and their particularly strong rejection of Jewish revolutionaries, coupled with the participation of populists and peasants alike in the pogroms of the early 1880s, is often cited as a primary reason for the turning of Jewish revolutionaries away from Russian movements and toward Jewish movements. Thus, Goldscheider and Zuckerman argue that

> Jewish intellectuals brought the political ideologies into the Jewish community . . . because they were excluded from the general society and not because the logic of the ideas pointed them in that direction or because of their commitment to the Jews. The Jewish revolutionaries worked among the Jewish masses only after the *Vai Narod* collapsed and the Russian peasants and workers rejected them. The Jewish liberals became nationalists only after the pogroms of 1881–2.[61]

Thus one root factor in the development of the post-1880 autoemancipatory responses focused on organizing Jews, such as the Bund (the Jewish socialist movement that emerged in the Northwest Pale in the 1890s) or the Am Olam, was the rejection of Jewish revolutionaries by Russian intellectuals, revolutionaries, and peasants in 1881.[62] Abraham Cahan, once a member of the Am Olam and later editor of the *Jewish Daily Forward* in New York, noted in his autobiography that some Jewish intellectuals "returned to the Jewish people" in response to the 1881 pogroms (although he and his friends did not).[63] Sidney Baily, a founding member of Odessa Am Olam and longtime resident of Alliance colony, New Jersey, recalled in his memoir that after the 1881–82 pogroms, "we sensitive Jewish students were embittered. We laid aside our studies and began to think of how we could aid the community in its slavish position."[64] H. L. Sabsovich, an activist in revolutionary circles in Odessa, found a distinct change in the reception he received from his non-Jewish comrades in this period. As his wife later recalled:

> My husband [had] counted among his friends as many Christians as Jews, and visited as many Christian homes as Jewish. The question of race and creed did not exist among the Intelligentzia [*sic*] at all. In the University the Jewish and Christian students were on the friendliest of terms. . . . The autumn of 1881 changed everything. The whole spirit of the country was altered. . . . The press, subsidized by the government, began a systematic hounding of the Jews, and denounced them as "the cause of all the trouble, inciting the people to riot and bloodshed." This cry found its echo in the universities. The Jewish students began to feel a change in atmosphere. They began to feel the animosity, not only of the Christian students, but of some of the professors as well.[65]

This change led Sabsovich to help found a Jewish self-defense league, which led directly to his activities as a leader of the Odessa Am Olam.

The experience of Baily and Sabsovich was not uncommon. Historian Nora Levin argues that the events of 1881–82 caused Jewish intellectuals, disappointed in the failure of the Russian Left to condemn violence against Jews, to return to the community to organize a Jewish defense.[66] For many, this Jewish defense activity ultimately led, as it did for Sabsovich, to involvement in autoemancipatory movements, such as Am Olam, Zionism, or the Bund. The image of secular Jewish students and intellectuals joining the traditional community in fasting and praying during the pogroms recurs in histories of the pogroms.

Although it is clear that the intelligentsia would play a key role in Jewish movements of autoemancipation after 1880, and that many Bundist and Zionist leaders had earlier been *maskilim* or Russifiers,[67] it is impossible to account for post-1880 responses so simply. Many intellectuals were disillusioned by the failure of liberalism in Russia. Most notably, Zionists articulated a program that denied the feasibility of *any* solution in which Jews remained a minority in another nation. However, others remained a part of Russian revolutionism, eventually identifying with the Bolshevik or Menshevik movements.[68] Indeed, the socialists leading the workingmen's circles that ultimately evolved into the Bund saw themselves as part of a *Russian* movement rather than a Jewish one for more than a decade after the pogroms.[69] Such an attitude is evident in the comments of one Jewish Socialist stating his goals for the Jewish proletariat: "We wanted them to assimilate as quickly as possible; everything that smelled of Jewishness called forth among many of us a feeling of contempt if not more. . . . We all believed that as soon as Jews began to speak Russian, they would, just as we had, become 'people in general', cosmopolites."[70]

Only by examining these varied responses and their constituencies separately is it possible to understand the development of each of the autoemancipatory movements. In analyzing three of the most significant varieties of autoemancipatory responses, the historical developments outlined above will explain how each response was rooted in a particular time, location, and constituency.

✳✳✳

The most common response to arise in the early 1880s was also the least self-consciously ideological: migration. Although the 1881–82 pogroms served as a catalyst for the mass emigration of Jews from eastern Europe, the causes of this migration were more complex. Anti-Jewish riots were not a new phenomenon in eastern Europe. For example, only ten years earlier, in 1871, a pogrom occurred in Odessa. Although this pogrom had dramatic social and cultural repercussions, it did not trigger a mass migration.[71] In addition, migration westward was not a new phenomenon, although the magnitude of the movement was. Jews had continually migrated from East to West in the seventeenth and eighteenth centuries. Moses Shulvass argues that these movements were started by the Cossack uprising in 1648 and the Muscovite-Swedish invasions following, but that the causes lay elsewhere:

> The reason why large numbers of Jews streamed westward throughout the seventeenth and eighteenth centuries was twofold: (1) the progressive decline and pauperization of the Polish commonwealth, and the perpetual persecutions of the Jews that resulted from them, and (2) the fact that during this period Western Europe began to develop into the political, economic, and cultural center of the world. Therefore, Jews who succeeded in overcoming the formidable obstacles of settling in Western Europe, were able to live under politically more secure and economically much more favorable conditions.

Setting the post-1880 migration in the context of continuing westward movement directs the search for causes at long-range demographic and economic trends, rather than at the sudden occurrence of anti-Jewish riots in 1881. Shul-vass's conclusion that "the theory that pogroms are the main factor which creates waves of Jewish emigration is exaggerated"[72] indicates the importance of looking beyond the pogroms.

A final piece of evidence supporting the argument that pogroms were not the primary cause of the migrations concerns regional differences within the Pale. It is clear that the pogroms of 1881 and 1882 centered in the southern Pale: "There was not a single case of rioting against Jews in the Northwest because the governor general of that region, Count E. I. Totleben, made it clear that he would not countenance such disorders." This "absence of anti-Jewish excesses in the Northwest" stood in stark contrast to the southern and southwestern Pale where "215 localities in the ten provinces of the Southwest experienced such disorders in the course of a few months."[73] Yet there is strong evidence that immigration of East European Jews to the United States, the nation receiving the most immigrants, was disproportionately made up of individuals from the *Northwest,* precisely where the impact of the 1881–82 pogroms was less direct.[74]

Because Jews from the Northwest Pale dominated the migration to the United States, the pushes in that region and pulls from the United States that shaped the migration flow must be examined. The northwestern Pale was the region suffering from the most severe crowding and pauperization, particularly in its cities. As Isaac Rubinow noted in his 1907 report on the condition of the Jews in Russia, "The congestion of Jews in the cities of Lithuania has been most acutely felt, especially since the May Laws of 1882 and the stringent regulations of 1891, and it is, therefore, no coincidence that the region that shows the greatest percentage of Jews in cities also gives the greatest number of immigrants."[75] The Northwest also had the most craft workers, the occupational group most severely hit by increased competition in the late nineteenth century. These craft workers dominated the migratory wave: fully 64 percent of the Jewish immigrants to the United States between 1899 and 1914 were classified in the "manufacturing/mechanic" occupational category, a percentage significantly higher than either the Russian Jewish figure of 37.7 percent or even the Northwest Pale figure of between 42 and 45 percent.[76]

The pushes that affected the craft workers of the Northwest coincided with pulls from the United States. Jacob Lestschinsky argues that it was this coincidence of pushes and pulls that increased the magnitude of the migration flow at this time, creating what has since been known as a "mass migration."[77] Thus, the occupational profile of Jewish migrants meshed with the need for industrial workers in turn-of-the-century America. Jewish migrants who had worked in the clothing industry in Northwest Russia before migration could gain rapid entrance into that trade in New York and other industrial cities.

Migrants with experience in the garment industry could make the transition to America more smoothly than many others, because that industry did not require knowledge of English, it was a home-based industry, it allowed participation of all family members, and it minimized religious impediments to employment because a family doing out-work could choose to work on Sunday rather than Saturday—an option not open to factory workers.[78] For merchants, the transfer of skills was more difficult. Although the rapid expansion of the immigrant Jewish community in the United States created opportunities for Jewish peddlers and merchants, capital was required to set up permanent operations, and a knowledge of English was more essential than in the garment industry. For this reason, Jewish tradesmen leaving the Northwest Pale frequently relocated to the South Pale, rather than migrating to the United States.[79] Its specific workings are not entirely clear, but it is apparent that the interaction between the needs of the host country and the occupational background of the migrants had a role in shaping this wave of migration as one dominated by Northwestern craftsmen and their families.

✳✳✳

The development of the second autoemancipatory response, revolutionism, was similarly shaped by economic, demographic, and regional factors. Jewish intellectuals and revolutionaries, and ultimately the Jewish proletariat, gravitated to a number of different revolutionary movements, both Jewish and Russian. The development and dominance of particular movements in particular regions, and their attraction for certain types of persons can be best understood by examining the social, cultural, and religious appeal of the various movements.

As discussed above, increasing numbers of intellectuals were attracted to Russian revolutionary movements in the 1870s. While disappointment with the *narodnik* experience led some of these revolutionaries to turn their attention to the Jewish proletariat as a potential revolutionary force, others continued their involvement in Russian movements. The different paths of revolutionaries are examined by Robert Brym in *The Jewish Intelligentsia and Russian Marxism*. Brym endeavors to demonstrate how class and regional differences affected the affiliations of Jewish radicals, both to account systematically for these variations and to dispel the notion that it was the marginality or rootlessness of these Jews that led them to revolutionary movements and ideologies. He asserts, "The ideologies of the intelligenty I examined were produced largely by the patterns of social mobility they experienced through changing social structures over time."[80]

Brym argues that, as they educated themselves and joined the intelligentsia, individual Jews became estranged from Jewish tradition and community. Many came to scorn the "backwardness" of their families and communities, and aspired to join the Russian middle class. Yet because avenues for mobility in Russian society were so limited, particularly for Jews, many found a home instead in the radical movements. The movement in which a person became involved depended on the degree that he was "embedded" in the Jewish community, as measured by the strength and number of his economic and social ties to the community. Those deeply embedded in the Jewish community gravitated to specifically Jewish groups; those less embedded, to secular Russian organizations. Brym emphasizes, "In a situation of conflict, persons will attempt to align themselves in such a way that the least possible damage is done to their basic values and to their important personal relations."[81]

The degree of embeddedness depended on occupation, class, and region. Areas with low Jewish population density were more likely to produce assimilated intelligenty, for social and economic interaction with gentiles was more necessary in these areas. In accordance with this, Brym found that Jewish Bolsheviks and Mensheviks had a low degree of embeddedness in the Jewish community and tended to come from areas with lower Jewish population densities and from more assimilated communities. Thus, in his sample, 68.5 percent of Jewish Bolsheviks lived outside the Pale, where Jewish populations were small and highly assimilated. An additional 21 percent lived in the South. Similarly, 45 percent of Jewish Mensheviks lived outside the Pale, and 45.8 percent in the southern Pale. In contrast, more than 73 percent of the leadership of the Bund, a movement focusing on activity among Jewish workers, was recruited from the northern Pale, where the Jewish community tended to be more traditional, community ties tighter, and Jewish population density higher.[82]

Just as economic and regional factors influenced individual radicals, the location and timing of the development of the Jewish socialist movement, the Bund, was also shaped by such objective factors. Ezra Mendelsohn attributes the early development of Jewish labor movements relative to Russian movements to these factors. Mendelsohn argues that the Jewish occupational structure, educational system, and guild tradition were the impetus to the development of a vanguard Jewish labor movement. In contrast to Russian factory workers, who were former peasants, Jewish workers had a long history as artisans. This craft background, claims Mendelsohn, is typical of labor pioneers. Additionally, the Jews' higher rate of literacy made them easier to propagandize, and their guild structure provided an organizational base for labor activities, as well as a cultural precedent.

Mendelsohn stresses that the conditions for the development of a Jewish labor movement existed primarily in the Northwest, where there was a large, unassimilated Jewish population that made up most of the proletariat. Similarly, in tracing the development of Jewish labor movements, including Labor Zionism and the Bund, Moshe Mishkinski emphasizes regional economic differences as a key factor. Mishkinski demonstrates that the Northwest region of the Pale was the center of the movement because it was the region that experienced the greatest degree of Jewish proletarianization. Because the Northwest was the region most heavy in Jewish industry and lowest in commerce, the beginnings of industrialization affected it greatly. Competition with factories and the great concentration of Jewish industry (crafts/sweatshops) contributed to the pauperization of Jewish workers.[83]

Thus the development of a specifically Jewish labor movement was a consequence of the unique characteristics, cultural and structural, of the Northwest. First, there was a high ratio of Jewish to non-Jewish workers, making Jews more important to a labor struggle in the region. Because the Jewish community was old and ties were thick, Jewish workers tended not to speak Russian, Lithuanian, or Polish, making agitation in Yiddish necessary. Additionally, the Jewish intelligentsia was more closely linked with the community in this region—Vilna had been the center of the Hebrew enlightenment, as opposed to a Russian enlightenment, and its many *yeshivot* supplied the "semi-intelligentsia," who were integral to the agitation phase of the Bund's development. Finally, Mishkinski argues that a Jewish majority in Lithuanian cities and towns "stimulate[d] its unique social self-determination."[84] This confidence was boosted by the relative lack of active anti-Semitism among Byelorussians and Lithuanians, as evidenced by the lack of pogroms there during the outbursts in 1881 and 1882. According to Mendelsohn, "This combination of a dominant Jewish proletariat and an intelligentsia more likely than elsewhere to be sensitive to its needs made possible the emergence of a specifically Jewish labor movement."[85]

The unique characteristics of Jewish life in the Northwest Pale that gave birth to a Jewish labor movement are amplified further by comparison with the South, where the labor movement was less distinctively Jewish and where many Jewish radicals joined Russian movements. The differences between the regions can be traced to their development as areas of Jewish settlement in Russia. The Northwest Pale was incorporated with a Jewish population intact in the late eighteenth century; the South was only settled by Jews after it came under Russian domination. As a new area of settlement, the proportion of Jews in the total population in the South was lower than in the Northwest. Thus in 1897, Jews represented 14.7 percent of Lithuania and 13.6 percent of White Russia, but only 9.0 percent of the South. Because the Jewish population in South Russian grew at the rate of 60 percent from 1881 to 1897 (owing, in part, to migration from the Northwest), it is clear that the disparity between the regions had been even greater before 1880. The proportion of

Jews in South Pale cities contrasted even more sharply with the situation in the Northwest: although Jews represented 50.0 percent and 55.2 percent of Lithuanian and White Russian urban populations (including towns and villages), they made up only 28.2 percent of the urban population of the South. The presence of Jews in the South in rural areas and their lower concentration in the cities increased the likelihood of contact with non-Jewish populations.[86]

As indicated earlier, the differences in population and population density in the two regions had a direct effect on occupational distribution. As Rubinow noted, "The larger the proportion of the Jewish population to the total population, the larger is the proportion of artisans to the Jewish population." Thus Jews of the South Pale were more likely to be involved in commerce than their counterparts in the Northwest. This occupational distribution also contributed to greater contact with non-Jewish populations, as merchants were likely to deal with peasant populations.[87]

Among workers in the South, Russians predominated, which meant that the Social Democratic workers' circles had "a Jewish complexion, but not quite to the same extent as in the Northwest." In addition, in the South, Jews tended to speak Russian, so there was little need for Yiddish propaganda. The intelligentsia there had "assimilated for two generations and [been] brought up in a thoroughly Russian cultural-linguistic atmosphere."[88] This profile of southern, and particularly Odessan, Jews and Jewish intellectuals as relatively assimilated in Russian language and culture had a profound effect on the development of the Am Olam that is examined in chapter 2. The first Am Olam chapter emerged in Odessa, was led primarily by Russified intellectuals, and was inspired chiefly by Russian agrarian ideologies. Am Olam Sabbath sessions revolved around readings in Russian of both Russian and western radical thinkers.[89]

The way in which such objective factors as Jewish population density, newness of settlement, and occupational profile come together to shape the various revolutionary responses reinforces Goldscheider and Zuckerman's emphasis on the importance of the varying density of ties in different Jewish communities. Here it again becomes apparent that where ties were older and thicker, the community and people in that community were more likely to confront new situations in a manner consistent with Jewish traditions. Applying this framework, it becomes apparent that, *in general,* Jewish intellectuals and workers in the Northwest, living in cities and towns with a majority Jewish population, more likely to have attended Jewish *hederim* and *yeshivot,* and less familiar with the language of non-Jews, responded through organizations that clearly identified themselves as Jewish. In the South, where communal ties were less dense, *in general,* where the intelligenty considered themselves Russian, where workers were likely to speak Russian, and where Jews were a minority, both in the cities and in the proletariat, responses were less clearly Jewish.

※※※

A third strand of autoemancipatory response can be found in territorialist solutions, including, but not limited to, Zionism. Early formulations of territorialism usually combined nationalism with agrarianism and socialism, focusing on the rejuvenation of the Jewish people through productive labor, particularly as cooperative agricultural activities. The early leaders of these movements, like their counterparts who formed the Bund, were influenced by the populist strand in Russian revolutionism. Goldscheider and Zuckerman argue that though the failure of the *narodnik* movement led some Jewish revolutionaries to turn to industrial laborers as a potential base of the future revolution, others

> who retained the belief in the virtues of tilling the soil and of collectivist agriculture . . . had no peasantry. Their work among the Russian *narod* had resulted in abject failure . . . In response, many turned to their people, the Jewish masses. But they had to create *de novo* Jewish peasants. How and where to do that became their central problem. They opted to establish Jewish collective farms, and chose emigration as the means to transform themselves and their people.[90]

Thus for action-oriented groups, such as Am Olam and the BILU, in the 1880s and 1890s, territorialist solutions combined strands of both the migration and the agrarian responses. Both of these small groups focused on settlement in agricultural colonies, Am Olam in the United States and the BILU in Palestine. In these early years, the question of destination was not central: "The choice between Palestine and America was a minor question in a generally agreed-upon agrarian socialist philosophy."[91] The emphasis on rectifying Jews' minority status through a national solution (whether political or otherwise) later became central in certain strands of Zionism, whereas the Am Olam saw itself as part of an emerging internationalism.

As the Zionist movement began to take shape as the most important territorialist movement in the late 1890s and early twentieth century, the movement became very broad-based. Unlike Jewish socialism, Zionism required neither a class identity nor a secular outlook. In fact, Zionism developed a strong base of supporters among the middle classes, who were alienated from the Bund and other socialist movements.[92] Among the Hibat Zion clubs that spread through the Pale beginning in the 1880s, "middle-class Jews with some Hebrew background" were the strongest component.[93] Rather than scorning traditionalism, Zionism drew on messianic imagery and gained a following among the religious, with synagogues often supporting the movement: "In some synagogues the custom was introduced of having special collection plates on the eve of Atonement for the benefit of the colonies in Palestine. . . . Zionist leaders sought to obtain [the rabbis'] good will and participation."[94] Thus the Zionist constituency was already quite mixed in the 1880s, as seen in the variety of Hibat Zion groups: "Some consisted mainly of orthodox Jews, others of radical students who got their inspirations largely from the then fashionable *narodnichestvo* [populism]. Some took the question of emigration very seriously, preparing themselves for immediate departure, while others were mainly philanthropic in character."[95]

This diversity in constituency led to a wide array of Zionist ideologies. Besides the BILU and Hibat Zion, new strands of Zionist ideology sprang up in the late nineteenth and early twentieth centuries. A religious Zionist movement, the Mizrachi, was formed in 1902, followed shortly by the establishment of a Labor Zionist movement, Poalei Zion, in 1906. Cultural Zionists, though not creating a political movement, put forth a program focusing on cultural rejuvenation and the Hebrew language.[96]

Because of the diffuse nature of the movement, it is difficult to account for its varied constituencies through attention to regional, economic, and demographic factors. Indeed, because it crossed both religious-secular and class lines, its supporters were less confined to one area than were the members of the Bund or the Am Olam.[97] Brym has suggested that Zionism was attractive in the South Pale because in this region there were many Jews who were merchants rather than industrial or craft workers, and therefore did not identify with class-based movements, whether Jewish or general. Yet, he claims, Zionism was also popular in the Northwest, because of its attraction for persons deeply embedded in the Jewish community.[98] Just as movements like BILU and Am Olam appealed to radicals attracted by populism and socialism, other strands of Zionist thought had great appeal for particular constituencies. For example, former activists in the Hebrew Haskalah, such as Eliezer Ben Yehudah and Perez Smolenskin, became active in the Zionist Hebrew press, stressing cultural and linguistic rejuvenation. This focus on language was only one intersection between enlightenment thought and Zionist ideology. Others included a stress on practical training for productive employment, and appeals to western ideals of liberalism and nationalism.[99] The ability of Zionists to appeal to a variety of groups enabled them to compete effectively with rival groups, such as the Bund, which were also in competition with the Russian and Polish socialist movements. By 1914, with the Bund suffering after the failure of the 1905 revolution and divided between coalitions stressing nationalism and those stressing socialism, Zionists outnumbered Bundists in Russia by ten to one.[100]

The autoemancipatory responses that emerged among Jews in the Pale in the post-1880 period represent a departure from an earlier faith in western-style emancipation. Yet migrants, revolutionaries, and territorialists were not breaking with their pasts. Rather, they were drawing on their experiences and beliefs to construct responses to their increasingly desperate situation. These responses, although different from previous actions, were firmly rooted in their individual experiences as well as in the social structure of East European Jewry, and they varied in nature according to cultural and economic differences, corresponding to local conditions.

Those who responded to conditions in Russia by migrating to America made a drastic break with the world that was familiar to them, leaving behind their homes and communities. Yet they did not break with their past completely. Their aspirations, values, and worldviews were a product of their experiences in Russia, experiences that varied greatly among Jews of different regional backgrounds and would shape their thoughts and actions upon arrival in America.

Those who journeyed to America as members of Am Olam, intending to establish agrarian settlements, differed from other Jewish migrants in the same period. The emphasis on the varying conditions within the Jewish Pale of Settlement and the contrasting responses to those conditions by different constituencies of Jews provides a background for the discussion in chapter 2 of the development of the Am Olam and the emergence and evolution of the Jewish agricultural colonies. The variety of experiences and responses within the Pale makes apparent the need to analyze the specific premigration origins of this movement to understand the goals, worldviews, assumptions, and human capital that its adherents brought with them, and which shaped the communities that they created.

2

The Am Olam
Members, Philosophies, and Experiments

> Am Olam, arise from the dust, cast off the scorn of the
> nations, for it is high time!
> >   —Am Olam call to action

> Our motto is a return to agriculture, and our aim, the
> physical and spiritual rehabilitation of our people. In free
> America, where many peoples live closely in peace and am-
> ity, we Jews, too, shall find a place to lay our heads; we shall
> demonstrate to the world that we are capable of manual
> Labor.
> >   —Am Olam member, B. Dubnow[1]

ALTHOUGH THE AM OLAM is the least known of the autoemancipatory movements discussed in chapter 1, it had in the early 1880s a following larger than that of the emerging Zionist movement.[2] Combining elements of the three autoemancipatory responses—migration, territorialism, and revolutionism—the Am Olam focused on productivization through agricultural labor in colonies to be established in the United States. Yet, although Am Olam members were unified in their desire to establish colonies and demonstrate to the world the productive ability of the Jewish people, there was much disagreement as to the shape these colonies would take. Those that were established varied from purely communal, agrarian colonies to settlements based on private property and combining agriculture with industrial or commercial occupations.

Ultimately the Am Olam was responsible for the establishment of only a handful of settlements that survived their infancy. The most lasting of these, in which both Am Olam adherents and nonmembers settled, were the New Jersey colonies. In this chapter, the development of the Am Olam is traced from its beginnings in the South Pale through the early settlement experiments in the western United States. Ideological differences within the Am Olam, and within the early settlements, are analyzed along with the policies of financial sponsors as the central factors that influenced the development of these western colonies. This focus on the dual impact of settler population and sponsor policies on the development of colonies is continued in chapters 4 through 6, which analyze the composition and character of the New Jersey settlements.

Like all the autoemancipatory responses reviewed in chapter 1, the Am Olam was a product of specific circumstances and conditions. Although the movement was influenced greatly by both the Haskalah and Russian populism, the incorporation of elements of these movements into the Am Olam ideology was shaped both by the background of members and by objective factors in the region in which the movement emerged.

As a product of the early 1880s, the Am Olam reflected many aspects of the three major autoemancipatory movements. Like both territorialists and migrants, Am Olam adherents firmly believed that a secure future could not be achieved in Russia. Like the Jewish revolutionaries who eventually joined the Bund, many members of the Am Olam saw themselves as part of an international movement advocating the ideals of socialism. Like the early Zionists, they believed that their communal, agrarian experiments would not only serve the practical purpose of "productivizing" individual Jews but would also demonstrate to the world the rejuvenation of the Jewish people.

The Am Olam was founded in Odessa in the spring of 1881, and, though several chapters were later formed outside the South Pale, the specific circumstances of that region had the greatest influence on its development. As a new and expanding city in a new area of Jewish settlement, Odessa emerged as one of the leading cities of the Haskalah movement in the mid-nineteenth century. Because Jews could participate both economically and politically in Odessan life, the Odessan Jewish community's development was like that of its western European counterparts. Thus Odessan Jewish leaders placed much emphasis on the tenets of the Haskalah, such as the belief that practical, secular education would enable Jews to gain acceptance in the larger, non-Jewish society. In Odessa, *maskilim* seized control of Jewish communal institutions as early as the 1830s, and, like western Jews, they began to establish modern Jewish schools and Reform-style synagogues.[3] The acceptance of enlightenment ideals is reflected in educational statistics: by the mid-1870s, nearly 70 percent of Odessa's Jewish students were studying in Russian schools, in contrast to 14.7 percent in Vilna.[4]

The legacy of this strong commitment to the Haskalah became one cornerstone of the Am Olam movement. The central tenet of the Haskalah, "normalization" of Jewish economic life, was a key element of the Am Olam program. Unlike the early Zionists who increasingly saw the Jewish problem as cultural and national, the Am Olam leadership "regarded the Jewish problem as essentially socio-economic and political." Like the *maskilim,* Am Olam members believed that anti-Semitism was caused by the concentration of Jews in "unproductive" occupations.[5]

The influence of the Haskalah on the Am Olam can also be found in the distinctly western orientation of the movement. The emphasis on things western among the Odessan intellectuals who came to form the Am Olam can not only be seen in their attachment to western philosophers but also can account, in part, for the selection of a western destination for the migration. Indeed, America had long been accepted by a large group of western radicals, including Fourier and Owen, as the logical location for radical agrarian settlement. It is clear that the western-oriented Am Olam leadership was familiar with this tradition. Cofounder Sidney Baily mentions Owen and Fourier, along with Tolstoy, as the primary influences on the group. Unlike the Zionist BILU movement, which was inspired by specifically *Jewish* as well as populist sources, among Am Olam members there is little evidence of specifically Jewish sources of inspiration.[6] Even the names of the two organizations reflect this difference in orientation. BILU is an acronym for the Hebrew "*Bet Yaakov Lechu ve Nelcha*" ("O house of Jacob, come and let us go"), a verse taken from Isaiah; Am Olam (the Eternal People), also in Hebrew, was the title of an article by Peretz Smolenskin, published in 1872 in the *maskilic* monthly, *Ha-Shachar.*[7]

The founders of the movement, all of whom came to live in the New Jersey colonies, were a part of this strong Odessan tradition of Haskalah. Monye Bokal, born in the 1850s into a religious home, had a rather traditional upbringing in Uman in the South Pale. He attended *heder* and was being groomed to become the local rabbi when he discovered the Haskalah. Converted to "the cult of labor," Bokal moved to Odessa to learn a trade, and became the center of a circle of like-minded people. By the early 1880s, Bokal had severed ties with his earlier religious upbringing. His father-in-law, a rabbi, dissolved Bokal's marriage shortly after the birth of Bokal's son, because he considered Bokal an unbeliever. In his memoirs, Sidney Baily recalled the clash between Bokal's earlier life and his new one in Odessa:

> It happened that Bokal's father paid a visit to Odessa to see his fine son. The father came to his lodgings and found a bunch of pranksters—his son's good friends. Bokal wore a short coat and long hair, and his friends wore their shirts over their pants, in gentile fashion . . . We were all embittered over *heder* [and were] against the practices laid down in the *Talmud,* and we dis-

1. Moses Herder, Am Olam leader and early settler at
Carmel. Before settling in Carmel, Herder participated in
the failed Arkansas colony. Herder remained in Carmel
until his death in 1911. *Courtesy Faith Klein.*

cussed Jewishness with the old man. We were aware of the fact that we were
hurting the old man, very much so, with our objections to and criticisms of
the Jewish code. I confess that I told him that in addition to our dissatisfaction with tradition, *Talmud, Shulchan Aruch* . . . customs and laws, we even
had some serious disagreements with the *Toras Moshe* (the Five Books of
Moses).[8]

Bokal, less a scholar and philosopher than a charismatic leader, devoted his
life's work, as well as all his savings, to the movement.

Bokal's two cofounders,[9] Sidney (Schneur) Baily and Moses (Moyshe)
Herder, were also of *maskilic* background. Herder had worked as a tutor in
wealthy homes and knew several languages, including German, Russian, and
Hebrew, the three languages of the different factions of the Russian Jewish
Haskalah.[10] Both Baily and Herder had, like Bokal, come from religious
households and rejected traditionalism in favor of the Haskalah. Baily's hostil-

2. Rachel Herder, wife of Am Olam leader Moses Herder.
Rachel Herder was a veteran of the Arkansas colony before
settling in Carmel. *Courtesy Faith Klein.*

ity toward traditionalism, apparent in his confrontation with Bokal's father,
permeates his memoirs. For example, Baily tells of attending a *heder* that was
"crowded, dirty, and full of offensive odors," in a community in which he was
beaten for associating with an "unbeliever." After being caught in *yeshivah*
with a heretical book (a pro-Hasidic tract written by a teacher from the
Zhitomir Rabbinical School), Baily was expelled and began his life as "an
infidel," entering *maskilic* circles in Odessa and studying in a Russian gymnasium and later in university.[11]

Of the three cofounders, Baily best represented the *maskilic* current in Am
Olam thought. By 1879, Baily was firmly implanted in the Odessan Haskalah,
then experiencing tremendous changes in the aftermath of the 1871 pogrom.
Baily's friends included intellectuals, such as Jacob Gordin and Moshe Leib
Lilienblum, founder of the early Zionist movement, Hovevei Zion.[12] He
joined a circle of *maskilim* in Odessa and studied Russian novels with them.
During this period, Baily met future Am Olam adherents, such as Bokal,

Mordechai Woskoboynikoff, and Moshe Freeman—all of whom would later join him in migrating to the New Jersey colonies. Before the founding of the Am Olam, this group met as a study circle at Woskoboynikoff's house, where Bokal was a boarder. There, on the Sabbath and holidays, "we would gather . . . young men and women, to read Russian and have discussions."[13]

The strong influence of the Haskalah on the Am Olam program was complemented by Russian and western radical ideologies. In response to both the reversal of liberal policies during the second half of Alexander II's reign and the increasing anti-Semitic fervor in Odessa in the 1870s, *maskilim* began to turn away from western models of emancipation and toward more revolutionary ideals. Their disillusionment peaked after the 1881–82 pogroms, which centered in the South Pale and which directly triggered the formation of the Am Olam. Although relatively few early Am Olam members were directly involved in Russian revolutionary movements, such as populism,[14] the influence of such radical ideologies on intellectual Jews in general, and on the Am Olam leadership in particular, is clear. As the Jewish intelligentsia moved away from faith in western-style emancipation, radical ideologies, such as Russian populism and western socialism and communism, increasingly permeated their circles. Thus, although Am Olam members shared the *maskilic* belief in normalization of Jewish economic life, they believed that such normalization required Jews to engage in agriculture exclusively, exhibiting a reverence for agriculture common among Russian populists, but not shared by the Haskalah movement. These beliefs had resonance in the South Pale, where Jewish students had been active in the populist movement and where there was some history of Jewish agricultural colonization. Similarly, the belief of many Am Olam members that "mere colonization was not sufficient and that the root of the evil lay in the system of private property" went well beyond the scope of the Haskalah, which aimed at making the Jews a productive element of the economic system.[15]

Several accounts of the Am Olam clearly demonstrate both the Russian and the western roots of the radical ideologies that joined with the *maskilic* faith in productivization to create the Am Olam belief in productivization through agriculture and in communal organization of society. In their memoirs, Am Olam members demonstrate a clear familiarity with both Russian and western radicals. Sidney Baily, for example, writing of the early Am Olam in Odessa, discusses the wide variety of intellectual influences—ranging from Russian novelists and critics to leaders of the Russian and Hebrew enlightenment movements to John Stuart Mill.[16] The movement was also shaped by the stress on agrarianism in the Russian populist movement.

In Russian thought, immigration to America to create an egalitarian, agrarian society was a familiar topic of debate in the work of intellectuals, such as Herzen, Bakunin, and Chernyshevsky.[17] Many of the Russian *narodnik* intellectuals believed that "democratic America would be fertile soil for the establishment of collective agricultural communes."[18] The strong identification with Russian intellectuals, and with populists in particular, was demonstrated by the Odessa Am Olam group, which, while passing through Brody en route to the United States, spent time discussing how to force the release of Russian *narod* philosopher G. G. Chernyshevsky from imprisonment in Siberia. A more concrete link between Russian populism and the Am Olam can be found in the decision of William Frey, a well-known Russian radical and member of the 1870s Russian émigré agricultural colony, Cedar Vale, to join the Am Olam colony in New Odessa, Oregon. Frey, a non-Jew, became the central figure at the New Odessa colony.[19]

The influence of radical ideologies on the Am Olam was furthered by members, such as H. L. Sabsovich, who brought to the group an awareness of socialist and communist systems. Sabsovich, a gymnasium graduate and university student in Odessa in 1881, had been active in "self-education centers" made up of Jews and Christians united by their concern with "the good of Russia, of its working masses, of its peasants."[20] Sabsovich brought to the group a thorough understanding of radical philosophies, both western and Russian. His involvement led to more serious consideration of a communist plan for the agricultural settlements.[21] The connection of persons like Sabsovich to the organization made it a target of the police, who raided several of the Odessa meetings, searching for terrorists and revolutionaries.[22] Baily writes that "the leaders who were politically suspect would avoid those small group meetings." In January 1882, a meeting was raided and members were held by the police for a day. After that, Baily recalls, "raids began occurring in every house; they were searching for politically subversive materials. We remained under police surveillance for a whole year and would have to report each month to the police."[23]

Although the Am Olam ideologies stemmed from both western and Russian radical movements, the connection of most Am Olam members to these movements was rather emotional; the specific content of their radicalism was somewhat vague. Except Sabsovich, even members who had extensive experience in Russian revolutionary movements had only an informal education in socialist theory gained through reading and discussion. Thus Abraham Cahan, who joined the Balta Am Olam determined to propagandize them in socialism, later admitted that at the time he "had no practical understanding of socialism."[24] The typical Am Olam member had not been directly involved in the Russian radical movement, and was therefore "more a revolutionary type than he was the bearer of a coherent ideology of revolution," as historian Ezra Mendelsohn explains. This ideological vagueness resulted both from the indirectness of contact with these philosophies—most members were exposed through populist literature rather than through practical experience—and from a general ignorance of socialist theory among Russian radicals themselves in the 1870s.

Mendelsohn writes, "What the Jewish intellectuals acquired from their acquaintance with Russian populist tradition . . . was a certain mood of revolutionary dedication and enthusiasm. The ideological content was, indeed, vague; what was clearly expressed was the revolutionary form, as manifest in the desire for rapid change, an end to oppression, a love for the 'people', a hatred for authority."[25]

The ideological vagueness of the movement can also be attributed to the heterogeneity of the membership. Among the early members of Odessa Am Olam were a mix of *maskilic* intellectuals, students, and craftsmen. Although all three of the founders shared a negative assessment of traditionalism, and had all been exposed to *maskilic* thought, none was a great social theoretician. Herder and Bokal functioned in the group more as "comforters" than theorists—neither had a clear plan for social organization of the colonies.[26] Baily's discussion of his secular education reveals more exposure to novelists than to social philosophers. Although intellectuals and social theorists joined the movement, the charismatic Bokal drew in ordinary craftsmen as well. Bokal pulled members into the organization with his magnetic personality: "The plain, reverent people believed in him as a messiah, and he had the trust of the people."[27] A believer in the workingman, Bokal was somewhat suspicious of the more intellectual members; as one member recalled, "There is the danger that the students who joined the organization may confuse the honest working-men with their bookish theories. . . . Bokal admitted these intellectuals into his circle only very reluctantly. These gentlemen, he said, wish to be privileged and to manage everything, for they believe that nobody but they understands anything."[28]

Moshe Freeman, an early member of the group, reported that Sabsovich's focus on communist and socialist systems brought conflicts between the intellectuals and the workers to the fore. In one case, the leader of one of the circles told Sabsovich that his circle's membership assumed that land in their future settlement would be divided among the colonists. At this suggestion, Freeman reported, Sabsovich ground his teeth, shocked at the suggestion that he should fight and sacrifice to assure a Jew individual ownership. Rather, Sabsovich argued that the colony must be a commune and that he would not tolerate individual ownership.[29] This diversity of opinion within the Odessa Am Olam led to strife within the group: "The tradesmen and workers were imbued with strong Jewish feelings and regarded the movement as nationalist, whereas the student faction was essentially Russianized and stressed the social and even the socialist aspect of it."[30] In the Odessa group, the students, better organized, prevailed. In his autobiography, Abraham Cahan observed that, by the time of their migration, the first Odessa Am Olam group "acknowledge[d] openly its communist intentions."[31] Given that Bokal, the leader of the nonintellectual faction, was apparently willing to accept this arrangement—he apparently placed little importance on private property, giving all of his own money to the movement and subsisting on bread and tea[32]—it can be surmised that those interested in private holdings were never well represented in the group. In fact, Freeman writes that cooperation was practiced by the group members in preparation for the migration—members in Odessa bought and sold goods cooperatively, the profits going into the communal fund.[33]

The heterogeneity of the Odessa group was replicated in new Am Olam circles founded in cities throughout the Pale in 1881 and 1882. Although many of these groups formally affiliated themselves with Odessa Am Olam, others operated as independent emigration associations. Of the affiliated groups, the second largest (after Odessa) was in Kiev. This group was focused specifically on productivization through farming and "was little interested in socialism or collectivism." Although this group proposed that its colony would at first operate "on a somewhat collectivist plan," their constitution stipulated that later "private ownership is to replace the collectivist system." Like the Odessa group, the Kiev Am Olam had a mixed membership: "Most of them [are] young people, former students at the universities and institutes of technology, true idealists who have renounced their careers in order to become good farmers. . . . The older members include former wealthy merchants with their families."[34]

Like the Kiev group, Balta Am Olam was concerned more with the establishment of an agricultural colony than with collectivism. When Abraham Cahan met the leader of the Balta group and asked whether the colony would be communist, he received no clear answer. "Though their idealism was deep and genuine," he reported, "they gave little thought to the doctrines of communism and socialism. They were determined only to start colonies in which life, a new kind of life for Jews, would be beautiful."[35] Cahan, who identified himself as a proud socialist, joined the group, hoping to propagandize them.

Yet the Odessa group was not the only one with collectivist aims. Despite the intention of the Kiev group to move toward private ownership, this group agreed to sponsor the Vilna Am Olam, which was dedicated to the establishment of a cooperative settlement. En route to the United States, Cahan learned that his socialist friends from Vilna had joined the Kiev Am Olam group.[36] The Vilna group sent three parties of settlers to the United States, one led by a former activist in a Russian revolutionary group. One group member, Alexander Harkavy, reported that the majority agreed while on the ship to

America that it would not be desirable to establish synagogues in the new colonies.[37] According to Abraham Menes, a historian of the movement, of the five or six groups arriving in 1882, three—the Vilna, Odessa, and Kremenchug groups—had "pronounced socialist leanings," while the Kiev and Balta groups "had no definite attitude in the matter, but they too wanted to begin life anew in America 'on a just social basis.'"[38]

Although there was much variation among Am Olam groups regarding the exact organization of the colonies they were to establish, an emphasis on agricultural labor and on the importance of demonstrating the productive abilities of Jews were consistent themes. The centrality of agriculture to Am Olam ideology is demonstrated in virtually every account of the movement. Thus Alexander Harkavy, a Vilna Am Olam member and later a renowned Yiddishist, wrote of gymnasium students "who abandoned their studies in order to take up farming." Sidney Baily wrote of the Am Olam goal to "leave Russia, to become farmers in 'the land of the free and the home of the brave.'"[39]

Accepting the view that anti-Semitism was a result of the concentration of Jews in unproductive occupations, the intellectuals who came together in the Am Olam argued that agricultural labor was the only means through which Jews could be normalized. In making this argument, Am Olam members, like the *maskilim* and later the Zionists, were accepting the argument of anti-Semites that Jews were a parasitic people. To rectify this situation, they argued that productive labor would enable them to be accepted among other peoples. Thus, reasoned Monye Bokal, the movement would allow Jews to "disperse among the free nations in a new world. We shall be compelled to become agriculturalists and we shall be like other people—we will live like other people."[40] Moses Freeman explained the group's goals in similar terms: "To settle on the land and live from our own work, and serve as an example to others. There in the colony, close to the tilled soil and in nature's bosom, the local storekeeper, middleman and 'luftmentsh' will be transformed into a useful member of society, for himself and for the world."[41]

The emphasis on demonstrating this transformation to the world community was a second central theme in Am Olam ideology. Members were concerned not only with productivizing the Jewish people but also with making their experiment an example. Am Olam members saw their migration as a movement of missionaries. In comparing themselves with the mass of Jewish migrants, Am Olam members emphasized their higher purpose: "They are not like us, we thought. We are not journeying to America for ordinary reasons: are we not idealists, who will demonstrate to the nations of the world that the children of Israel are capable of being farmers."[42] One member wrote, "Our motto is a return to agriculture, and our aim, the physical and spiritual rehabilitation of our people. In free America, where many peoples live closely in peace and amity, we Jews, too, shall find a place to lay our heads; we shall demonstrate to the world that we are capable of manual labor."[43]

The desire to demonstrate their achievement to the world was usually tied to the belief that the colonies would be communal. In establishing communal agrarian colonies, some members emphasized, the organization would be furthering internationalism and communism. As one member explained, their purpose was "to demonstrate to the world that Jews are capable of being agriculturalists; and as progressive, advanced and intelligent humans—live on communist principles."[44] Some members, emphasizing the establishment of communal colonies, believed that their experiment would not only demonstrate to the world the productive abilities of Jews but would also serve as a model communal society. Thus, cofounder Bokal wrote, "we Jews have given to the world its loftiest ideas of morality. . . . perhaps we were destined to show the world that life could be established on the basis of the highest truth and justice."[45]

✳✳✳

Most Am Olam chapters failed to survive the journey to the United States intact. The lack of definite plans and conflict over colony structure, as well as the practical difficulties of obtaining land and organizing colonies, led to the collapse of the Am Olam as an organization soon after arrival. As contemporary George Price explained, "it is clear that without a solid organization and without a clear perspective as to the proper steps which they would take upon their arrival in the new land, it was impossible to undertake anything so radical."[46]

Several Am Olam groups, realizing the impracticality of their plans, dissolved almost instantly upon arrival in New York. Among these were the Kiev, Balta, and part of the Vilna group. Although they abandoned their agricultural aims, many remained true to their social goals, establishing communes in the city. The Odessa commune in New York "housed some fifty to sixty people on a collective basis."[47] Abraham Cahan located his radical friends in the Vilna commune, where they "settled themselves in an apartment with several rooms at 48 Essex Street, near Grand. The leader of the commune was Menaker. They all lived communistically." Cahan recalled sessions at the Vilna commune, when Bokal, sojourning temporarily in New York before joining the Alliance colony, would address the group. Cahan described commune life: "One of the women stayed in the apartment during the day, doing all the housekeeping chores. The other commune members went to work. All earnings were turned in to the general treasury. This included the considerable earnings of two members who had become expert ladies' tailors in the old country. They gave all they earned to the commune. There was a warm bond among the members."[48]

Although members of the Vilna commune had apparently abandoned their plans to establish a colony, other Am Olam groups and members, like Bokal, saw the urban communes as an intermediary step toward their dream of colonization. Some members of the Odessa group worked on farms outside the city to gain experience and earn money, which they contributed to the group's communal fund. Similarly, members of the Kremenchug group worked on farms and gave their earnings to the communal fund. Efforts to move from this transitional stage to colonization were thwarted both by the slow rate of growth of the communal treasuries and by the often disappointing first experience with farm labor.[49] George Price reported on these difficulties as a correspondent for the Russian Jewish periodical, *Voskhod*.

> The Jews among the intelligentsia, who had been students in gymnasia, Real-schulen, universities and others, became farm-hands at the outset and despite the difficult work and their being unaccustomed to labor for fifteen or eighteen hours daily—work which they imagine to be as fatiguing as 'prison' labor—remained on the farm for several months and at times for a year or more. The writer of these lines is personally acquainted with many such persons who showed their devotion to agriculture, and, even he, not having known what physical labor meant, worked sixteen hours a day for four months on a Connecticut farm, where he got calluses on his hands, plowed, planted, threshed grain, gathered in the harvest, and even fed hogs and cows, until, finally, his enthusiasm for colonization cooled off.[50]

Some of the colonists, such as Sidney Baily who worked on a Shaker colony in Connecticut before joining Alliance, and Harris Rubin who wrote of the isolation and physical hardships he experienced on a farm near Albany before joining Carmel, were unshaken by these difficulties.[51] Yet for many, this encounter with reality dissuaded them from pursuing an agricultural life.

Members abandoned colonization plans not only because of practical difficulties but also because they were overcome by the lure of the city. Abraham Cahan, after traveling to the United States with the Balta Am Olam group, recalled in his autobiography: "After my arrival it took me just three days to realize that the establishment of communal colonies was not really my dream. I was not fascinated by village life, by the prospect of laboring on the soil. On the contrary, I felt strongly drawn to the life of the city. My heart beat to its rhythms, and as the heart feels so thinks the head."[52] Like Cahan, many Am Olam members chose to pursue their revolutionary goals in New York. By the late 1880s, much of the former Am Olam leadership "discovered" the Jewish proletariat in America's eastern cities and began to transform themselves into labor leaders. Like Cahan, who came to prominence as the editor of the Yiddish language socialist paper, the *Jewish Daily Forward,* these intellectuals turned away from Russian-oriented populism and toward a specifically Jewish labor movement. They came to recognize the need to propagandize in Yiddish, a language that most of them had formerly scorned: "In 1887 Nikolai Alenikov, the former leader of the Kievan Am Olam, made a speech urging Jewish Russian radicals to enter the Jewish labor movement . . . in 1887, another Am Olam alumnus, Rayevsky, made the point that the place of the Jewish intelligentsia was in the Jewish labor movement, and that the use of Russian should give way to the use of Yiddish."[53] This experience of former Am Olam members in New York parallels that of Jewish radicals who remained in Russia and turned to the Jewish proletariat, forming the Bund.

Although the Am Olam quickly disbanded as an organization, and most of its members never fulfilled their ambition of establishing agricultural colonies, a few did proceed with their plans. As former members like Cahan remained in New York to organize urban laborers, those who held fast to the movement's original goals set out to establish colonies throughout the country. Between 1881 and 1884, about twenty-four Jewish agricultural colonies were established in the United States.[54] Despite the organization's dissolution, almost all these attempts emerged through the efforts of Am Olam members.[55]

The first of the Am Olam–related colonies to be established on American soil was founded in late 1881 on Sicily Island, Louisiana, in the Mississippi River. Although the migration of this group was too early to allow it to be formally considered an Am Olam chapter, it was clearly a part of the same response.

The Sicily Island group comprised primarily families from Elizavetgrad, the site of the first of the 1881 South Pale pogroms. During the fall after the pogrom, twenty-five families aiming "to engage only in farming on a cooperative basis" began their journey to the United States. The group was augmented by an additional nine families from Kiev.[56] These migrants, arriving in Brody in October of 1881, made a positive impression on the officials of the French Alliance Israélite Universelle (AIU), stationed there to direct migration. The Alliance, struck by the group's "concrete and limited plan" to establish agricultural colonies, and faced with a fait accompli, in that they "had simply taken their fate into their own hands and left Russia," paid for their passage to the United States. This aid was continued on the American side of the Atlantic by the short-lived Hebrew Emigrant Aid Society (HEAS), formed to cope with the sudden influx of Jewish immigrants. HEAS provided money to purchase the colony's land, through its New Orleans chapter, enabling the establishment of the colony on December 28, 1881.[57]

This success in securing aid can be attributed in part to the leadership of Herman Rosenthal. Rosenthal, who arrived in New York several months before the group, was a wealthy and well-educated merchant from Kiev who believed that productive labor on the land would eliminate anti-Semitism. He described his analysis of the Jewish problem:

> Long ago I had come to the conclusion that so long as we have no toiling class that produces its own bread there will be no end to our tribulations. A people that lives at the expense of the labor of others cannot continue to exist indefinitely. Similarly, the Jewish problem will not be solved by the non-Jewish world. Since this is a problem of life and economics, it will eventually spring up also on the soil of America. What has befallen the Chinese in America [the Chinese Exclusion Act had just been passed] may also befall our brethren if our leaders do not take steps betime to anticipate this peril. In my opinion, one of the best means of averting this danger would be to establish a class of half a million farmers and workers living by the sweat of their brows.[58]

Through Rosenthal's efforts both the New York Committee (of HEAS) and the New Orleans Jewish community were enlisted in the project. A committee that included the governor of Louisiana was formed, and the Sicily Island site was selected.[59]

The involvement of HEAS and the New Orleans Jewish leadership in the project proved to be a mixed blessing. Although these groups raised the necessary money and provided a warm welcome to the migrants upon their arrival in New Orleans,[60] the selection of the Sicily Island site doomed the colony to failure. The reason for this error was a subject of much controversy. George Price insisted that the selection of the Louisiana site was forced by Moritz Ellinger of HEAS in New York, who "had some political and private interests in mind." According to Price, Ellinger, even after being shown publications that demonstrated that the soil and climate were unsuitable, advocated the Louisiana site because "some 'politicians' wanted to colonize Louisiana. Somebody owned a deserted place somewhere at the world's end. It was there, through Mr. Ellinger's insistence that thirty families were sent in 1881."[61] In contrast to Price's interpretation, others insist that the poor choice of land was because of ignorance: "The originators of this settlement [the New Orleans committee] were not farmers themselves, but were city dwellers who had no desire to go out onto the farm land such as it was in Louisiana."[62] Whatever the reason for selecting the Sicily Island site, "all agree," according to a historical article about the colony in the *Jewish Tribune,* "that a more injudicious choice could not have been made."[63]

The Sicily Island location could not have been less conducive to colonization. The colony was isolated, surrounded by deserted plantations, which made it difficult to obtain provisions. The tremendous mosquito population and swampy conditions led to outbreaks of malaria and yellow fever among the colonists.[64] Finally, before the grain harvest in the spring of 1882, the Mississippi flooded, ruining the crops, washing away equipment, and inflicting damage to the colony amounting to twenty thousand dollars.[65] The colony was abandoned less than one year after it was founded.

Despite its swift demise, the Sicily Island colony left a legacy for subsequent colonies. First, while the disastrous outcome disheartened potential colonists and sponsors alike, it did in later years demonstrate the importance of site selection in colonization projects (although many later failures resulted from unfavorable project sites, only one other attempt was made in the Deep South). Equally important, veterans of the Sicily Island colony, including Rosenthal, served as the core of a second colony, established in 1882 in South Dakota; others joined Arkansas and Kansas colonies. Thus understanding the workings of the Louisiana colony can shed light on later colonies.

The Sicily Island group, consisting of fifty-one men, thirty-four women, and sixty-six children under the age of fifteen, was quite heterogeneous. The Jewish newspaper, *American Hebrew,* reported that the group included twelve merchants, eleven farmers, three teachers, one lawyer, one carpenter, one bookkeeper, one typesetter, one cigarette maker, six clerks, one student, two tobacco cutters, one tinsmith, one saddler, one professor, and one tobacco manufacturer. All "had strong desires to go into agriculture and had been interested in agricultural pursuits while yet in Russia."[66] Yet though the colonists shared an agrarian dream, their motives and plans reflected the heterogeneity that had been part of the Am Olam, even in Russia. George Price wrote that the colony was made up of four types of members: intellectuals who were devoted to the ideal of colonization; average people from southern and southwestern Russia "who were not afraid of work and who wanted to become farmers in the new land"; young enthusiasts; and people "who had no particular qualifications or any desire to colonize and who joined the group only because they did not know what to do with themselves."[67]

The heterogeneity of the group undoubtedly contributed to the mixture of communalism and private ownership in the colony's constitution. Although the constitution specified that all resources were to be communal and that all business was to be conducted by the group as a whole, "the intention was to establish each farmer on an individual basis as soon as the colony was on a strong foundation."[68] As one colonist wrote to the Hebrew Russian newspaper, *Ha-Melitz,* in January of 1882, members of the colony were given the opportunity to work on the land without charge for two years, after which "each person will be able to purchase his share of the land with money."[69]

The constitution was a thorough document, covering many aspects of colony life. The purpose of the colony, stated in the constitution, was "the improvement of the moral and intellectual condition of its members and their families, to promote their welfare by united and harmonious action on their part, and to afford mutual assistance to themselves." To insure the desired morality, members of the colony were forbidden to "sell or deal in spirituous or malt liquors within the limits of the colony."[70] Reports on community life demonstrate a concerted effort to achieve these moral and intellectual goals: "At night the colonists gathered in the 'big house' and indulged in debates and discussions lasting until after midnight. One Borowick, who had been in the United States before, and Rabinowitz, a linguist, taught English. A small school was organized for the children. Rosenthal regaled the colony with his poems. Borowick, for many years a member of an operatic company, entertained with song. A weekly news bulletin written in Russian was issued."[71] The concern about morality was apparently unrelated to religious concerns. Although the constitution stipulated that houses, a school, and a library were to be built, no mention was made of a synagogue. In a report on the demise of the colony, a sponsor noted, "Judaism was a mere by-word, the people were fed with ham, and Sunday substituted for Sabbath."[72]

Dedication to mutual assistance was demonstrated in the colony's rules. For example, if a male member should die, the group pledged to care for his widow's farm for five years. The constitution also bound members to support the family of a sick member. Similarly, the group was to "supply money, farming utensils, or other articles of husbandry, household furniture and stock to its members, and generally do and provide for their mutual support or for the furtherance of their aims and purposes aforesaid whatever shall be necessary."[73]

Communal tendencies in the constitution were tempered by a recognition of individual property rights. Thus, though the constitution stipulated that members' own money deposited with the New Orleans committee was to be used as a general fund for the colony, such members were entitled to "a special credit on the books of the colony for the amount so deposited less the cost incident to his voyage and his support." Similarly, although the constitution stipulated that all land was to "remain the property of the colony" and that "no member of the colony can dispense of the same until the debt of the colony to the Immigrants' Aid Association is paid," it recognized each member's right to his own private property.

The colony was to be governed by a board of governors, made up of seven members elected by the colony members. The board was responsible for keeping accounts for the association, and reporting to the membership. Disputes were to be settled internally by the board of governors, with a right to appeal to the New Orleans Committee. Members bringing such disputes before the civil authorities were to be expelled from the colony. Members could amend the constitution by a two-thirds vote and could elect to dissolve the colony by a four-fifths vote. In the case of dissolving the colony, any assets remaining after debts were paid were to be divided among members in proportion to their interest in the association. In addition, a two-thirds vote was required for approval of any business venture undertaken by any member.

Because the failure at Sicily Island was attributed to unfavorable climate and soil conditions and not to the design of the colony, it is not surprising that the Cremieux, South Dakota, colony, founded by Rosenthal and twelve families from the Louisiana project, imitated the earlier colony's mixed socialist-private constitution. After the failure in Louisiana, some of the Sicily Island colonists joined new settlements in Arkansas and Kansas, and Rosenthal returned to New York to begin plans to establish a colony in Dakota Territory.[74] A northern location was chosen to avoid the heat and disease that had plagued the Sicily Island colony. The opening of a former Indian reservation near Mitchell, South Dakota, for settlement by homesteaders made the Dakota site feasible for colonization.

In New York, Rosenthal enlisted the aid of Michael Heilprin, the enthusiastic supporter of many colonization projects, and Benoir Greenberg, a young, wealthy, and idealistic Russian immigrant. In addition, several Am Olam members, waiting in New York for just such an opportunity, joined the project.[75] Lazar Mashbir, a member of the Balta chapter of Am Olam, joined this group, as did his sister Esther, the future wife of Sidney Baily.[76]

The first two families arrived in Mitchell on July 5, 1882, and attracted much attention from the townspeople when they "celebrated the event by procuring a large can of boiling water and brewing and drinking Russian tea, right in the streets of Mitchell."[77] By the fall of 1882, the colony had twenty families, and, as word of the black, fertile soil spread, other families joined the settlement, which at its peak was home to two hundred.[78]

Because the land was obtained under the Homestead Act, claims had to be filed by individuals, so the communal ownership of property that had existed on Sicily Island was not replicated. Members filed claims for quarter sections (160 acres) at $1.25 per acre. Rosenthal and Greenberg, who were well-off financially, bought their land outright—Rosenthal purchasing four quarter sections, a complete square mile.[79] Because the constitution for Cremieux has not survived, it is unclear how much of the Sicily Island format was retained, but it is apparent that in farming cooperatively and in their social and intellectual life, Cremieux colonists replicated many aspects of the earlier colony.

As in Sicily Island, where social and cultural activities had centered on the "big house" (in that case the abandoned big house of an earlier plantation) occupied by Rosenthal, in Cremieux, Rosenthal built a house that served as the community center. Both Rosenthal and Greenberg built large houses of eight to ten rooms that served as their homes and as community centers, used for frequent dances, lectures, and parties.[80] Rosenthal owned a piano, and concerts were common: "The colony had its own glee club and choral organization. Native farmers who came to the concerts marvelled at the artistic ability displayed in these affairs." Rosenthal's home also served as a school, as he invited all the colony's children to benefit from the services of a tutor he hired for his offspring.[81]

In Cremieux, as in the Louisiana colony, religion apparently played no role in the settlement's cultural life. No mention is made of religious services in the records of the colony, and no synagogue was ever built. The colony had no religious leaders. Hogs were raised and eaten in the colony, and "a young couple married in the colony received a litter of pigs for a wedding gift."[82]

The first year in Cremieux was successful, the colonists bringing in respectable harvests of oats, wheat, rye, barley, and flax. Subsequent years proved disheartening, because of both the colonists' inexperience and natural conditions. Their location in the Dakotas assured that they would not be plagued by malaria, yellow fever, and floods, but it did not make them immune to natural disasters. In its first year, the colony was barely saved from a prairie fire. The Dakota winters were as harsh as the Louisiana summers: "The cold was so intense that the kerosene would freeze in the lamps, and one's very breath congeal on his pillows at night. . . . [There were] blizzards of such intensity as to make even a short trip from house to barn a hazardous journey."[83] After triumphing over these hardships in the first year, the colonists faced destruction of the wheat crop by parasites and a severe drought in the second year. The following year, severe thunderstorms destroyed the crops.[84]

These natural disasters thwarted the colonists' ability to repay their debts, debts ultimately responsible for the demise of the colony. Accounts differ concerning the cause of the colonists' indebtedness. A posthumous account published in the Detroit *Jewish Chronicle,* long after the colonization idea had passed out of favor, blamed the financial woes of the colonists on inexperience and extravagance. This report claims that a committee of colonists sent to Milwaukee to buy supplies "engaged in a reckless orgy of extravagant buying. They bought beyond their means and their needs. They bought the best horses, paying as much as 800 dollars for a single team. They bought quantities of fancy lumber for their houses." The settlers then built houses beyond their means, according to the *Chronicle.* This extravagance, according to this account, was made worse by the colonists' ignorance: "Only after the livestock had arrived at the colony did they wake up to the fact that they had made no provision for its housing, and no preparation for its feeding. Worst of all, only then did it dawn upon them that animals needed water, of which there was a woeful shortage."[85] In contrast to the report in the *Chronicle,* colonization supporter George Price argued in his contemporaneous account that the colonists' debts were caused by insufficient sponsor support and natural disaster:

> The money of the Committee was spent for transportation, payment for land, purchase of necessary tools and the building of houses. When at the end of the first year, on account of the drought, the crop was not good and means were needed for sustenance, the colonists were forced to borrow and pay an exorbitant rate of interest. They did not have good tools; they had insufficient livestock, and all their endeavors to procure assistance from the Committee were in vain. . . . For several years, the colonists were patient and worked hard, and during all these years, they had to deprive themselves of essentials. But finally, when they saw no way out of their misery and indebtedness, some of them, and, later, those remaining, sold their land and moved to various cities.[86]

It seems unlikely that a group of colonists, many of whom had participated in the semicommunal settlement at Sicily Island and all of whom were devoted enough to the ideal of colonization to abandon the city for the harsh conditions of the Dakota prairies, would sabotage the colony through extravagance, as stated by the *Chronicle* account. The overspending was probably because of the colonists' ignorance of prices and inexperience at farming, as historians Orlando and Violet Goering argue. They demonstrate that most of the colonists' debt was incurred when the third summer's crop was lost to poor weather conditions and the farmers were forced to mortgage their lands at "extortionary" interest rates.[87]

The indebtedness, whether incurred through greed, ignorance, or lack of support, caused the colony to begin to dissolve by 1885. Although a few families remained and eventually gained title to their land, most returned to New York. Rosenthal, who exchanged part of his holdings for a grain elevator in Mitchell, eventually moved to New York, where he became head of the Slavonic department of the New York Public Library.[88]

✳✳✳

The first colony founded by a self-proclaimed Am Olam group was also in South Dakota, only three miles from Cremieux.[89] This colony, Bethlehem Judea, was founded in September of 1882 by members of the Kremenchug Am Olam chapter. The twelve members who established the colony were soon joined by the remainder of the group, bringing the total to thirty-two colonists. Members of this group had gained experience upon arrival in New York by finding work on farms outside the city. The monies earned through this labor were given to the group's communal fund until a colony site was found.[90]

Upon arrival in South Dakota, the Kremenchug group established a colony that differed in several ways from the earlier Sicily Island and Cremieux projects. First, the group was made up entirely of Am Olam members. Second, except one married couple, the group consisted of young, single men. Thus, the Bethlehem Judea group lacked the heterogeneity observed in the earlier groups and was more unified ideologically. The single-mindedness of the new arrivals was noted by a Cremieux colonist: "Seeing these brave youths taking so eagerly and without inner conflict to hard physical labor and looking toward their future with confidence, one comes to the conclusion that the great spirit of Israel is still alive, that faith in their own strength has not yet been destroyed among the children of Israel."[91]

The ideological unity within the group led to the establishment of a colony thoroughly socialistic in design. Members lived together as one household and all property was communal. The fourteen who originally worked on the farm labored communally; the others, who temporarily worked in cities, gave their earnings to the colony's communal fund.[92] In their constitution, the colonists voiced the Am Olam concern with demonstrating to the world the productive abilities of the Jewish people and outlined their purpose and design:

> The colony Bethlehem Judea is founded . . . to help the Jewish people in its emancipation from slavery and in its rehabilitation to a new truth, freedom, and peace. The colony shall demonstrate to the enemies of our people the world over that Jews are capable of farming. . . .
>
> All members of the colony Bethlehem Judea must engage in farming. Only when all work on the farm is finished may they engage in other productive occupations. Commercial activity is absolutely forbidden. (This point cannot be revised.) All members of the colony form one family enjoying the same rights and privileges. . . .
>
> The colony considers it its duty to continue the colonization of Russian Jews in America through the establishment of new colonies.
>
> The new colonies thus established form one community with the mother colony and are subject to its regulations . . .
>
> Women shall enjoy equal rights with men.[93]

The constitution of the settlement exemplifies the major themes of Am Olam ideology. First, the concern with productivizing Jewish economic life and demonstrating this productivization to the world is emphasized as the key purpose of the colony. The sense of mission is further demonstrated by the emphasis on the colony's role in enabling additional colonies to be founded: one-third of the colony's income was to be set aside as a colonization fund.

The Am Olam belief in farming as the sole means to achieving this productivization is expressed in the clause stipulating that all colony members must farm. The utopian and socialist elements of Am Olam ideology are demonstrated in the clauses emphasizing equality among members, and the stress on family and community as the models for the colony.

Despite their lofty ambitions, the communal way of life proved too much for the Bethlehem Judea group. As conditions improved, disagreements among the colonists about work assignments and agricultural decisions increased.[94] After eighteen months, the colony was divided into private holdings. The president of the colony, Saul Sokolovski, explained that, after the initial period in which members were dependent upon one another, collective life became difficult as members began to conclude that they could manage their own affairs. Although Sokolovski insisted that collective projects could be successful "with select human material," he moved to a position that emphasized the importance of Jewish farming over the specific socioeconomic design of a colony.[95]

As private farmers, the colonists of Bethlehem Judea succumbed to the same difficulties that plagued their neighbors at Cremieux. Their agricultural endeavors were stymied by natural disasters, including drought, storms, and insects. The experience that the settlers had gained on eastern farms before migrating to South Dakota did not prepare them for prairie conditions or prairie crops. Finally, the support that they received from the Jewish community was insufficient. The colony, like Cremieux, was disbanded in 1885.[96]

The emphasis on collective life in the Bethlehem Judea colony was replicated in a second Am Olam colony, founded in Oregon in January of 1883. This colony, known as New Odessa, was established by the first group of Odessa Am Olam and was the most successful western settlement, lasting five years.[97] The relative success at New Odessa resulted from a combination of support from the established Jewish community, well-suited human capital, and location.

From the beginning of their odyssey, the Odessa Am Olam group had attracted attention from potential sponsors. Although some western Jewish leaders were so dismayed by the group's liberal views on religion that they wrote letters to America warning of the colonists' radicalism, the group impressed enough of the Jewish leadership to obtain good support. Arriving in Brody in November of 1881, this group, like the Elizavetgrad group that had preceded it, impressed the Alliance Israélite Universelle with its concrete plans. Because they were too late to be included in the AIU-financed transport on which the Elizavetgrad group had traveled to the United States, the Odessa group could have been returned to Russia, but "the combination of its youth and its agrarianism appealed to various individual leaders in the Jewish communities in the West, particularly to Dr. Landsberg [the rabbi of Lugmitz] and to Professor Bernstein [of the alliance in Berlin]."[98]

Upon arrival in the United States, the group was aided by Michael Heilprin and other Jewish leaders, including Jacob Schiff.[99] According to Herman Rosenthal, leader of the Sicily Island and Cremieux settlements, the colony's New York supporters had been impressed by "the order and discipline which prevailed among them" while they lived communally in New York. These supporters "admired their modes of behavior in finding work for their members, and their rejection of all assistance from the various immigrant aid societies which were founded in those days."[100] Heilprin was instrumental in obtaining aid for the colonization project.[101] In a letter written in November of 1883, Heilprin justified this aid. Claiming that the failure in Louisiana resulted from "hasty action and improper choice of the locality," Heilprin wrote, referring to the New Odessa group, that among the Jewish immigrants "there were not a few whose firm determination or ardent desire to devote themselves to agricultural pursuits, in the land which was to become their new home, deserved special attention." The aid, Heilprin reported, had been used for initial expenses on land, animals, implements, and travel, but further maintenance was not required. His assessment of the group's future was optimistic: "The young men have done a great deal of hard work, their zeal has not abated, and the future of the colony is promising. It is able to maintain itself in spite of trying privation and scantiness of means—even if no further aid whatever is afforded it; generous assistance could rapidly make it flourishing and promote its expansion."[102]

The actions of the New Odessa group gave their sponsors much reason for optimism. The group demonstrated its unity and determination while still in New York, members building the communal fund through work as farmhands, longshoremen, and railroad men. Those in the New York commune practiced the collective style of living that they hoped to establish in the colony. Meanwhile scouts were sent to find a favorable location for the settlement. The scouts sent to the Pacific Northwest, led by William Frey, a non-Jewish former Russian nobleman, military officer, and professor of mathematics who had experience in a Russian communal agricultural settlement in America, located a site in Douglas County, Oregon. The site consisted of 910 acres, 700 of which were covered with forest.[103]

Upon locating the site, owned by a wealthy, local Jewish merchant, and placing as a down payment money raised by Heilprin, a group of twenty-five men and nine women were selected from among the three Odessa Am Olam groups that had arrived in New York by July 1882. The colonists journeyed to Oregon via Panama, a particularly arduous journey in the days before the

Panama Canal. While slightly more than half of the group remained in Portland to work, eight or ten proceeded directly to the colony.[104] According to Rosenthal's account, a number of colonists became discouraged at this point, and left the group.[105] Others, apparently, were only too eager to begin work in the colony—one who was assigned to work in Portland became so impatient that he left the city and traveled 250 miles by foot to the colony site.[106]

By the spring of 1883, the colony was home to between forty and fifty people. Most of the membership consisted of young, single males. Of the forty-seven people who resided in the colony by August, there were thirty-six men (four of whom were married), seven women, and four children. The adult membership ranged in age from nineteen to thirty-eight.[107] Although the colonists made several errors at first—after planting corn in an area more suited to cattle, they found themselves priced out of a grain market dominated by the railroad interests—they soon achieved economic stability by signing a contract to supply lumber to the railroad. The colonists concentrated their energy on the fulfillment of the railroad contract, which would provide the first installment payment on the farm. In the first two years, four thousand cords of lumber were cut, and sold for between seven thousand and eight thousand dollars. On the land cleared, colonists planted additional crops that were primarily for consumption within the settlement. Meanwhile a few colonists with specialized skills worked outside the settlement, placing their wages into the communal fund.[108] Title to the land, which had been bought in the name of colonist Simon Krimont in March of 1883 for twenty-eight hundred dollars (at 8 percent interest), was transferred to the New Odessa Community in 1884, after the colony was legally incorporated.[109]

Life in New Odessa was strictly communal, with an emphasis on moral and intellectual development. From the beginning, this group of Odessa Am Olam members had been socialist in orientation, adopting the motto "United we stand, divided we fall," which was engraved in English on their seal. Sokolovski, of the Bethlehem Judea colony, wrote of the New Odessa colonists: "The life of the colonists is fully established on a cooperative basis, with the national basis completely lacking. The colonists are permeated by cosmopolitan tendencies and regard the colony as an international organization."[110] Colonists lived together in a large, two-story building with sleeping quarters upstairs and dining room, kitchen, and assembly hall below.[111] A reporter for the *Overland Monthly* who visited the colony found that the colonists had fully embraced the communal life-style. He observed that, except the few married couples, all the community members slept—and spent most of their time—in a large common room, with a corner reserved for the women. The accommodations were rough, and all the sparse furnishings homemade. The food was equally plain; most meals consisted of "bean soup and hard baked biscuits of unbolted flour called after the name of that wretched dyspeptic Graham."[112]

The reporter emphasized the moral tone of the community. The colonists had rejected religion, he reported, and had no formal code of behavior, but instead concentrated on simply being good: "One of their young women once replied to me, when I remonstrated her for some unusual act of courtesy, exclaiming 'You are too good!' 'Why we cannot be too good.'" The principal colony activity was intellectual—the settlers engaged almost constantly in debates, discussion, and reading, mainly on philosophical issues.

The communal philosophy was clearly stated in the articles of incorporation filed at the Douglas County Court House in late 1883. The object of the corporation was "mutual assistance in perfecting and development of physical, mental and moral capacities of its members." The economic basis for the colony was also elaborated: "Said corporation has no capital stock and no shares. The money and labor voluntarily offered by the members shall never be credited for the individual benefits of donators nor claimed back by withdrawing members but used only to promote the object herein specified."[113]

In accordance with both the Am Olam philosophy and with the stated policy of earlier settlements, all members of the community were considered equal. Whether the theoretical equality between the sexes held true in practice, either at New Odessa or at Bethlehem Judea (where equality between the sexes had also been established in principle), is not entirely clear. Both settlements had few female members, and there are few glimpses of women in the accounts of these colonies. The observations that are available present a picture of a group of people who, while not achieving full equality between the sexes by modern standards, were clearly questioning and attempting to reform the norms that dominated their society. As one New Odessa member wrote, "In the beginning the women had demanded full equal rights. They had gone to work in the forest, with the men taking their turn in the kitchen and laundry. Soon, however, the women realized that they were not yet fit for that type of work and they returned to their previous tasks. Now they assure us that they have acquired the necessary physical strength and endurance for working in the forest."[114] There is no evidence that the transition of women back into the more physically demanding jobs occurred before the colony's demise. However, the men did continue to take turns serving as cook on Sundays.[115]

The lengthiest account of women in the colony is found in the *Overland Monthly* description of a wedding at New Odessa, an account clouded by the author's rather traditional and romantic view of women (he repeatedly refers to the women as "charming flowers," and calls their sleeping quarters a "nest of maidenhood"). Here we see that the bride and groom were marrying out of love, and that the decision to marry was made jointly. The free choice of the bride in marrying was also stressed in the words spoken to the bride in a ceremony performed by a fellow community member:

> Oh maiden, let no fear
> Of aught now keep thee here,
> Only confidence in him
> That he will his life so trim,
> As to bring both joy,
> Joy, joy, only joy
> If you think this,
> If you hope bliss
> If thou lovest him only,
> And without him art lonely,
> If thou wilt bless his strength
> To his virtue give length
> And ever be truest wife
> Yielding to him thy sweet life,
> Then prepare the pledge to say,
> Or if not, thou mayst speak nay.[116]

Here, though the freedom of the bride in making her choice is stressed, it is also recognized that in marrying, she will be giving up her freedom—a legal fact that they could hardly ignore. It appears that New Odessa colonists, though perhaps not achieving full equality between the sexes, were striving earnestly to achieve that goal.

Over time, the colony's social, cultural, moral, and intellectual life was increasingly led by William Frey, whom the colonists, feeling "that they needed people who were experienced communitarians who could guide the future teachers of humanity as to how to achieve their goals," persuaded to join them.[117] The selection of a non-Jewish leader is a further indication of the colonists' self-image as internationalists.

Frey, a devotee of both communism and positivism, not only had experience in agricultural colonization but also had developed strong ties with the Am Olam groups in New York. In his autobiography, Abraham Cahan recalls Frey's lectures to the group "in which he argued for brotherhood, communism, vegetarianism, non-resistance, and against violence and revolution." Frey's faith "was compounded out of communism and Comtism; to these he added vegetarianism, and ate only fruits and vegetables." In Cahan's view, Frey was a fanatic, but Cahan was impressed by his devotion to his ideals and his high level of morality. "I never left him," writes Cahan, "without feeling the way a *hasidic* Jew feels after visiting his *rebbe*."[118]

Frey's arrival in Oregon was, according to one colonist, "a milestone in the history of our 'commune'." Although the colony had no constitution, a strict regimen emerged under Frey's leadership, as recorded in a letter from a colonist:

> We work from six o'clock in the morning till half-past eight in the morning . . . [then] we have breakfast. Work is resumed at ten o'clock and continued to four o'clock in the afternoon. [Next] is dinner, followed by a rest period and intellectual activity. Monday, Tuesday, Thursday, and Friday are devoted to the study of mathematics, English, and to Frey's lecture on the philosophy of positivism. On Wednesday, current matters are discussed and on Saturday, the problems of the 'commune'. On Sunday we rise . . . and immediately a lively discussion begins on the subject of equal rights for women. . . . After breakfast, one member goes to survey the farm, another reads a newspaper or a book, the rest sing, shout and dance. [Later] dinner is served. Two men wash the dishes, the choir sings, the organ plays. . . . [Then] begins a session of mutual criticism; then the work for the week is assigned."[119]

The structured life that emerged at New Odessa was noted by visitors. Many visitors praised the colony's cleanliness and discipline. Even critics praised these aspects of colony life. For example, Herman Rosenthal, an outspoken critic who referred to Frey as "this narrowminded man," wrote, "The settlement 'New Odessa' became an agricultural model to its neighboring farmers. Their work was organized and regimented." Similarly, another critic, Rabbi Judah Wechsler of St. Paul, Minnesota, commented, "The colonists are the most intelligent Russian immigrants I have ever encountered." He marveled at their library and noted, "the cleanliness of their houses and the order of all their activities pleased me greatly."[120]

Despite their praise for the colony's achievements, such critics, as well as a growing group of colonists, were troubled by Frey's philosophy and dominance of the settlement. Not surprisingly, Rabbi Wechsler was concerned that "they do not observe the Sabbath. They desecrate the Holidays and they told me directly that they are completely disinterested definitely in Judaism." Wechsler's observations were accurate—Frey himself reported that although the colonists "are proud of their nationality," they had abandoned Judaism as a religion.[121]

Disinterest in Judaism was hardly unique to the New Odessa colony. Am Olam as a movement had little Jewish content and none of the earlier colonies had instituted any religious ritual. Yet even secularists were concerned that Frey's "Religion of Humanity" was having a detrimental effect on the colonists. Thus, Herman Rosenthal—the leader of the two nonreligious colonies of Sicily Island and Cremieux—expressed concern that Frey's teachings were resulting in Jewish self-hatred. According to Rosenthal, Frey taught that 'the Jew is narrowminded and self-centered," and that "no faith is able to exist without Jews believing in it." Rosenthal claimed that Frey's teachings led his followers to regard themselves "as the twelve disciples of Jesus."[122]

As Frey's followers became increasingly devoted to him "with a zeal and fervor approaching hero worship,"[123] a rift developed between them and a second group of colonists, led by Paul Kaplan. According to Rosenthal, Frey and his followers began to impose his philosophy on the group: "His sermons, which were as fresh dew to his disciples, were a source of derision for those who did not accept this faith; others paid no attention at all to his talks. All of this angered Frey and his disciples, and they would attack and bitterly criticize their opponents."[124] Robert Rosenbluth, son of colonists Selig and Annuta Glantz Rosenbluth, who were married in New Odessa in 1883, confirms Rosenthal's account, pointing to the rift between Frey and his followers, and the Kaplan group, as the principal cause of the colony's eventual dissolution.[125]

Abraham Cahan, a friend of Kaplan's, also documented this rift as a primary cause of the demise of the colony. According to Cahan, "Frey was determined to impose a positivist character on the colony, with the members following the tenets of Comte's religion of humanity and, in addition, not eating meat." Kaplan, who disagreed with Frey's philosophy and methods, was angered by many of his innovations. Observers reported that when the group gathered around Frey's organ to sing positivist songs, Kaplan would "stand aside, disturbing the peaceful mood with a bitter sardonic smile on his face." Most of the colonists, according to Cahan, did not agree with Frey's philosophy, but they had so much respect for him that they did not challenge him until, because of his growing influence, "his positivism became more burdensome" and, with Kaplan's open opposition, "peace diminished."[126]

These ideological clashes, rather than the natural disasters and debt that plagued earlier settlements, were responsible for the demise of the colony. As Rosenthal noted, "Had it not been for the controversy regarding the various ideals, differing aspirations, and false visions, they would have succeeded; they would have acquired a great deal of wealth and would have served as a model for wandering exiled brethren."[127] In assessing the demise of New Odessa, Abraham Cahan also focused on ideological problems, although he looked beyond the differences between Frey and Kaplan to a larger problem with communalism. Cahan, who saw the failure as a confirmation of his belief "that socialism could come only as the result of a social revolution and that such a revolution would have to be on a world scale," believed that the New Odessa failure demonstrated the difficulties inherent in communalism within a capitalist system. Although recognizing the important role of the schism between Frey's followers and detractors in the demise of the colony, Cahan argued that tensions were increased by resentment about inequities in labor performed by different members, lack of privacy, rural isolation, and sexual jealousies. These tensions were increased because the colonists, as victims of a capitalist system, had to work too hard. Frustrations grew, according to Cahan, because some "insisted that communism required literal togetherness: eating from the same bowl, sleeping in the same bedrooms." None of these difficulties resulted in outward clashes until the opening of the fissure between Frey and Kaplan provided the opportunity to vent frustrations openly. The mutual criticism sessions became a forum for such conflicts.[128]

Whether these ideological clashes were an inherent problem of a communal experiment within a capitalist system, as Cahan believed, or incidental to this specific project, as Cahan's friend, Kaplan, argued,[129] they succeeded in tearing New Odessa apart. Frey and his followers left the settlement in an emotional departure, apparently without enmity on either side. Shortly afterward, a fire destroyed the community building and library—the heart of the settlement—hastening the departure of the remaining colonists. Some of the members remained together, starting short-lived communes in San Francisco and New York.[130]

An additional, poorly documented Am Olam colony was an unnamed settlement in Arkansas. No organizational records of this colony remain and only one firsthand account, an unpublished memoir written by Kate Herder, who was a young child when she lived in the settlement, survives.[131] Like the first colony in the Deep South, Sicily Island, the Arkansas colony folded within one year.

During the spring of 1883, a group of about 150 people left New York for Arkansas after receiving a tempting offer to settle on a tract of land and supply staves to a lumber company. At first, the thickly forested site looked promising to the colonists, who wrote back to New York of the Eden they had discovered. Although the connection of the first group of settlers to the Am Olam is unclear, their letter was received by one of the Odessa Am Olam groups waiting in New York for just such an opportunity. A group of about thirty Am Olam members, including three families, quickly moved to Arkansas and, with their own money, purchased land near that of the first group.[132]

The Am Olam group included cofounder Moses Herder, his wife, and four young children, including Kate. A second Am Olam member, Goldstein, who, like Herder, later joined the Carmel, New Jersey, settlement, also joined the Arkansas colony. Besides the thirty Am Olam members who journeyed from New York, two former Sicily Island colonists joined the Arkansas settlement.[133]

The exact organization of the colony remains unclear, but the memoir of Kate Herder, about seven years old when her family moved to Arkansas, provides some detail on the work and hardships in the colony. Herder's memoir indicates that the families lived in a group house: "We lived in that house for some time and we were not the only family neither [*sic*]. There must have been about four more besides ours." Similarly, it appears that the group made purchases as a unit, as Herder writes that "all the families scraped together all the money they had. They coaxed the owner of the house to let them have the horse and wagon only to the store and back because they were going to buy a big supply of the most necessary things they needed." The memoir also records the gathering of the staves to fulfill the lumber contract: "Father would go around with an ax and chop around the twigs and bushes around the big trees, and we children would pick all the twigs together and make a big pile of them. And for this work that all the family did from the oldest child to the youngest including Father and Mother, we got instead of money from the man that owned ever so much land, cows, pigs, and horses, yellow corn meal, matches, and the water that drips off the cheese." Although Herder does describe a makeshift Passover meal, in which coffee had to substitute for wine, the acceptance of pigs in payment for work indicates that, as on the other colonies, Jewish ritual was quite lax. Herder's memoir also makes note of the heavy rains, floods, and frequent visits to the colony by rattlesnakes.[134]

The general conditions of the settlement described by Herder's memoir are confirmed in the only other account of the colony, a *Jewish Tribune* article written in 1929, based on interviews with a few of the Arkansas survivors.[135] This account focuses on the difficult conditions in the colony, caused primarily by the harsh climate. Efforts to bring staves to market were thwarted by frequent floods. Summer temperatures higher than 100 degrees made daytime work impossible. Only two log shacks and a barn provided shelter, as construction on a larger building was never completed. Because of the shortage of living quarters, there was only room for the women and children to sleep inside; the men had to sleep in the open. Snakes were a common problem, as were frequent rainstorms. The climate made the colony a perfect breeding ground for mosquitoes, who brought with them not only discomfort but also disease. The *Tribune* account records that 90 percent of the colonists caught malaria or yellow fever, and eighteen to twenty of the settlers died. According to this account, the smaller group of Am Olam members returned to New York first, and brought with them a letter from the others to the Am Olam leadership in New York, "describing the sufferings and misery of the colonists and begging for aid to get away from the plague infected country."[136] Accounts differ on the time it took the Arkansas colony to be abandoned, but its lifespan was definitely less than two years, and, in all likelihood, less than one.[137]

Except the New Jersey settlements that are the focus of this study, the remaining colonies founded in the early 1880s were extremely short-lived and are not well documented. Many of them differed from the earlier attempts in several respects. First, for many of these experiments, such as the two colonies near Washington, D.C., and the Painted Woods colony in North Dakota, there exists no clear connection with the Am Olam organization, either ideologically or organizationally. Second, many, such as the Beersheba, Kansas, colony and the Painted Woods colony were not only financed by but were also organized by American Jewish sponsors, rather than by the immigrants themselves. Some of these colonies undoubtedly had members connected to or inspired by the Am Olam. For example, Sidney Baily, when discussing the various Am Olam activities in the West, mentions in his memoir that "the energetic Meeker was leading some [colonies] in Kansas."[138] However, Meeker's identity is unclear and it is not stated which colony he led. The existing records on these colonies make additional connections to the Am Olam difficult to establish.

Of these colonies, those in Kansas were the most significant in population and endurance. Seven colonies were established in Kansas, including Hebron, Moses Montefiore, Beersheba, and Lasker. Hebron, financed by Heilprin's Montefiore Agricultural Aid Society (MAAS), was founded by a large group of eighty families, about half of whom had their own means, but it was extremely short-lived. The remaining three, Gilead, Touro, and Leeser, were very small, with about 40 families among them, and were founded in 1886, after the dissolution of the Am Olam.[139]

The most interesting and well-documented of these efforts was the first of the Kansas colonies, orchestrated by Rabbi Isaac Mayer Wise of Cincinnati. Beersheba colony was founded on government land by sixty Russian Jews in 1882. Lasting four years, the Beersheba colony's history is most significant for the light it sheds on the difficulties of a sponsor-run colony. The tensions between colonists and sponsors foreshadowed many of the problems that developed in the New Jersey colonies. Although the demise of Beersheba colony was for many years attributed to the usual difficulties of drought, injudicious choice of location, and inexperience of the colonists, a more recent study by historian Lipman Goldman Feld concludes that the sponsors played a significant role in the Beersheba colony's failure.[140]

The Cincinnati Society played a much more prominent role in organizing the colony than did sponsors of the other western colonies, and, because of their unfamiliarity with farming, made several key mistakes early on. The site chosen was considered inappropriate by both a railroad agent and Jewish leaders in Kansas City. Kansas City's Rabbi Eppstein wrote in his diary, "We now learn that the land they had in view was situated near Dodge City, a sandy barren district which is not a fitting place for farming."[141] Charles K.

Davis, agent of the Cincinnati Society, traveled with the colonists to Kansas in late July 1882. In his diary, Davis admits that though many people were consulted about the proper site for the colony, none had seen the site.[142] Davis, not a farmer himself, also made errors in buying supplies for the colonists. For example, he purchased an expensive mower—a machine for cutting grass or wheat—before the land had been plowed or planted, but he failed to buy adequate machinery and farm animals to plant the wheat.[143]

Tense relations between the sponsor's agents and the colonists complicated the situation. Davis's patronizing attitude toward the colonists is evident throughout his diary. When colonists came to Davis with health and other problems, he wrote that they "act like a lot of children." On several occasions, Davis, a young man himself, patronizingly referred to the male colonists as "the boys." During the journey to the colony site, Davis worried continually about the impression his charges were making on the non-Jews with whom they came in contact. Thus he supervised the colonists in cleaning up their temporary quarters in town twice daily, remarking, "I don't want the landlords to make any remarks about their habits." Similarly, when some of the colonists took sardines from the group's supplies, Davis wrote, "They almost worry me to death as I want to hide their conduct from the people of Kansas City, especially the Gentiles who have never seen Russians before because I don't want them to form a poor opinion of our people."[144] Despite Davis's concern, the colonists were warmly welcomed by the farmers near the colony, and the townspeople of nearby Ravanna took a great interest in the colony, even allowing the Jews to bury their dead in the town cemetery.[145]

The supervision of the Cincinnati Society continued after the establishment of the colony, and caused increasing resentment among the colonists. A Hungarian farmer, Joseph Baum, was appointed supervisor of the colony, ruling the colony "with terror" and expelling those colonists he considered undesirable. The resentment of Baum by the colonists was recorded in Rabbi Eppstein's diary: "By all those members of the colony who retraced their steps and came here [to Kansas City], Mr. Baum was spoken of as a man who acts partial and in some respects dishonest not only toward the colonists but also toward the general committee." The Cincinnati Society disregarded such reports, believing Baum's claims "that all these he has sent off were lazy and would not work and that with such men no soil could be made a success."[146]

Despite the tendency of both Davis and Baum to regard the colonists as lazy or childlike, the immigrants proved to be industrious in their money-making efforts. Indeed, the colonists became increasingly interested in business ventures and "began to view their stay in Beersheba as nothing more than a stepping stone for another future." Without the knowledge of their Cincinnati

sponsors, the colonists opened a store in nearby Ravanna.[147] In 1884, the settlers seized an opportunity to earn cash by leasing a right-of-way through their
land to the cattle syndicate.

The sponsors were outraged at the colonists' independence in agreeing to
this transaction, "for the Society resented having the colonists doing anything
without their approval first."[148] Despite the fact that the colonists still had more
land than they could cultivate and a report by Davis defending the legitimacy
of the transaction, the sponsors responded by taking from the colonists their
stock and implements. A receipt given to one Beersheba colonist listed the
possessions taken: "One pair oxen, two cows, one calf, one wagon, one yoke,
one chain, one well bucket and rope, axe, shovel, churn, twelve milk pans,
two milk buckets, hatchet, wheel-barrow, hand saw, file wrench, corn knife,
one pair boots, one straw hat, one bale of wire."[149] The vindictiveness of the
sponsors in taking the colonists' possessions—down to their buckets, hats, and
boots—amounted to a deliberate effort to ruin the colony.

Despite the wrath of the sponsors, the colonists' deal with the cattle syndicate provided them with enough cash to replace their possessions and continue the settlement. In 1885, several local papers published favorable reports
on conditions in the colony. In that year, many of the colonists took on new
occupations, either besides or instead of farming. Most of the colonists did
move on to pursue careers as merchants in larger cities in subsequent years, as
Ravanna became a ghost town.[150]

Thus the ultimate demise of Beersheba colony resulted neither from poor
conditions, the inexperience of the colonists, nor the vindictive actions of the
sponsors, but from a gradual decision by the people involved to move on to
other ventures. As Feld notes, "They utilized this period of their residence in
the colony to become Americanized and acquire assets that could help them in
these pursuits. After leaving Beersheba, several borrowed money on their
homestead titles to go into business."[151] Because there is no evidence that the
Beersheba colonists shared the Am Olam's goals or philosophies, it is difficult
to pass judgment on the colony. It did not succeed as a colony, but it clearly
acclimated the colonists and provided them the financial start to strike out on
their own. Depending on what their initial goals had been, it might be that
the Beersheba colony was successful by the colonists' standards.

In contrast to Beersheba, the remaining Kansas colonies never achieved
economic stability. At first, Moses Montefiore colony, named for the famous
English, Jewish banker-philanthropist, appeared to hold great promise, but its
significance lies not in any success it achieved but in the connections of its
members to other colonization projects. Montefiore colony, sponsored by
Michael Heilprin, included a few of the survivors of the Arkansas colony,
demonstrating that it did have at least a tentative connection to Am Olam.[152]

In addition, a few of its survivors went on to settle in the Alliance colony in New Jersey.[153] The Montefiore colony itself never got off the ground, because when, in April 1884, a group of thirty settlers arrived from New York to join the earlier settlers, they found that there was not enough desirable government land. Others, who had obtained land there, found the soil unsuitable and were soon forced to sell.[154]

Seventeen of the Montefiore families, again with the help of Heilprin, soon settled on another site in southwestern Kansas, which became Lasker colony. Colonists made claims on quarter sections of 160 acres under the Homestead law. The colony never achieved economic stability—their efforts were thwarted by lack of water, poor crops, low prices, and wild horses. While still in New York, the group decided that members would rotate between colony and city; those in the city would contribute to the colony fund. Although this plan was followed only in part, those in the city did continue to contribute, but their help was not enough to save the settlement.[155]

Despite the colony's economic difficulties, it did achieve an active social life and a unique organization. At first, the colonists lived in one large sod house, but soon six houses were built to house six groups. This heterogeneous group of colonists decided on this living arrangement because they were "fearful lest divergent religious or economic viewpoints might disrupt the colony." Thus each living group "was composed of people of like temperament and was granted autonomy in the conduct of its affairs." The groups met together in the evenings for discussions and debate. A library was established using all the books that the members had brought with them. Differences among the groups did not disrupt the social life of the settlement: "One group was religiously orthodox in its practice—the others, if not irreligious, were nonreligious. Still they all fraternized." Even the nonreligious helped to form the *minyan* (group of ten men necessary to perform a religious service) on the High Holidays.[156]

This harmonious existence ended with a combination of a poor colony economy and a land boom in the area. As a land company bought tracts for an irrigation project in 1886, land prices boomed. The colonists, faced with a serious economic situation, could not resist selling out at inflated prices, and the colony was quickly abandoned.[157]

✳✳✳

Efforts to establish agricultural colonies in the United States in the early 1880s demonstrate dedication to the central tenets of the Am Olam. All the colonies established emphasized the importance of introducing Jews to productive agricultural labor and of demonstrating this productivity to the world.

Yet despite their unity in emphasizing these goals, the colonies that were established exhibited much variation, particularly in economic organization. Much of this uncertainty can be traced to the Am Olam itself—the membership agreed on the centrality of productivization through agriculture, but the organization's position on communal versus private ownership was quite vague. Despite the outspoken communal stance of students and intellectuals who came to dominate the Odessa group, this chapter contained a contingent who believed that their labor on the land should lead to private ownership. Outside Odessa, there was no clear economic program shared by Am Olam chapters.

The vagueness within the Am Olam as to the socioeconomic design of the colonies was compounded upon arrival in America by the participation in colonies of persons not part of the organization. The indecisiveness about the economic structure of the colonies led to much variation in design, from the strict communism of New Odessa and Bethlehem Judea to the mixed communal-private design of Sicily Island and Cremieux, and the even less communal Beersheba.

Variations among colonies were directly linked to the degree of heterogeneity within each group of colonists. In New Odessa and Bethlehem Judea, the most communal of the settlements, colonists were primarily young, single, male students and intellectuals who were all Am Olam members. In contrast, in those settlements with mixed populations, including Am Olam adherents and nonmembers, single people and families, and intellectuals and workers, mixed economies emerged. Finally, in the sponsor-led effort at Beersheba, the colonists, none of whom had any clear link to Am Olam, were oriented not only toward private ownership but also toward trade rather than agriculture.

Besides influencing the socioeconomic design of the colony, the mix of colonists had an impact on the fate of each colony. Aside from the colonies where natural disasters or weather conditions led to colony failure (as in the Louisiana and Arkansas experiments), the cause of the dissolution of each colony was influenced by the composition of its population. In the two most homogeneous, doctrinaire colonies, New Odessa and Bethlehem Judea, philosophical differences and intellectual isolation took a heavy toll. Disputes among the colonists at Bethlehem Judea did not bring the colony to an end, but they did cause the settlers to abandon their original design and divide the colony into private holdings. At New Odessa, the philosophical differences between Frey's followers and detractors produced a severe schism in the colony. In both colonies, the disproportionate number of males led to social difficulties, and cultural isolation frustrated the intellectually oriented settlers. Thus the loss of the New Odessa library dealt the final blow to that colony.

In contrast, the more heterogeneous colonies that were not ruined by natural disaster apparently did not experience the degree of division over philosophical issues that developed at New Odessa and Bethlehem Judea. In Lasker, philosophical differences were accepted as a vital part of colony life, and the group-living plan allowed colonists with different philosophical and religious orientations to live together harmoniously. The failure of Lasker as a colony resulted from the decision of the economically strapped settlers to take advantage of inflated real estate prices and to move on to other ventures. Similarly, the Beersheba colonists abandoned their colony not because of internal differences but because they found more lucrative opportunities in other fields.

The experiences of these settlements have strong parallels in the New Jersey colonies. As in the western colonies, where the choice of location was central in determining the outcome of the experiment, the location of the New Jersey colonies played a crucial role in their development. The New Jersey colonies, in a temperate region, avoided the extremes of heat and cold that plagued colonies in both the Deep South and the northern plains. In addition, the convenient location of South Jersey to both markets and cultural life in New York and Philadelphia enabled the colonists to avoid the social and economic isolation of the western settlements.

The South Jersey location had drawbacks as well as advantages. Although the settlements' convenient location provided access to cultural and economic opportunities, it made the project attractive to settlers who, though helping bolster the economy, greatly altered the character of the colonies, and caused them to deviate significantly from the original Am Olam goals. In addition, the proximity to the large Jewish communities of New York and Philadelphia, though providing access to increased financial aid from sponsors, also increased the ability of sponsors to oversee the daily life of the colonies, resulting in some of the same sponsor-colonist tensions that plagued Beersheba. Despite the temperate climate, the location did not guarantee ideal farming conditions. As in Arkansas and Louisiana, where the presence of thick forests deceived the settlers into overestimating the productive capacity of the land, the New Jersey land, covered by pine forest, was soon revealed to be composed of sandy soil, ill-suited for the grain crops the settlers had planned.

The location of the Jersey colonies had a tremendous impact on the composition of the settler population. Although none of the New Jersey groups were ever as homogeneous as the New Odessa or Bethlehem Judea settlers, the Jersey colonies were dominated at first by an Am Olam contingent, sharing an intellectual orientation and a South Pale background. Yet the proximity to New York and Philadelphia made the colonies an attractive destination to new settlers who wanted to leave the city for reasons unrelated to ideological agrarianism. The increasing heterogeneity of the settler population had a tremendous influence on development in New Jersey. As the colonies grew and became increasingly heterogeneous, with Am Olam members and those of South Pale origin losing ground to new groups of settlers, the Jersey colonies were transformed from agrarian, semicommunal colonies into mixed agricultural–industrial settlements based on private ownership.

This transition in the character of the colonies, and the related change in the type of settler arriving in the colony after the initial period, was influenced greatly by the colony sponsors. As in the western colonies, the sponsors enlisted to support the colonies had an impact on the outcome of the New Jersey experiment. The extent and type of sponsorship could determine a colony's chance of success and the direction that colony life would take. In the next chapter, the motives and goals of the philanthropists who took on sponsorship of the New Jersey colonists are examined. Their influence and that of the changing settler population in shaping the colonies are examined in chapters 4, 5, and 6.

3

Colony Sponsors

THE IDEALISTIC ENTHUSIASM of the Am Olam pioneers who migrated
to the United States during the early 1880s could not alone ensure the
successful establishment of the proposed colonies. The settlers had to secure
land, and to buy seed, agricultural implements, work animals, and supplies to
support their colonies until the first harvest. The groups that sent their members out to earn money for their communal funds found their earnings to be
woefully inadequate.

The lack of capital made the outcome of the Am Olam's projects dependent on the aid of European- and American-Jewish relief organizations. These
organizations, responding to the westward flow of refugees in 1881 and subsequent years, were enlisted as sponsors for the various Am Olam projects. Aiding the colonies for various reasons seldom coinciding with the colonists' own
goals, these sponsors played a major role in determining the outcome of the
colonization experiments.

Established western Jewish communities, inundated with refugees in the
aftermath of the 1881 and 1882 pogroms, reluctantly began to accept responsibility for aiding the migrants during the decade after the crisis. A series of
organizations was established to direct the migration and aid the mass of refugees, which included the Am Olam colonists. Yet these western sponsors seldom shared the objectives of their Am Olam clients, and the forms of aid that
they offered were determined by their own needs, motives, and goals. Shaped
both by their experiences as western Jews and capitalists, and by prevailing
western philosophies of philanthropy, these sponsors developed aid policies
that, although saving the colonies from extinction, caused them to deviate
significantly from their original blueprints. In this chapter, the sponsors' motives and their goals for their immigrant clients are explored. The specific
impact of sponsor policies on the New Jersey settlements is analyzed in the
chapters that follow.

The level of involvement of American and European Jewish leaders as colony sponsors varied. The French Alliance Israélite Universelle played a central role in enabling the Am Olam groups to proceed from Brody to the United States. Once in America, although the Am Olam colonies of Cremieux and New Odessa appear to have received only financial support and encouragement from their sponsor, Michael Heilprin's Montefiore Agricultural Aid Society, sponsors of other colonies were more active in planning the colonies and supervising daily affairs. For example, the New Orleans chapter of the Hebrew Emigrant Aid Society had a tremendous impact on the outcome of the Sicily Island colony, for this sponsoring group selected the unsuitable Mississippi River site. Colonies, such as Beersheba in Kansas and, later, Woodbine in New Jersey, both of which lacked clear connections to the Am Olam, were dominated by colony sponsors who selected the settlement sites and inhabitants, and directed daily affairs through on-site supervisors. Although such direct supervision of colony life proved fatal for the Beersheba colony, and led to major disruptions at Woodbine, lack of sponsorship could also doom a colonization experiment.[1]

The inconsistency in colony sponsorship by Jewish immigrant aid organizations was a result of both discrepancies between the goals of the Jewish philanthropic leadership and those of the colonists, and disagreements among the sponsors themselves. Although some members of the Jewish leadership shared with the colonists a romantic desire for a return to agricultural pursuits, the primary aims of the sponsoring organizations contrasted sharply with Am Olam goals. Thus sponsorship of colonization projects was undertaken by organizations with clear agendas of their own. When sponsor and colonist goals clashed, settlers found themselves either without enough money or dominated by sponsor policies and supervisors.

The response of the western Jewish leadership to the Am Olam's plans was rooted both in the circumstances of the post-1880 migration and in the life experiences and values of the leadership. As the situation of Jews in Russia became desperate in the early 1880s, western Jews found themselves faced with a refugee problem that they felt might threaten their position in western society.

Because of their proximity to the crisis, the German-Jewish community was among the first of the western communities to face the refugee problem. As the migration took shape, Germany became the major country of transmigration, and German Jewry took on the responsibility of directing the refugees' journey on the eastern side of the Atlantic.[2] Yet the unique circumstances of German Jewry made this involvement difficult.

In Germany, Jews had been debating the relationship between Judaism and citizenship for a century before the refugee crisis. The argument that Jews would have to abandon all, or at least part, of their Jewish identity to achieve acceptance in Germany was widely accepted. The Reform movement, which blossomed in Germany during the nineteenth century and which emphasized the compatibility of Judaism with German citizenship, was one response to such pressure. A second response was conversion to Christianity, and many German Jews, including members of leading Jewish families, chose this option. In a letter to his daughter upon her conversion to Protestantism, Abraham Mendelsohn (son of *maskilic* leader Moses Mendelsohn), who had raised his children as Protestants, wrote, "By pronouncing your confession of faith, you have fulfilled the claims of society on you."[3]

The pressure of the citizenship debate left several legacies for German Jews that affected their response to the refugee crisis. Faced with an abundance of anti-Semitic literature and sentiment, the German-Jewish community became very internalized, with few organizations to represent the community to the outside world. This insulation left the Jewish community in a defenseless position: "Nearly a century of German pressure had rendered them incapable of any public affirmation of their Jewishness. To fight anti-Semitism would violate the terms of the emancipation."[4] The limited activities of late-nineteenth-century German-Jewish organizations revealed this weakness. For example, the first national German-Jewish organization, the Deutsch-Israelitischer Gemeindebund (German-Israelite Community League, 1869–81) responded to the influx of Russian Jews during a cholera epidemic and famine with plans to resettle the refugees in the Russian interior. Similarly, the community responded to the 1873–74 wave of anti-Semitism within Germany with appeals to the courts, apologetic literature, and internal self-criticism, rather than attempting to counter the attacks with self-affirming measures. Not until the formation of the Centralverein Deutscher Staatsburger Jüdischen Glaubens (Central Union of German Citizens of the Jewish Faith) in 1893— well after the refugee crisis—did German Jewry begin to reverse its passive and apologetic position.[5]

Although the Russian refugees' ability to find aid in the German-Jewish community was complicated by the German Jews' passive posture, their position was further compromised by a deep-seated prejudice against eastern Jews, or *Ostjuden,* among German Jews. Because German-Jewish assimilation was "not merely the conscious attempt to blend into new social and cultural environments but was also purposeful, even programmatic disassociation from traditional Jewish culture and national moorings," traditional Judaism increasingly became identified as backward, or even pathological. German Jews identified the *Ostjuden* as "dirty, loud, coarse . . . immoral, culturally backward."[6] These attitudes can be seen in the increasingly antagonistic attitude of German Jews toward traditional religious orthodoxy and the use of Yiddish.

The influx of Russian-Jewish refugees in the early 1880s only confirmed many of the German Jews' prejudices. The desperate condition of the eastern Jews reinforced German Jews' patronizing attitudes: "More than ever, the relationship was defined in philanthropic, 'welfare' terms."[7] As quarantines of migrating Jews became necessary because of cholera epidemics among them, the stereotype of the eastern Jew as dirty was confirmed. Such attitudes, compounded by the fear that an influx of Jewish refugees would result in increased anti-Semitism, led German Jews to focus on aid that would prevent mass settlement in Germany. The German government's hostile attitude toward the migrants, which rested on the stereotype of Jews as exploiters, confirmed the Jewish community's fears.[8] Popular stereotypes that linked the refugees with German Jews threatened the position of the German Jews by intimating that, like the refugees, German Jews were also immigrants and fundamentally alien. German authorities believed that dealing with Jewish migrants was "an act of saving their country from a horde of dangerous invaders bent on subverting the economic, political, and social life of the Reich." In their efforts to control the migration, German authorities created policies ranging from expulsion of immigrants to restrictions on residence, employment, and naturalization.[9]

Although somewhat more distant from the events in eastern Europe, the superior organization of the French-Jewish community led to their high level of involvement during the refugee crisis. The French Alliance Israélite Universelle (AIU), the largest and wealthiest Jewish organization in the world, was seen as the logical agency to take charge. As migrants began to cross the border from Russia into Brody, Galicia, in 1881, the AIU sent a representative, Charles Netter, to direct the housing, feeding, and transport of the refugees. Yet like their German counterparts, the French Jews had attitudes toward the migrants that were shaped by their own struggle for emancipation and fear of anti-Semitism. Soon the leadership of the AIU began to question the wisdom of its assumption of responsibility for the refugees and to shy away from aiding the migration.[10]

Although the emancipation of French Jewry had been achieved more smoothly than that of German Jewry, the French experience had created similar attitudes toward the refugees. As in Germany, Jews in France regarded eastern Jews as alien and uncivilized. This view can be traced, in part, to the values of the French Revolution, through which French Jews had achieved citizenship. Strongly influenced by this Revolution-era perspective, French Jews held "a view of society that emphasized the power of education and reason to destroy religious superstition and defined equality not in terms of individual freedom but as the sharing in the heritage of *la patrie*. From this point of view, those who chose to retain Old World traditions were perceived not only as ignorant, but also dangerous to society." Drawing on both this scorn of the traditionalism so rife among Russian Jews and pride in their own emancipation, there was a strong current in both French-Jewish opinion and AIU policy that "called upon Russian Jews to remain in their homeland and to struggle for their rights much as French Jews had done a century before."[11] Indeed, Baron Maurice de Hirsch, a member of the AIU Central Committee and ultimately one of the primary supporters of colonization projects, remained convinced until the mid-1880s that aid to Russian Jews in their homeland was preferable to migration. Hirsch hoped that by giving Russian Jews aid in Russia, he would provide them the opportunity to advance and assimilate in their home society. He believed that such assimilation would ultimately be rewarded with citizenship. The baron was prepared to donate hundreds of millions of francs to education and manual-training programs in Russia toward this end.[12]

Given this sentiment toward eastern Jews, it is not surprising that the AIU, so instrumental during the early days of the refugee crisis, withdrew from aiding the migrants in subsequent years and resisted settlement by the refugees in France throughout the crisis. Besides sharing with German and other western Jews a scorn for their traditional eastern brothers, French Jews were, like their German counterparts, increasingly threatened by anti-Semitism in the late nineteenth century. The fear of anti-Semitic backlash, which peaked during the Dreyfus affair of the 1890s, motivated French Jewry to discourage migration of additional Jews to France.[13] The Franco-Russian alliance, which was solidified shortly after the initial crisis in the early 1880s, further inhibited the ability of French Jews to aid their Russian coreligionists' migration, for many felt that speaking out on persecution in Russia would be embarrassing to the French government.[14]

The attitudes of French Jewry toward Russian Jewry, their concern about a possible anti-Semitic backlash, and their desire to support French foreign policy vis-à-vis Russia, are all evident in the AIU response to the 1881 crisis. Although the 1881 pogroms received much attention in the French press, and prominent Frenchmen joined in protesting the atrocities, the AIU maintained a low profile. Despite the popular outcry against the persecution of Russian Jewry, which would have supported action by the AIU, the organization refused to plan a protest meeting in Paris or to take any other large-scale action. Thus the AIU decided in early 1882 not to push for a parliamentary interpellation. Such inaction by the principal French-Jewish organization most certainly contributed to the decision of the prime minister not to intervene in the affair. Thus the French-Jewish community demonstrated that "in their concern for Jewish rights in Eastern Europe, the first consideration of the western group was the interest of their government's foreign policy."[15]

The reluctance of organized French Jewry to foster migration was exhibited in AIU policy from the moment of Netter's arrival in Brody. At first, Netter aided only those willing to return to Russia by furnishing them with train tickets and cash.[16] Only when the refugees demonstrated that they were unwilling to return did the AIU begin to design alternate plans. Once it became clear that it was impossible to either return the refugees to Russia or to maintain them in Brody, the AIU's primary goal became to divert migration away from France "at all cost."[17] Even as the AIU decided in July 1882 to aid migrants to America, it continued to promote plans to foster the transmigration of Jews into the Russian interior.[18]

The decision of the AIU to direct the migration toward America was consistent with a long-standing belief in the potential of America as a refuge for Jews. As early as 1866, the AIU proposed a large-scale migration of Jews to the United States, but the cool reception the plan received in America prohibited the pursuit of this course of action. After the 1881 crisis, even before the AIU Central Committee voted to appropriate a million francs for migration to America, the AIU sponsored the migration of more than fifteen hundred of the refugees to the United States—with two Am Olam groups among them.[19] Even in the face of the crisis, however, migration plans remained limited—only those refugees already in Brody were to be sent to the United States, according to the AIU policy. By December of 1881, the AIU considered the crisis over, and liquidated its Brody committee.[20]

Yet soon after Netter returned to Paris, Brody was again packed with refugees, many of whom had heard that the AIU would provide free passage to the United States. By early 1882, there were an estimated twenty-four thousand refugees in Galicia, with an urgent need for immediate aid.[21] While appealing for help from German and Austrian philanthropists, the AIU, which found itself spending twenty-five thousand francs a week to clothe and feed the refugees, determined that closing the station was the only way to stem the tide of migrants: "They were morally convinced now that it was the willingness of the Western philanthropic agencies to provide funds—not poverty and persecution in Russia—which was principally responsible for the swelling tide of emigration. They were determined, therefore, to close the dam gates before the tide swamped all orderly procedures."[22] In its effort to liquidate the Brody station, the AIU enlisted the aid of Jewish relief organizations worldwide, developing a plan to allow limited migration of the refugees in Brody to America and other western countries, while returning others to Russia. Returning to Russia was strongly resisted by the refugees, some of whom were returned by force.[23] The end of the Brody crisis in late 1882 marked the end of the AIU's role as the central figure in the aid of eastern refugees.

Although playing less central roles in the refugee crisis, Jewish relief organizations from other European nations expressed similar resistance to migration. In England, where anti-Semitism was of less concern than in either France or Germany, the small Jewish community discouraged immigration largely through neglect. Some immigrants settled in England, but any communal effort to systematically aid immigrants was resisted: "For fear of appearing too hospitable, the major charitable bodies resolutely left immigrants to their own devices."[24] Although English Jews offered minimal amounts of aid for a limited period to those who arrived independently in English ports, organized English Jewry took steps to prevent further refugees from arriving. Thus the London Relief Committee made it clear to the AIU that "none of the Brody refugees were acceptable in England and it would be best to return them to Russia."[25] The committee even published announcements that told refugees directly that they should not come to England. As in France and Germany, leaders of the major Jewish relief organization in England, the Mansion House Relief Fund, saw North America, rather than their own country, as the logical destination for the refugees. In less than three months in 1882, the Mansion House sent 4,422 adults, 1,325 children, and 527 infants to the United States and Canada.[26]

Because of the refusal of the western European Jewish communities to accept refugees, AIU officials were forced to suspend plans to distribute the refugees among European countries. The response of the Austrian community, citing a fear of anti-Semitic backlash, was typical.[27] When the American HEAS representative, Moritz Ellinger, met with the leadership of the Viennese-Jewish community in March of 1882, he found much resistance to the idea of aiding the refugees. Ellinger reported that leaders of the Wiener Allianz feared that a public campaign in support of the refugees would result in an anti-Semitic backlash. As in France and Germany, it is clear that the problem of reconciling Judaism with citizenship was central to the reluctance of Viennese Jews to support the refugees. One community leader argued, according to Ellinger, that "no appeals for co-operation should be made to Jews in favor of persecuted Jews, as he considered himself above everything a loyal citizen of Austria, and one of the peers of the empire at that, and he did not think it proper to help inaugurate a movement that might be looked upon as an international movement of Jews as such." Ellinger met with similar resistance elsewhere in Austria-Hungary.[28]

As the magnitude of the refugee crisis became clear, European Jewry increasingly looked to America as the logical destination for the migrants. Yet like their European counterparts, the American-Jewish leadership was not enthusiastic about the prospect of receiving large numbers of refugees. American-Jewish leaders, predominantly of Reform German background, shared with their European coreligionists a negative view of the Russian Jews. In addition, Jewish leaders in the United States expressed concern that the financial burden of absorbing the refugees would be overwhelming, and that the arrival of a large number of migrants would increase anti-Semitism.

In America, Jews had not had to struggle to achieve citizenship. Yet because the American-Jewish community was dominated in the late nineteenth century by Reform Jews of German descent, the American-Jewish leadership shared with German Jewry a collective memory of the German-Jewish struggle, a pride in their own acculturation and modernness, and a scorn for the more "backward," traditional communities of the East. In fact, Reform Judaism had taken a firmer hold in the United States than in Germany. In both their outward ritual—use of English in synagogue, use of a choir and organ—and in their ideological assumptions, American Jews had moved a good distance away from the traditionalism that still dominated among East European Jews. These modern, German-American Jews recorded their attitudes about citizenship and religion officially in the Pittsburgh Platform, adopted by the American Reform movement in 1885. The platform, written in German, rejected all laws and rituals "not adapted to the views and habits of modern civilization." In addition, the platform maintained that Judaism was not a race or nation, but a progressive religion comparable to other American sects:

> We consider ourselves no longer a nation but a religious community, and therefore expect neither a return to Palestine, nor a sacrificial worship under the administration of the sons of Aaron, nor the restoration of any of the laws concerning the Jewish state.
>
> We recognize in Judaism a progressive religion, ever striving to be in accord with the postulates of reason. . . . Christianity and Islam being daughter religions of Judaism, we appreciate their mission to aid in the spreading of monotheistic and moral truth. We acknowledge that the spirit of broad humanity of our age is our ally in the fulfillment of our mission, and therefore we extend the hand of fellowship to all who co-operate with us in the establishment of the reign of truth and righteousness among men.[29]

Although pride in the progressiveness of the American Reform movement was communitywide, it was particularly pronounced among the elite of the Jewish community. This group of wealthy New York Jews, who became the core leadership group in the face of the refugee crisis, prided themselves on their acculturation and spectacular success in America. Their Reform temple, Emanu-El, was the symbol of these achievements, "hailed by the *New York Times* as one of the leading congregations of the world, 'the first to stand forward before the world and proclaim the dominion of reason over blind and bigoted faith.'"[30]

Given their pride in their triumph over traditionalism and their successful Americanization, it is not surprising that American Jews looked at the refugees with disdain, seeing them as dirty and uncivilized. Even before the mass migration began, organizations like the B'nai B'rith and the Young Men's Hebrew Association excluded East European Jews from their ranks.[31] American Jews, as they began to perceive the potential magnitude of the immigration, expressed concern that they would be overwhelmed by the newcomers. The *Jewish Messenger,* the newspaper of wealthy, Reform, East Coast Jews, revealed this apprehension when it warned that the influx might lead to the "Russianization of American Judaism." As early as May 1881, the *Messenger* used such fears to argue against the immigration: "It is very philanthropic to desire the Jews of Russia to leave that Empire, now that riots have broken out in the Ukraine, but to suggest that three million of them settle in America, evidences more enthusiasm than common sense. A better way, perhaps, would be to send American Jewish missionaries to Russia to civilize them there than give them an opportunity to Russianize us, in the event of such a colossal emigration."[32]

The fear that an influx of East European Jews would overwhelm the community was compounded by worries that such an influx would result in increased anti-Semitism. The established Jewish community expressed fear that the same negative qualities that they were so conscious of in the migrants would arouse prejudice against the Jewish community as a whole. Thus upon his September 1882 resignation as secretary of HEAS, Augustus A. Levey commented in the *Jewish Messenger,* "The mode of life of these people in Russia has stamped upon them the ineffaceable marks of permanent pauperism, only disgrace and a lowering of the opinion in which American Israelites are held . . . can result from the continued residence among us . . . of these wretches."[33] Increasing nativism in late-nineteenth-century America contributed to this fear of an anti-Semitic backlash, as even the most elite Jews began to be threatened by anti-Jewish policies. In 1877, Joseph Seligman, one of the most successful financiers in America, was turned away from the Grand Union Hotel in Saratoga Springs, and similar exclusions at other prestigious resort areas followed.[34]

Fearing that the immigrants would fan anti-Semitic sentiments and embarrassed by newspaper accounts of the filth and disorder in the expanding Jewish immigrant neighborhoods of New York, the elite German-American Jews took steps to distance themselves from the newcomers. Thus among New York's elite Jews, "to be identified as a Jew, along with 'those people,' became increasingly irksome. 'Those people' were loud, pushy, aggressive—'the dregs of Europe.' They made a bad name for everybody." Efforts to create a distance between themselves and the newcomers led to both Americanization campaigns and to a form of German-Jewish anti-Semitism:

> The Germans began to speak of the Russians as something akin to the Yellow Peril and Russian "Orientalism" became a repeated theme. The German

Jewish press echoed this, speaking of the "un-American ways" of the "wild Asiatics" and referring to Russian Jews as "a piece of Oriental antiquity in the midst of an ever-Progressive Occidental Civilization." The *American Hebrew* asked: "Are we waiting for the natural process of assimilation between Orientalism and Americanism? This will perhaps never take place." The *Hebrew Standard* stated it even more strongly: "The thoroughly acclimated American Jew . . . has no religious, social or intellectual sympathies with them. He is closer to the Christian sentiment around him than to the Judaism of these miserable darkened Hebrews."[35]

Despite the antipathy that many members of the American-Jewish community felt toward the refugees, sympathies were aroused by the suffering of the Russian Jews. Even the *Messenger,* despite its early and strong opposition to immigration, advocated support of the AIU appeal to aid the refugees and soon reversed its antiimmigration position as the seriousness of the crisis in eastern Europe was revealed.[36] As the scope of the refugee problem became apparent, American Jews, demonstrating confidence and pride in their country, grudgingly recognized that America offered the best hope for the refugees. Relief committees began to form throughout the United States, indicating the acceptance of sentiments expressed by the Board of Delegates of the Union of American Hebrew Congregations that "it is America, the haven and refuge for the oppressed of all nations, to which the afflicted outcasts look with longing and hoping eyes and where they are sure to find that protection which a despotic government denies them."[37] The reluctant acceptance of this position led the newly formed Hebrew Emigrant Aid Society to send Moritz Ellinger as its delegate to Europe in 1882, to gain financial support for a plan that would settle the refugees in agricultural colonies in America. The ambivalence of the American position is clearly articulated in Ellinger's account of his statement to a group of Jewish leaders in Hamburg:

We did not invite the emigration; we are fully aware of the endless troubles we were bringing upon our heads by the immigration of a large number of Russians to our country, and would rather assume the position of Europe in simply raising means for the settlement of the exiles anywhere else but in the United States. But we are actuated by no selfish motives. In the face of all the difficulties that presented themselves in the immigration of these exiles to the United States, and fully cognizant thereof, we recognize the fact that America, or rather the United States, is the only land which has room enough, is free and generous enough, which offers an unobstructed field for all occupations and handicrafts, and which knows neither prejudice nor intolerance, but welcomes the laborer and enables him to develop all his faculties. Of all the countries on earth, America would form the Mecca of these persecuted people, and the only country in which they can hope to succeed in founding by their toil and labor homes worthy of freemen, and enjoy that protection to which every man, who is a good, loyal citizen, is entitled by right divine.[38]

Although the American-Jewish leadership gradually acknowledged that the United States was the logical destination for most of the migrants, they insisted that the Europeans must accept an appropriate share of the financial burden. As early as May 1881, the United Hebrew Charities began preparing to receive the refugees in the United States by forming the Russian Relief Committee, which cared for the first arrivals in September 1881.[39] As they began to recognize the scope of the potential migration, members of the Russian Relief Committee advocated the establishment of a permanent society to focus on immigrant relief. As a result, the Russian Emigrant Relief Committee was formed in September 1881. This committee's predictions that five hundred refugees would arrive soon proved to be short of the actual numbers, and by late November a meeting was called to establish an "organized, permanent, incorporated society." Despite objections from prominent members of the community, including Jacob Schiff and Myer Isaacs, who considered the plan too radical, the Hebrew Emigrant Aid Society (HEAS) emerged from this meeting.[40] Local branches of the society were soon established in cities throughout the United States.

One of the first actions of HEAS was to send a representative to Europe to garner financial and organizational support. Moritz Ellinger sailed for Europe as the HEAS representative in early January 1882, barely one month after the formation of the organization. His trip commenced as complaints grew in America that the Europeans were "dumping" refugees on the United States without adequate support. By the time of Ellinger's mission, European relief organizations had established a procedure for dealing with the Russian Jews gathering in Brody. At Brody, the refugees were sorted, and the able-bodied were sent on to Lemburg, to be shipped to the port of Hamburg, where ships destined for the United States were available.[41]

Ellinger traveled throughout Europe, meeting with Jewish leaders in England, France, Germany, and Austria, and trying to win support for HEAS relief efforts. Although Ellinger's report to the society emphasizes the cordial reception he received, the outspoken condemnation of the atrocities in Russia, and the enthusiastic support offered him, the optimism in his report was exaggerated.[42] Despite Ellinger's satisfaction that all of those with whom he met had promised support, he found it difficult to translate these promises into cash: "Paris went to work after the Mansion House meeting, but it took weeks before active steps were initiated, and Germany seemed asleep and unmindful of the terrible drama reaching so close to its door. It is true, the Mansion

House meeting had created a sensation, a pleasurable one, but no one had moved to translate that sensation into active measures of relief."[43]

As Ellinger's mission in Europe continued, he received telegrams from the society in the United States, complaining that immigrants were arriving rapidly and bemoaning the lack of material support from Europe. In an attempt to coordinate the relief efforts, an International Jewish Conference met in Berlin in late April 1882. There Ellinger emphasized that "Europe has been told" of the need for "large sums, whereof the largest proportion must be furnished by Europe."[44] Although the European committees failed to allocate the support requested by Ellinger and refused to give HEAS in New York full control over the migration, the conference did successfully divide labor among the involved parties. According to this division of labor, Berlin was made responsible for the continental journey of the refugees; Vienna was to cooperate in selecting which refugees should be granted passage; London would preside over the trans-Atlantic voyage and the financial coordination, as well as work with New York on the principles of settlement; New York was to receive the immigrants and distribute them throughout the United States; and Paris was to study migration to other countries.[45]

The formation of HEAS and Ellinger's mission to Europe indicated acceptance by the American-Jewish community of its role in the crisis. However, the fear that the absorption of so many refugees would present an overwhelming financial burden led not only to pleas for European financial support but also to insistence that the migrants be properly sorted and screened. HEAS officials were willing to assume responsibility for able-bodied migrants, but they feared that without proper screening their resources would be overwhelmed by the demands of needy refugees. In addition, American Jews feared that the arrival of large numbers of paupers would arouse the anti-Semitic sentiment that they so wanted to avoid.

Because of both financial concerns and fear of an anti-Semitic backlash, the American-Jewish leadership insisted that only able-bodied refugees be forwarded to the United States. HEAS' somewhat naïve instructions to Ellinger outlined this policy:

> The selection of emigrants must be systematic and must be controlled by the European Committee from the departure from the Russian town until the arrival at an American port. The shipments must be regulated according to the ability of the American Committee to receive and distribute emigrants. Only those having a trade or able and willing to settle on the lands of the Society or to work as laborers on railways or otherwise should be selected for emigration. The aged and the helpless should remain in Europe at least until those upon whom they are dependent have been successfully established

in their new homes. Absolute paupers must on no account be chosen for emigration. Before sending emigrants to America, the difficulties of settlement in the new country must be clearly set forth and only the willing must be transported and these must abide by the decisions of the American Committee.[46]

While in Europe, Ellinger received a telegram from HEAS in New York, complaining that unfit immigrants were arriving: "Many emigrants arrive daily; majority incapable of supporting themselves; will be permanent burden on community." The telegram reported that HEAS officers were resigning in frustration and instructed Ellinger to "insist on careful selection of emigrants and prompt remittance of funds."[47] Thus at Ellinger's insistence, the International Conference adopted a resolution that "in future only such Russian refugees shall, as a rule, be accepted who possess the ability of being presumably capable of earning their support in the country of their new settlement." The resolution faulted past disregard for such principles: "Europe thus admits the grievous wrong which it commits in sending to America people that, by their very helplessness and physical inability, must become a permanent burden upon the community."[48] When asked by the Europeans what to do with "the weak, the aged and the children," he replied that their fate "is a problem which you must endeavor to solve." Ellinger explained:

> We in America must positively refuse to receive a large number of people who will remain a perpetual burden upon the community. We must refuse to serve as an Almshouse where paupers are deposited like the foundling by his unnatural mother, for us to take care of. Our duty as American citizens forbids us to swell the pauper population of our country, and it would be a crime against those who will form the nucleus of an army of freemen in the future, were we to listen for a moment to appeals which should never be made to us.[49]

Concerns about selectivity persisted after the Ellinger mission. In HEAS reports during the early 1880s, selectivity was a frequent theme. For example, the 1883 report complained that the burden of support was increasingly serious "owing partly to the arrival of a large number of persons unable, by reason of age, chronic disease, or extreme youth, to earn a livelihood."[50] Similarly, the Philadelphia-based Association for the Protection of Jewish Immigrants, established in 1884, resolved to "prevent the landing of paupers in this port" and to "facilitate the landing of such persons as are able and willing to help themselves by honest and useful labor."[51] The screening of the migrants would remain a persistent theme for years after the initial refugee crisis. Later aid organizations, such as the Baron de Hirsch Fund (established 1891) and the

Jewish Agricultural and Industrial Aid Society (established 1900), provided aid only to the able-bodied, and much of their aid was in the form of loans and training, in an effort to help only those who could help themselves. Both organizations, reflecting the disdain for almsgiving among American relief organizations in general, strongly discouraged charity in any form.

The fears of the American-Jewish leadership about the possible ill effects of the migration led them to advocate colonization projects as an outlet for the migration. Once it became clear that repatriation to Russia was unfeasible, and that migration to the United States was the best way to deal with able-bodied refugees, aid officials turned to agricultural colonization experiments because they believed that such projects were the only way to absorb large numbers of the refugees into America, while avoiding the potential downfalls of mass migration. First, the channeling of migrants into colonies would disperse the refugees across America and avoid the build-up of large, unhealthy ghettos, which were likely to arouse anti-Semitism. Second, establishing able-bodied Jews in agricultural colonies would provide immediate employment for the refugees. Providing agricultural employment for the migrants would not only minimize the financial burden of supporting refugees but would also counteract anti-Semitic stereotypes of the unproductive or parasitic Jew.[52]

Even before the establishment of HEAS, the Russian Relief Committee of the United Hebrew Charities had proposed the establishment of agricultural colonies in the southern and western United States. The Russian Relief Committee's successor, the Russian Emigrant Relief Committee, organized the Russian Emigrant Relief and Colonization Fund, whose purpose was to collect fifty thousand dollars to aid refugees and transport them "to points West and South."[53] Upon its establishment, HEAS also focused on colonization efforts and developed a colonization plan, which Ellinger presented to the European-Jewish leadership during his 1882 mission.

During his European mission, Ellinger garnered support for the HEAS position that "a disposal of greater numbers is only feasible by establishing colonies."[54] The American plan for colonization met with some resistance, particularly in France. There the experiences of the AIU in Palestine and with the refugees in Brody had convinced many that the migrants were not good material for successful colonization. Nevertheless Ellinger managed to convince the Europeans that "colonization would offer the only outlet for disposing of large masses, such as we had to expect in the spring."[55] Ultimately Ellinger won endorsement for his colonization plan at the International Conference in Berlin.

Although pecuniary support from Europe did not match Ellinger's optimistic predictions, the colonization plan gained widespread endorsement among many of the European committees. Indeed, some AIU officials had demonstrated an inclination toward colonization schemes even before Ellinger's mission, as the support of the AIU for the two Am Olam groups that passed through Brody in the fall of 1881 indicates.[56]

In America, HEAS immediately began taking steps to implement colonization plans. The Sicily Island, Louisiana, colony was established by the New Orleans branch of HEAS, although the parent organization apparently did not lend its direct assistance. The Alliance, New Jersey; Cotopaxi, Colorado; and Beersheba, Kansas, colonies were all assisted by HEAS.[57]

Support for colonization efforts was buoyed in America by the agrarian ethos, work ethic, and bias against almsgiving, shared by American Jewry, as well as by the desire to disperse the immigrants and demonstrate their productive abilities.[58] Such motives frequently led colony sponsors to ignore the communal philosophies of some of the Am Olam groups, despite the fact that these philosophies clashed directly with the sponsors' reverence for capitalism and private property. Michael Heilprin, whose Montefiore Agricultural Aid Society (MAAS) took on the role of principal colony sponsor in the early 1880s, expressed his personal belief in capitalist principles, but supported and encouraged avowedly communistic settlements, such as New Odessa, Oregon. MAAS' support for New Odessa was aided by the millionaire banker-investors Jacob Schiff and Jesse Seligman, who signed a MAAS advertisement that stated: 'New Odessa is based on communistic principles . . . but neither has the Montefiore Society endeavored to make converts for any social doctrine. . . . Its object is to help struggling and deserving Jewish farmers, and to foster agricultural pursuits among Jewish immigrants; but it leaves the choice of internal organization of each colony to the settlers, reserving for itself no kind of control or supervision.'[59] The independence of the colonists was also endorsed by Ellinger, when addressing concerns of a different nature in Europe. When questioned as to whether migrants to the United States would be forced to work on Shabbat, Ellinger stated that "the colonists are at full liberty to arrange their mode of living as suits their own inclinations."[60]

Despite the initial emphasis on agricultural colonization as an outlet for the migration, an extensive network of colonies did not materialize in America. HEAS, which had presented to the Europeans a colonization scheme as the centerpiece of its program, never developed a concrete colonization plan. HEAS aided several colonies, but the poor condition of the arriving refugees forced it to focus instead on the immediate relief of immigrants in port cities, such as New York.

The optimism that Ellinger expressed in Europe concerning the potential of agricultural colonies to absorb the refugees was challenged even before his return. Critics of the mass colonization plan argued that few among the refugees were equipped for such an undertaking. Thus AIU officials in Paris with "intimate knowledge . . . of the material which crowded to Brody in their flight from the house of slavery," tried to convince Ellinger that the refugees lacked the necessary human capital.[61] Even a contemporary supporter of the colonization idea, George Price, concurred with the notion that the refugees were unsuitable for agricultural colonization: "Anyone who saw those masses, transported on the freighters, suffering privations, particularly upon their arrival on the shores of the United States, does not need any clarification or explanation why this mass could not even think of colonization."[62] Michael Heilprin, who continued to support colonization projects until his death in 1888, argued that though there were refugees suitable for colonization projects, they were greatly outnumbered by migrants who were clearly unfit for colonization:

> [In locating potential colonists] We had . . . to contend with an anti-Russian prejudice, an outgrowth of ignorance and self-over-estimation kindred to anti-Semitism. But few understood the language, the sentiments, the aims and inclinations of the strangers. But few would believe that among the wrecks of distant communities which a storm of persecution had driven to our shores, there was material for construction which might become an honor to this country and to all Israel.[63]

The desperate condition of most of the refugees not only caused officials to doubt their potential as colonists but also forced HEAS to devote most of its means to immediate relief, despite the distaste of officials for charity. As impoverished refugees poured into New York, HEAS officials scrambled to provide them with housing, food, and employment.[64] As Price recalled, "No one could think of such grandiose colonization schemes, when such a multitude of tattered, impoverished, and famished families had to be saved from hunger and cold. All efforts of the committees were directed toward the amelioration of the fate of those unfortunate paupers."[65]

The perception that the refugees were unfit for colonization and the concentration of HEAS funds on immediate relief, combined with the lack of concrete colonization plans, severely restricted the implementation of large-scale colonization. Despite HEAS' faith in colonization, the organization had laid no practical plans before Ellinger's trip. While Ellinger was in Europe, a second HEAS representative, Julius Goldman, was sent to the Dakotas to assess the logistics of a colonization plan. Goldman's report concluded that "to settle the refugees in lands in the West in masses . . . is entirely infeasible." Although he remained convinced that successful colonization could be achieved on an individual basis, he ruled out the possibility of successful colonization "upon the communistic or co-operative plan." Goldman's conclusion that large-scale colonization was beyond the means of the society put a damper on the HEAS plans.[66]

Goldman's negative assessment of the viability of mass colonization projects, coinciding with Ellinger's return from Europe with approval for just such a plan, created much turmoil within HEAS. After a short time, however, Goldman's recommendations won out. At a national conference in June 1882, only one month after Ellinger's report was filed, HEAS voted against a large-scale colonization project in a resolution that stated: "Organizations now existing should not be called upon to perform the work of colonization upon any large scale; while they may assume the task . . . in exceptional cases, of providing facilities for independent agricultural employment."[67]

HEAS' focus on immediate relief, as well as continued financial disputes with European aid societies, led to the organization's rapid demise. Assailed by local aid society branches that protested that they could not absorb any more refugees, and by the immigrants themselves who denounced the deplorable conditions at the HEAS Ward's Island station in New York, HEAS repeatedly turned to Europe for aid. By the summer of 1882, when aid from the European committees proved not to be forthcoming, HEAS reached a crisis point and called for a discontinuation of the migration. At a July 1882 conference, HEAS made this position clear, agreeing to accept only the refugees remaining in Brody, with European financial aid. The coincidence of this agreement with the end of the 1881–82 pogrom crisis in Russia, led the relief committees to evacuate and close the Brody refugee station by the end of the year. HEAS itself was disbanded soon after, in March 1883, leaving the United Hebrew Charities in New York and local relief societies in other cities to care for the refugees.[68]

Because both HEAS and the AIU were effectively out of the immigrant aid and colonization business by the end of 1882, prospects for large-scale agricultural colonization were doomed. Although local relief committees and Heilprin's underfunded MAAS stepped in to sponsor isolated colonization projects, not until the 1891 establishment of the Baron de Hirsch Fund did a major funding organization reenter the colonization arena.[69] Heilprin's support for New Odessa, Cremieux, Bethlehem Judea, Carmel, and the Kansas colonies was enthusiastic, but the MAAS budget was never large-enough to support a large scale colonization scheme.[70]

Despite the cessation of the pogrom crisis in 1882, mass emigration from Russia continued during the following decades and spread to communities, both within the Pale and in other East European countries that had not directly experienced pogrom activity. Indeed, worsening political and economic conditions led the migration flow to *increase* in the years after the crisis. Although Jewish immigration to the United States averaged 22,700 per year between 1881 and 1889, the yearly average increased to 40,700 between 1890 and 1898; to 53,500 between 1899 and 1902; to 123,000 between 1903 and 1907; and to 93,800 between 1908 and 1914.[71]

As during the initial migration crisis, the goals and policies of the American-Jewish relief organizations that tried to cope with this flow of migrants were shaped by the attitudes and values of the leadership of the organized Jewish community. As in 1881 and 1882, these leaders had a negative view of the migrants and feared that their uncivilized behaviors would provoke anti-Semitism. This fear and suspicion led philanthropists to focus on the twin goals of preventing the build-up of large concentrations of migrants in the urban ghettos and reducing the characteristics of the migrants that they found strange or threatening. Thus "removal" of immigrants from urban ghettos and Americanization of the refugees became the cornerstones of relief policy in the years after 1882.

Although the feelings of established American Jews about the immigrants were influenced greatly by the attitudes toward religion and citizenship that they shared with their western European brethren, the economic success of the leadership group in America also shaped their feelings toward the migrants and their endorsement of particular types of relief. The persons who dominated the Baron de Hirsch Fund ("the fund") and its subsidiary, the Jewish Agricultural and Industrial Aid Society (JAIAS), were among the most financially successful Jews in America, and their achievements provided them with tangible evidence that America was a land of opportunity and that the American economic system provided the means for men of humble beginnings to achieve riches.

The list of trustees of the fund and the JAIAS reads like a who's who of New York Jewish society. Jacob Schiff, Oscar Straus, Jesse Seligman, Abraham Abraham, Leonard Lewisohn, and others who fill the pages of *Our Crowd* dominated the fund's board of directors.[72] A few of these persons had arrived in the United States with good means, such as Jacob Schiff, whose family had once shared a double house in Frankfort with the Rothschilds.[73] However, many of these bankers, department store magnates, and investors had achieved the rags-to-riches dream. For example, Solomon Loeb, whose daughter married Schiff, arrived in the United States as a steerage passenger in 1849, bringing with him his one pair of shoes. Working his way up from a position as a helper in a Cincinnati dry-goods store, Loeb became a founding partner of the huge Kuhn, Loeb and Company investment firm. The Straus and Seligman empires similarly began as small-scale peddling ventures. Straus became the head of the Macy's retailing business, as well as secretary of commerce under President Theodore Roosevelt. The eight Seligman brothers were spectacularly successful in the banking business.[74]

The financial achievements of these Jewish leaders led them to place tremendous faith in the value of hard work and in the possibility for success in America. The enthusiasm they felt for their adopted country was illustrated in the extreme by the Seligman family, which had a virtual obsession with Americanization. Like many in their social group, several of the Seligman brothers had Americanized their names—Jesse, one of the original Baron de Hirsch Fund trustees, had changed his name from Isaias. In the second generation, their passion for American names reached an extreme: "Joseph's sons (Jesse's oldest brother and the leader of the family) included George Washington Seligman, Edwin Robert Anderson Seligman (after Robert Anderson, the defender of Fort Sumter), Isaac Newton Seligman, and Alfred Lincoln Seligman—a quaint compromise. Joseph planned to call the boy Abraham Lincoln Seligman, but decided that the name Abraham was too Judaic to perpetuate in America."[75] The passion for Americanization went beyond names—many of the second-generation Seligmans were educated in Joseph's home by Horatio Alger, the author of popular rags-to-riches novels, who served as a live-in tutor. The Seligmans hoped their sons "would all acquire the red-blooded standards of 'Tattered Tom,' 'Ragged Dick,' and Alger's other newsboy-to-riches heroes."[76]

This belief in assimilation and the possibility of advancement through hard work was shared by Baron Maurice de Hirsch, the major non-American figure involved in aiding American colonies after the 1881–82 crisis. Hirsch, an international banker and one of the wealthiest Jews in Europe, came from a family that had long revered agriculture and had a long tradition of philanthropy.[77]

Hirsch's philosophy on relief was like that of the American-Jewish leadership. In an 1891 article entitled "My Views on Philanthropy," Hirsch underscored the obligation he felt, as a wealthy man, to help others. Yet, he explained, "I contend most decidedly against the old system of alms-giving, which only makes so many more beggars; and I consider it the greatest problem in philanthropy to make human beings who are capable of work out of individuals who otherwise must become paupers and in this way create useful members of society."[78]

Hirsch's belief that philanthropy must be used to inspire productivity rather than to encourage dependence was tied to his conviction that the "Jewish problem" was a result of the abnormal Jewish occupational profile. Thus Hirsch, like many of his American counterparts, saw assimilation and occupational "normalization" as the solution to the problem. Hirsch's philanthropic activities included involvement in the AIU—he was elected to the AIU Central Committee in 1873—as well as many non-Jewish causes. His belief that nonwestern Jews would achieve citizenship through assimilation and productivization led him to focus his early efforts on educational activities. He was a major supporter of the AIU educational program in Turkey, and his first response to the pogrom crisis in the Pale was to suggest an extensive secular education program.[79] As late as 1887, Hirsch proposed an educational plan for Russian Jews, which he was prepared to finance through a gift of 50 million francs. Hirsch hoped that these schools would help normalize the Jewish occupational profile and ultimately lead to the granting of citizenship. Only after it became clear that the Russian government was unwilling to cooperate with his plans did the Baron begin to advocate emigration for Russian Jews.[80]

In supporting migration, Hirsch emphasized that the movement must be more than simply a physical transplantation of people. Rather, his belief that assimilation and, specifically, normalization of the Jewish occupational distribution would result in acceptance led him to advocate agricultural colonization and manual training. As one of Hirsch's biographers explains, "He had always believed that Jews were subjected to indignities and special disabilities because the only education they received was concentrated entirely in the study of *Talmud,* which did little to prepare them for the difficult task of earning a living and resulted in Jews becoming peddlers or petty traders."[81] Hirsch's confidence that, by providing manual training or the opportunity to farm, Jews could be "normalized" and absorbed in the western democracies led him to donate 10 million dollars to establish the Jewish Colonization Association, which supported agricultural colonization in the West, particularly in Argentina.[82] Subsequently, Hirsch, at the urging of Michael Heilprin, donated 2.4 million dollars for the Baron de Hirsch Fund in the United States, which, according to the Deed of Trust, had eight purposes:

1. Loans to immigrants from Russia and Roumania, actual agriculturalists, settlers within the United States, on real or chattel security.

2. Transportation of immigrants (after arriving at an American port) to places where they may find work and make themselves self-supporting.

3. To teach immigrants trades and contribute to their support while learning such trades, and furnishing them necessary tools to enable them to earn a living.

4. Improved mechanical training for adults and youths.

5. Instruction in the English language and the duties of American citizenship; technical and trade education; establishment of special schools and workshops.

6. Instruction in agricultural work and improved methods of farming.

7. Cooperation with established agencies in the United States for the purposes of relief and education.

8. Other methods of relief and education which the Trustees may, from time to time, decide.[83]

The strong belief of both the American-Jewish leadership and the baron in the value of working one's way to success, combined with their distaste for the foreign habits of the refugee, led immigrant relief efforts to emphasize training and Americanization. Thus the major relief organizations, including the Baron de Hirsch Fund, sponsored programs that taught English and skills to enable the immigrants to succeed through their own efforts.[84] Central to the beliefs of the sponsors was the conviction that the refugees must be enabled to help themselves—once given the means to work, the eastern immigrants would be able to follow in the German-Jews' footsteps and achieve success. Thus the Baron de Hirsch Fund's provisional charter targeted money for education and training; "furnishing craftsmen with tools and implements necessary to earn a livelihood"; and in other ways enabling the recipients to support themselves. While encouraging self-help, both the fund and the JAIAS specifically discouraged charity.[85]

The emphasis on self-help evident throughout the policies of the fund and the JAIAS reflects not only a belief in the work ethic and confidence in the opportunities available in America but also contemporary American thought on philanthropy. During the nineteenth century, American philanthropists had increasingly moved toward an emphasis on individual responsibility and away from almsgiving.[86] Belief in the unlimited opportunity available in America, represented by the expanding frontier in the early portion of the century and the explosion of business and industry later, made American poverty seem a paradox. Like Seligman and Straus, who looked at their success and concluded that anyone who worked hard could achieve riches, American popular culture began to emphasize that, in a land where anyone could rise to fame and fortune, those who remained poor must be responsible for their own failure: "In a society where self-sufficiency is available to all people of ordinary talent and reasonable energy, poverty reflects a personal weakness."[87]

The tendency to see the roots of poverty in individual failing was reinforced by the needs of the industrializing economy. As historian Michael Katz notes, this "redefinition of poverty as a moral condition . . . served to justify the mean-spirited treatment of the poor, which in turn checked expenses for poor relief and provided a powerful incentive to work."[88] Thus the emphasis on individual failure was reinforced by belief in the rags-to-riches dream and also served the needs of both an overtaxed relief system and the developing industrial sector's need for cheap labor.

The tendency to blame poverty on the poor combined with societal changes, such as urbanization, immigration, increased mobility, and population growth, which disrupted traditional communities and mechanisms for dealing with the poor, resulted in the development of new, punitive styles of poor relief during the nineteenth century. The development and spread of the almshouse as a way of reforming paupers was accompanied by the reduction of outdoor relief.[89] Thus as many historians argue, desire for social control or "the preservation of social order and discipline" was another reason for the increasing emphasis on individual failure among the poor and for more punitive relief measures.[90]

Historians have argued that one reason for this transition in relief policy is the breakdown in traditional relations between rich and poor. During colonial times, strict settlement laws insured that "dependent neighbors made up the ranks of the poor. The town recognized a clear obligation to them and officials were not especially concerned with possible malfeasance."[91] In contrast, as cities grew, populations expanded, and traditional relationships between classes broke down in the nineteenth century, poor people were increasingly regarded with suspicion:

> The colonists, assuming that the bulk of the local poor deserved support, had not let the potentiality for abuse, the possibility that loafers might profit from the arrangements, color their perspective on relief. To their successors, however, the chance of corruption overwhelmed all other considerations. Now that the poor were not brothers in the community but stood as next of kin to criminals, one could not help be too careful to guard against dishonesty. Rejecting the slothful took precedence over relieving the needy.[92]

The concern about abuse led a quarter of America's largest cities to completely abolish outdoor relief between 1878 and 1893.[93] The parallels between this general suspicion of the poor and the German-American Jews' suspicion of "alien" East European Jewish refugees are striking.

Although German Jews did not create almshouses for the Jewish immigrants, their relief policies, like their attitudes toward poverty itself, reflected the policies of nineteenth-century American philanthropy. During the period of mass Jewish migration to the United States, two groups of reformers dominated the poverty debate. Their diagnoses of the problem and their solutions differed, but both reemphasized the distinction between worthy and unworthy poor and reinforced the belief that the pauper class was primarily made up of undeserving persons, and both influenced the approach of American-Jewish aid organizations.

Social workers represented the more conservative of the two groups of reformers. Their dedication to psychiatric casework reinforced the tendency to see the roots of poverty in the individual. Concern for the morals of the undeserving is clear in their harsh critique of outdoor relief. As Josephine Shaw Lowell, the founder of the Charity Organization Society (COS), explained, "No amount of money scattered among people who are without character and virtue will insure even physical comfort."[94] COS workers spearheaded the attack on outdoor relief. Lowell even argued that the worthy poor must sometimes suffer in this effort to improve the morality of others: "Many good people call it a cruelty to refuse help to the family of a drunkard, but where the father and mother are cruel, no outside help will save the children from suffering, while to refuse outside help may do so."[95]

In contrast to the social workers' focus on the individual roots of poverty, Progressives in the late nineteenth and early twentieth centuries saw poverty as a result of social ills. Although still affirming their belief that many paupers were unworthy, these Progressives focused on the working poor, arguing that despite moral habits, working families were vulnerable to poverty. Thus Progressives emphasized the environmental causes of poverty, arguing that by improving the working-class environment, poverty would be reduced. Robert Hunter, one of the more radical Progressives, argued that if the economic system could work only with a reserve labor and capital pool, "then the poverty of this large mass of workers must continue unrelieved until the system is reorganized."[96] Yet most Progressives failed to challenge the structure of the economy as Hunter did. Thus policies of the Progressive reformers focused primarily on improving the slum environment, in an effort to uplift the city. The Progressive reform consisted of "coercive" measures, such as ridding the slum of gambling, alcohol, and prostitution, and the workplace of dangerous conditions; and "environmentalist" measures, such as the building of parks, playgrounds, and community centers. Although the individual character-molding approach of the COS was scorned by the Progressives, these new reforms had an equally moralistic tone, and sometimes an even more ambitious one: "They conceived of their mission in far broader terms, dreaming not just of pulling slum dwellers up to some minimal standard of respectability, but of purging the entire moral climate."[97]

In this societal approach, very little change was made in dealing with dependents. As the Progressives concentrated efforts on purifying the city for the benefit of all, they did little specifically to aid those who had already fallen out of working-class life. Many Progressives even affirmed traditional views of the pauper class, whom they distinguished from the working poor. Even Robert Hunter asserted that "there is unquestionably a poverty which men deserve, and by such poverty men are perhaps taught needful lessons." Hunter also believed that outdoor relief could lead people into poverty: "In nearly all cases, he who continually asks for aid becomes a craven, abject creature with a lust for gratuitous maintenance."[98] Thus while Progressive reformers focused more on the environment than on the individual roots of poverty, distinctions between deserving and undeserving poor were maintained.[99]

Besides these two primary strains in American philanthropic thought, the industrial education movement emerged in the post–Civil War era to deal with a specific type of client: the poor black. Spearheaded by Booker T. Washington, this movement aimed at training blacks for useful trades. At Tuskegee Institute, the central educational institution of the movement, Washington's students were encouraged "to work hard, save their money, invest in property [particularly a home], and have a strong moral character." In a striking parallel to the *maskilic* ideology that influenced the Am Olam, Washington emphasized the importance of demonstrating to the world the productive ability of his people. Thus according to historians Mary Berry and John Blassingame, Washington "ultimately . . . felt that as the black person became a useful part of the southern economy, political and personal freedom would follow."[100]

All these currents in nineteenth-century relief policy were reflected in the major Jewish relief organizations that developed to cope with the immigrant crisis and continued to direct relief efforts well into the twentieth century. As time passed after the crisis of 1881–82, policies of these organizations became more rigid and more self-conscious in reflecting both the attitudes of the leadership and the larger trends in American philanthropy. If the entire family of Jewish relief organizations is examined, parallels with the COS, the Progressive, and the industrial education approaches emerge. For example, the casework performed under the auspices of United Hebrew Charities echoes the social work approach of the COS; the establishment of settlement houses and relief efforts focused on cleaning up the Jewish ghettos and tenement houses reflect the philosophy of Progressives; and the Baron de Hirsch Fund's manual-training programs parallel the industrial education movement. Within the Baron de Hirsch Fund and its subsidiary, the Jewish Agricultural and Industrial Aid Society, the two relief organizations dealing with colonization, these three strains are clear.

Like the COS social workers, Jewish relief officials firmly believed that aid to the lazy or unworthy was wasted. In directing aid to persons capable of helping themselves, the fund and the JAIAS scrupulously avoided paupers. From the early years of the migration, American-Jewish leaders insisted that only the able-bodied be selected by the European aid organizations for migration. Even the most sympathetic among the American-Jewish leadership insisted that aid should be channeled only to the worthy and that charity should not be dispensed. Thus Michael Heilprin wrote in an 1888 letter, which helped persuade Baron de Hirsch to become involved in American relief:

> Jewish charity has always justly been praised—perhaps slightly beyond its merits. Even anti-Semites would hardly dare to deny it. It is constantly doing a great deal of good. But it has also been productive of evil consequence. It

has fostered a habit of relying upon individuals and congregational institutions, and in proportion weakened the instincts of manliness, self-reliance, and honor. It is time to moderate this deleterious influence of a noble sentiment and practice. Jewish institutions ought to be founded on the principle of aiding those who aid themselves, of promoting and rewarding independent efforts and successful energy—not by gifts and distinctions, but by affording means for enlarging the scope of honorable efforts and the field of manly energy.[101]

Although the early relief organizations, such as HEAS, requested that only able-bodied refugees be selected for migration, the confusion of the crisis and the brief life of the organization prevented the full development of this policy. In the fund, exclusive aid to those capable of helping themselves led to the implementation of strict selectivity rules to govern relief. As the fund developed, it increasingly emphasized an applicant's finances as a measure of his ability to succeed in America. Only migrants who could finance their own transportation and had additional means "for establishing themselves at their new place of settlement" would be given cards of introduction to the fund by the fund's European counterpart, the Jewish Colonization Association (JCA). This requirement would help "check the immigration of people who would become a burden for the country of their settlement."[102]

Emphasis on assisting only the able-bodied was also apparent in the policies concerning aid to potential colonists. Means-testing was used in selecting colonists from the 1890s on, as both the fund and the JAIAS developed policies that required farmers to obtain a first mortgage in the private market before they could qualify for a second mortgage through either agency. Myer Isaacs of the fund instructed the JCA that Russian boys sent to the Woodbine agricultural school should come from families with means sufficient to purchase farms in America, "as only such a self-relying element can be expected to accomplish satisfactory results."[103] Additionally, sponsors tried to develop means for testing the aptitude of applicants for farming. Indeed, the plan developed in August of 1889 to determine policies of the fund specified that "[the giving of] alms to persons who will never be able to help themselves, is deemed foreign to the object of the Fund."[104] Fund and JAIAS records demonstrate that this restriction was enforced consistently, as many requests for charity were denied.

The COS philosophy of relief was reflected not only in the selectivity and anticharity stance of the fund and the JAIAS but also in the focus of many programs on individual improvement—programs that also reflect the industrial education movement's philosophies. Most of the fund budget was designated for such improvement programs as English and manual-training classes. These classes were designed to give the migrants the skills they would need to work their way up, as well as to encourage their Americanization.[105] In the colonies, the fund and the JAIAS sponsored many self-improvement and training activities, ranging from the cultural program of the Jewish Chautauqua Society to the establishment of the Woodbine Agricultural School and the Fels model farm in Alliance.

The emphasis on individual screening and disdain for charity reflected the Jewish leadership's belief in the work ethic, as well as their fear of arousing anti-Semitism and their absorption of COS and industrial education-style philosophies of relief. At the same time, Jewish relief was also influenced by the new policies of Progressive reformers. The most clear reflection of Progressivism can be seen in the concern of the Jewish leadership about the conditions in the growing Jewish ghettos.

In launching assaults on the ghetto, fund officials were influenced both by their own concern that poor ghetto conditions would trigger an anti-Semitic backlash and by the arguments of contemporary Progressives, who saw the ghetto environment as a breeding ground for poverty. When efforts to slow migration, early in the crisis, proved futile, Jewish aid organizations increasingly spoke of "removals" as a method of preventing ghetto growth. In such programs, immigrants would be removed from the ghetto and dispersed to communities with less Jewish concentration. Plans to establish colonies were integral to this strategy, for successful rural colonies would draw immigrants out of the city.

The desire to physically remove immigrants from the crowded urban ghettos is a constant theme in the Jewish relief literature from the beginning of the migration. From the HEAS colonization plan, which emphasized the scattering of migrants throughout the United States to avoid the expansion of ghettos to the later policies of the fund and the JAIAS, the need to "clean out the ghetto" was considered paramount. It was suggested by both fund and United Hebrew Charity officials that families refusing to relocate should be denied aid.[106] Fund records from local branches, such as Philadelphia, demonstrate that removals were the most favored form of aid. Thus the Philadelphia Committee records for the late 1890s show that in every year more of those aided received "transport to relatives or labor centers" than any other form of assistance.[107]

In the first decade of the twentieth century, efforts were made to organize these removal efforts more efficiently. The JAIAS, which itself aimed to further removal by granting loans to farmers establishing themselves in rural districts, organized the Industrial Removal Office (IRO), dedicated exclusively to dispersing immigrants nationwide. Working through a network of local relief societies and employment agents, the IRO succeeded in placing seventy thousand families outside New York by 1914.[108]

An even more ambitious removal effort was organized and funded in 1906 by a Baron de Hirsch Fund trustee, Jacob Schiff. Schiff's plan, which became known as the Galveston Movement, was to avoid the build-up of Jewish population in eastern ghettos by diverting immigrants to other ports. Galveston, Texas, was selected as the best potential port because it had both steamship service to Bremen and railroad access to the American West. This effort was cooperative, with the Jewish Territorial Organization handling both publicity in Europe and transportation to Bremen; the German-Jewish community organizing care for the migrants in Bremen and their departure on steamships; and the Industrial Removal Office directing immigrant placement in America. Immigrants were screened carefully, with a preference for young laborers who were not Sabbath-observant (it was believed that Sabbath-observers would be more difficult to place in jobs). Both internal disputes among the cooperating organizations and legal attacks on the program, which was accused of encouraging immigration, led to its demise by 1914, after bringing only ten thousand Jews through the port of Galveston.[109]

Although sponsors' initial enthusiasm for colonization faded rapidly, with HEAS abandoning such projects in favor of short-term relief, support for colonization remained a part of the immigrant aid program. Although sponsors increasingly recognized that colonization was not practical on a large scale, a few of the surviving colonies were maintained because they met the needs of the sponsoring organizations.

Goldman's 1882 conclusion that large-scale colonization was impractical led HEAS to turn away from its extensive colonization plans. The many colony failures in the 1880s did little to recommend such projects to the relief organizations. Colony after colony was abandoned because of unfavorable weather conditions, internal disputes, or poor site selection. Even in the New Jersey colonies, where temperatures were moderate and access to markets good, the settlers struggled through the 1880s and would not have survived without repeated intervention by philanthropists.[110] Except Michael Heilprin's MAAS, which actively supported colonization projects until Heilprin's death in 1888, none of the relief organizations focused on colonization activities from 1882 to 1891, when the Baron de Hirsch Fund was established.

Although the few Am Olam-linked colonies that survived until the establishment of the fund were saved by fund policies, the goals of the original settlers and of the fund trustees conflicted in several areas. Am Olam ideologies were fairly diverse, but all members shared a reverence for agricultural labor and saw engagement in farming as the primary goal of their enterprise. In contrast, though a few of the sponsors, particularly Hirsch himself, shared this romantic view of agriculture, farming was, for the sponsors, a means rather than an end.[111]

Clearly, colonization projects fulfilled a number of the goals shared by the baron and his American counterparts. First, the establishment of colonies would provide an outlet for removals, particularly if the colonies established provided opportunities for industrial, as well as agricultural, employment. Second, by providing both manual training and employment opportunities in the colonies, these projects allowed immigrants to become engaged in productive labor and to advance economically. Third, colonies in rural areas increased the contact of the immigrants with native-born Americans, thus furthering Americanization.

Sponsors' goals conflicted in several respects with the goals of the Am Olam colonists. First, Am Olam adherents had hoped to establish independent colonies, and few of the Am Olam intellectuals perceived a need to be supervised. However, for the sponsors, one clear benefit of colonization was that colonies lent themselves well to supervision. Thus potential colonists could be screened to ensure that only the deserving, hardworking elements received aid. By granting aid through loans that had to be repaid and by refusing to aid charity cases within the colonies, sponsors could continue to ensure that settlers were productive. Those failing to earn a living would default on their loans and be forced to leave the colony. In addition, sponsors could exercise a high degree of control over cultural life and encourage Americanization by selectively funding cultural, social, recreational, religious, and educational programs that they believed meritorious. Thus sponsors aided activities, such as cultural events, English classes, modern religious education for children, and manual-training programs.[112]

An additional potential sponsor-settler conflict was over the economy of the colonies. Many (although not all) Am Olam settlers hoped to establish colonies that were cooperative, or even totally communistic, but the sponsors believed that colonies could be used to instill individualism and economic independence in the immigrants. Thus sponsor loans were available only to single families and not to multifamily groups, to discourage communalism. Similarly, the insistence of the sponsors that colony affairs be run on business principles worked against communal tendencies.

Although the colonies could not have survived without the aid of American and European sponsors, the goals of the sponsors shaped colonial development in a direction at odds with the goals of the original settlers. Each time sponsors stepped in to aid the projects, beginning in the 1880s, their policies altered the path of the settlements. The coincidence of increased sponsor support with the dissolution of the Am Olam movement gave sponsors even greater influence on the colonies. As the Am Olam contingent in the New Jersey colonies diminished, the sponsors used recruitment and loan policies to bring in new types of settlers who differed from the settlements' founders. Once the Baron de Hirsch Fund established firm policies for colony aid in the 1890s, sponsor influence became a major force in determining the outcome of the colonization project. The development of the New Jersey colonies—the only Am Olam–related colonies to survive the 1880s—and the role of both sponsors and immigrants in that development are the focus of the remaining chapters.

4

The First Years in Jersey

Settlers and Sponsors, 1882–1890

T HE NEW JERSEY COLONIES of Salem and Cumberland counties, like the
Am Olam colonies in South Dakota and Oregon, began as communal,
agrarian settlements. However, while the short-lived Am Olam colonies in the
West remained isolated both from sponsors and from potential new settlers,
the New Jersey colonies were under the close supervision of New York and
Philadelphia sponsors, and were constantly absorbing new groups of settlers.
Despite strong similarities in origins to the western colonies, the influence
both of colony sponsors and of new groups of settlers led the New Jersey
settlements to rapidly move away from their communal and agrarian roots.
Within the first half decade they began their transformation into mixed agricultural–industrial settlements, with economies based on private ownership.

Alliance, the first of the New Jersey colonies, was founded in May 1882,
with the aid of HEAS of New York (also called the New York Committee)
and the French AIU. The initial group of settlers, which consisted of twenty-
five families, was quickly augmented by new arrivals, so that by the end of the
first summer between sixty and seventy families lived in the colony.[1] These
groups arrived at Bradway Station (later known as Norma) via the Jersey Central railroad, accompanied by the New Jersey commissioner of immigration, a
strong supporter of the colonization project.[2]

The early settlers had to quickly learn to cope with difficult and primitive
conditions. Their immediate need for shelter was met through the intervention of politicians from nearby Vineland, who procured more than a thousand
army tents for them by an act of Congress.[3] The land obtained by HEAS for
the settlement was virgin, sandy soil covered by scrub oak and pine, and had
to be cleared before planting could begin. Although HEAS supported the
settlers with a weekly wage during this period of clearing the land, many

colonists supplemented their income and gained practical experience by working for non-Jewish farmers in the area.[4]

During the first months in the settlement, the Alliance colonists appeared to be replicating elements of the communal blueprints that guided the Am Olam colonies at Bethlehem Judea, South Dakota, and New Odessa, Oregon. After a brief period of living in tents, several large buildings were constructed in which the colonists lived and dined communally. The barracks, divided into separate twelve-foot by fourteen-foot compartments for each family, was satirically called "Castle Garden" after the crowded immigrant station in New York harbor through which the settlers had passed. The Alliance colony's "Castle Garden" was described by a reporter from the *New York World* who visited the colony during its second month: "Two rows of compartments were on each side opposite one another with a narrow passage between them, the full length of the house. In each compartment lived a family with children. Two beds were in each room, a large one for husband and wife and a small one or cradle for the children. Other than this, very little furniture was to be seen in these drab rooms, except for a closet or wardrobe which stood in each room between the beds."[5] This account, the earliest contemporaneous observation of the colony, also includes a description of the communal dining system and of the settlers themselves:

> A bell announced time for lunch and about 200 or 300 people, men, women and children hastened quietly to the dining room. Each one was doled out his portion of chicken soup, broth and broiled meat. . . . When they sat down to eat I was able to observe these people as much as I wished. They were much healthier looking than the new immigrants which one sees in New York. Their bodies looked strong. . . . The veins in their intertwined fingers showed that they had strong arms. While they were eating they sat dressed in clothes like farmers and toilers of the soil at the time of work. The women were dressed up, but their garbs were plain and clean, dressed like farmers' wives.[6]

During the first months, work was organized on a communal basis. From the arrival of the first group in May, "the whole company work[ed] together on 30 acres of wild land."[7] When HEAS purchased an additional thousand acres, the group planted crops under the guidance of an instructor and superintendent appointed by the society. According to the *New York World* report, the work schedule was strict. Settlers arose at 4:00 A.M. and worked in the fields together until breakfast at 6:00. After breakfast, settlers resumed work until 9:00 A.M. They retired during the hottest hours of the day, from 9:00 until 2:00 P.M., and then returned to work until 7:00.[8]

The resemblance of the life-style at Alliance in this immediate postsettle-

3. Hirsh Coltun. He and his wife, Jennie, were among the founding families of Alliance. The Coltuns have been identified as members of Odessa Am Olam. *Courtesy Doris and Sanford Rosenman.*

ment period to the communal living and working patterns of the Bethlehem Judea and New Odessa Am Olam colonies was not coincidental. Although the exact number of Am Olam members among the original Alliance colonists is uncertain, a number of Alliance colonists had clear Am Olam connections. The Goldhafts, who remained in the colony for five years, were members of Am Olam. Tevye Goldhaft became interested while in Russia in the idea of productivization, believing that if Jews became farmers they would become "normal" and anti-Semitism would disappear. Similarly, Moses Bayuk, an Am Olam member who arrived with the original group and remained a community leader until his death, looked to farming as a way of normalizing the Jew. He was an assimilated, secularly educated lawyer, greatly inspired by Tolstoy.[9]

Various others among the original settlers had definite ties to Am Olam. The Coltuns, Crystals, Levins, Opachinskys, Rosinskys, Stavitskys, and Zagers were all members of the Am Olam. All of these families remained in Alliance

4. Jennie Coltun, wife of Hirsh Coltun.
Courtesy Doris and Sanford Rosenman.

through 1900.[10] The Coltuns traveled from Hamburg to New York City on the same boat as Am Olam founder Bokal, who later joined the Alliance colony. In addition, the Levins were closely related to the Levinsons, who also remained in Alliance through 1900, thus drawing the Levinsons into a circle of people connected to the Am Olam even though their membership in the organization cannot be verified. Traveling with the Levins and Levinsons on a boat from Hamburg were two additional founding families, the Mennies and the Strausnicks, both from Kiev.[11] Thus among the forty-three founding families who remained in Alliance for at least a few years, nine can positively be identified as Am Olam members, and for at least three others there is evidence of a connection. Because of the difficulty of positively identifying Am Olam members among the settlers (no membership list exists for the organization), it is very possible that there were additional Am Olam colonists who cannot be identified.[12] Even if there were not, these twelve represent an impressive proportion, 27.8 percent of the core group.

This core of long-lasting Am Olam settlers was augmented by a second group that arrived during the next three years. Between 1882 and 1885, many Am Olam members joined Alliance, including a number of the organization's leaders. For example, Monye Bokal, one of the organization's founders, arrived in Alliance after the first summer, but some time before 1885. Bokal was considered by many the guiding spirit of the organization. Abraham Cahan, briefly a member of the Balta chapter of Am Olam, recalled, "All respected him because Bokal lived like a hermit, free of egotism, honest, peaceful. He never showed anger and when he argued it was in a friendly tone and with an earnest, pale face illumined by a smile that gave a strong impression of saintliness."[13] Despite his leadership role in the Am Olam, Bokal's impact on Alliance was limited, because of his untimely death in 1886.

Also in this second group of Am Olam members were Sidney Baily and his wife, Esther Mashbir Baily. Sidney Baily, a founding member of Am Olam, had been the head of one of the Odessa Am Olam circles; his wife was the sister of the leader of Balta Am Olam, and an intellectual in her own right. Esther had joined her brother in settling one of the South Dakota Am Olam colonies, before marrying Sidney and settling in Alliance in 1885.[14]

Esther and Sidney Baily remained farmers in Alliance until their deaths, but the other Am Olam adherents who settled in Alliance during this period enjoyed much briefer stays. Moses Freeman's experience was typical. He joined Odessa Am Olam and traveled to New York with the second Odessa group in May of 1882. Soon he and his party were settled in Alliance by the New York committee of HEAS, but he and his wife did not adapt well to farming and left the settlement within two years.[15] His group included Chaim Spivakovsky (later Spivack), leader of the Kremenchug Am Olam group; George Seldes, Baily's cousin and an Am Olam activist and anarchist who subsequently attempted to found a more radical colony;[16] and a Katsovvey (Kasovich), who served as the head of Am Olam in Poltava. Other Am Olam settlers in this period included Konefsky, Feffer, Peisochovitz, Schwartz, Gartman, Freedman, and D. Steinberg. In his autobiography, Freeman recalled that there were about fifty families in his group, but because there are no comprehensive lists of Am Olam members and no records of settlement for persons staying in the colonies for only a brief period, it is not possible to identify those in this group not specifically mentioned in Baily or Freeman's memoirs. Of the thirteen positively identified here, all except Baily, Seldes, and possibly Steinberg, either died or left within the first few years.[17]

Despite the similarities between the early life-style at Alliance and the Am Olam colonies of New Odessa and Bethlehem Judea, the settlers at Alliance exhibited less radicalism than their western counterparts. This moderation was probably because, like the Am Olam-related colonies in Louisiana, Kansas, and at Cremieux, South Dakota, the Alliance settlement was not exclusively an

5. Harry Steinberg working his Alliance colony farm.
Courtesy Doris and Sanford Rosenman.

Am Olam colony. Although the most ideologically radical of the western colonies had been formed by coherent groups of Am Olam members, who organized in Europe and migrated as a group, the Alliance colony, like the other
less doctrinaire settlements, was heterogeneous in composition. Despite the
legend, common among descendants, that the "original 43" families migrated
together from Europe, there is no evidence to support this claim. Instead, the
earliest Alliance colonists arrived in small groups, and many migrated individually from Europe.[18] As outlined above, the settlers who were a part of the Am
Olam organization arrived in the settlement over a three-year period; the leadership group included Odessa Am Olam leaders Sidney Baily and Monye
Bokal, Kremenchug Am Olam leader Spivakovsky, and veterans of the western
colonies, such as Esther Mashbir Baily, arriving last—*after* the land had been
divided into single-family holdings and many community patterns had been
established. Thus although the colony included a core of Am Olam members,
other settlers, including many of the radical settlers' wives, were far more
traditional. Religious colonists, such as Isaac "the Hasid" Krassenstein, and

religiously observant wives of radicals, such as Moses Bayuk, were a moderating influence.[19]

Contrasts between Alliance and the purer, western Am Olam colonies can be seen in religious ritual and other aspects of daily life. For example, colonists at New Odessa were outspokenly nonreligious, observing neither holidays, the Sabbath, nor dietary laws, but the Alliance settlers did observe religious rituals. During the era of communal dining, meat was brought to the colony from a kosher Philadelphia slaughterhouse—a marked contrast to western colonies where pork was consumed. On the Sabbath, no work was performed and religious services were conducted. Many colonists also recited daily prayers.[20] Similarly, while free love was reportedly practiced at several of the western Am Olam settlements, where single people dominated, Alliance settlers, virtually all of whom arrived in family groups, "all slept in a great circle on the floor, with their clothes on, so there would be no mix-ups between husbands and wives" in "Castle Garden" until the partitions were constructed.[21]

Many of the most radical of the Am Olam members who settled in Alliance had strong religious educations and supported community religious institutions despite their own ambivalence, or even distaste, for traditional religion. Baily claimed that he and his Odessan group were "embittered over *heder* [and were] against the practices laid down in the *Talmud,*" and he has been characterized by his granddaughter as "vehemently" antireligious. Yet he and his wife participated as teachers in a somewhat unorthodox Sabbath school where she "read poems in Yiddish from Rosenfeld and others, and also in German from Schiller and Goethe," while he "spoke on Jewish current events and Jewish post-biblical history and on Jewish ethics generally, from the Scriptures and the *Talmud.*"[22] Similarly, Tevye Goldhaft "wasn't particularly pious, although he would go to the synagogue as a fairly regular thing," according to his son. "Mostly, he would go there for a good argument, taking the side that religion was superstition." Nevertheless Goldhaft observed the Sabbath and his home was kosher, apparently in deference to his wife.[23] Moses Bayuk, son of a rabbi and a learned talmudic scholar in his own right, attended synagogue out of respect for his neighbors, but he often went with a copy of Tolstoy tucked into his prayer book. His daughter reported that he made a point of smoking on the Sabbath and eating on Yom Kippur (both violations of traditional practice).[24]

This participation in religious life by nonreligious or even antireligious intellectuals led to the development of religious practice and institutions at Alliance that deviated from orthodoxy. Thus the religious school in which the Bailys taught contrasted sharply with the traditional *heder.* Similarly, in 1887, the Alliance colonists celebrated Chanukah, which began that year on December 11, on December 25—accommodating the holiday schedule of their new country.[25] By the late 1880s, it is clear that there were factions of varying religiosity in Alliance—two separate synagogues were established in the community by 1889, and, though there is no existing documentation explaining the reason for the split, it appears that the most traditional community members, such as Krassenstein ("the Hasid") and Solonsky, were affiliated with Tiphereth Israel (1889), while radicals, such as Sidney Baily and George Seldes, were associated with Eben ha-Ezer (1888). The Tiphereth Israel members dominated the Chevrah Kadisha (Burial Society).

Even before the split there was evidence of tension between the religious and secular factions in the colony. When Monye Bokal, leader of the radical faction died suddenly in March of 1886, his comrade Sidney Baily recalled bitterly, "The sanctimonious *chevrah kadisha* would not let us dig a grave in the graveyard row, and forced us to bury him outside the fence of the cemetery as Jewish communities used to bury one who committed suicide."[26] In subsequent years, as many of the most ardent Am Olam secularists left the settlement, or softened their views, divisions between religious factions in the community lessened. By the early 1890s, when the burial society was incorporated, Sidney Baily was listed as a member.

Just as Alliance proved more conservative religiously and socially than the Oregon and South Dakota Am Olam colonies, it also developed along less radical economic lines. Within the first few years, the communal work system was abandoned. Six months after the settlement of the colony, the land was divided into thirteen- to fifteen-acre single-family plots and distributed by drawing lots. These plots were at first arranged in clusters of four so that "four families working together might make use of the same horses and implements, thus saving capital and taking advantage of cooperative endeavor." Under this arrangement, "each man was given the work which he was best adapted to do." Yet even this limited communal ownership was short-lived, the partnerships dissolving and the horses sold within two years.[27] By 1884, the pattern of single-family farming was established in Alliance, and a house was constructed for each family on its own plot.

The reasons for the transition from communal living and working patterns to single-family farming are complex. Many accounts of the colony do not even mention the early, communal period. Accounts that do tell of this period are vague about its demise. A United States Immigration Commission report of 1911 says only that "the work was hard, the matured crops rather disappointing, and the communistic programme [*sic*] not entirely satisfactory."[28] Another account, written by the son of early settlers, notes that "in the beginning the colony . . . was going to be a sort of cooperative," but "as often happens with idealists, their ideas, basically workable, only work out later in some less idealistic form."[29] Many descendants of the colonists, brought up in the United States, tend to ascribe their value system to the settlers and assume that their ancestors aspired to private ownership.[30]

More satisfying explanations for the transition can be found both in the close relationship with sponsors in Philadelphia and New York and in the coalition of immigrants who founded and continued to settle in the colony. The proximity of Alliance both to sponsors and to the urban immigrant centers led to a high level of intervention by sponsors and a continuous influx of new settlers.

Unlike the western Am Olam settlements, Alliance was conveniently located to large Jewish population centers. In fact, the site was chosen precisely because it was on the New Jersey Central rail line, about fifty miles from Philadelphia and a hundred miles from New York.[31] The proximity to these cities and the availability of rail transportation provided the farmers with easy access to markets for their produce. In contrast, the western Jewish settlements lacked easy access to markets and were isolated from their sponsors. Settlers of New Odessa, Oregon, who were also aided by New York philanthropists, were weeks away from their sponsors; settlers in South Dakota were equally remote. The Sicily Island, Louisiana, colonists were sponsored by HEAS through its New Orleans office, but they were located four hundred miles upriver from New Orleans in an area so remote that it was "three days journey from a city with no train service."[32]

Although their proximity to New York and Philadelphia philanthropists yielded tremendous benefits for the Alliance colony in monetary support, this support was not unconditional. Sponsors supervised the colony closely and shaped its development in accordance with their own goals for the settlement. As discussed in chapter 3, sponsors feared the concentration of immigrants in urban ghettos and hoped that the establishment of rural colonies would draw Jews out of the ghetto. Sponsors felt that immigrants settled in rural areas would rapidly adopt American ways, for they would be surrounded by Americans rather than by other immigrants. An implicit part of the Americanization that the sponsors advocated was the acceptance of the ideas of self-reliance and independence, which they believed would be reinforced by the experience of single-family farming. Although the degree to which the sponsors believed that agricultural labor would "normalize" the immigrants varied, they did emphasize the value of economic independence, whether farm or home ownership. Sponsors argued that such holdings must be earned, and scorned charity as debilitating, believing that charity bred dependence. Similarly, they saw socialism and other challenges to the ideal of the independent, individual American entrepreneur as threatening.[33]

The impact of these goals and beliefs on the colonies was evident from the earliest days of Alliance. From its establishment, activities in the colony were coordinated by a supervisor appointed by HEAS, a non-Jew named A. C. Sternberger. The control of daily affairs by the sponsors set Alliance apart from most of the western Jewish colonies. Sternberger supervised work during the early period, running the settlement with a system of bells to call colonists to work or to dine. Sternberger's purpose was to "prove to the world that the Jews are capable of becoming farmers in America."[34] He defended the colonists to critics of the experiment, praising their ability and diligence, and demonstrated sensitivity to their needs by calling in a Philadelphia rabbi to consecrate a cemetery and preside over the burial when the first death occurred in July 1882.[35]

Sternberger's mission, however, was to establish the Jews as farmers, not to found a cooperative settlement. From the beginning, he emphasized that HEAS viewed the early communal living and working arrangement as an intermediate step in the effort to establish farmers on their own plots. During the second month of the colony's existence, Sternberger told a reporter that he expected HEAS to allocate parcels of land to the newly trained farmers by the end of the summer of 1882. He reported to HEAS in June 1882 that "in his thirty years of experience he had never had such diligent and attentive students as these and that they are all eagerly waiting to stand on their own feet and not to have to be dependent on the Committee."[36]

HEAS followed through on this plan in November of 1882, granting each family a thirteen- to fifteen-acre plot, on which a two-room house was built and a well dug. HEAS also allotted common land for schools, a synagogue, and a cemetery, and provided farm implements. In return, each colonist was responsible for a mortgage of between 321 and 443 dollars, including 125 dollars for the house and well, and 15 dollars per acre of land. These mortgages were offered only to single families; none were issued to unrelated multifamily groups or to persons without families. The mortgages were to be repaid over ten years, the colonists paying only interest in the first four years, and both interest and principal thereafter.[37] The mortgages were taken over by the Alliance Land Trust, a newly formed organization created to supervise Alliance colony upon the dissolution of HEAS in 1883. Trustees of this new organization included members of the HEAS leadership, such as Henry S. Henry, president of HEAS, and Isaac Eppinger, and future leaders of the Jewish Agricultural and Industrial Aid Society and the Baron de Hirsch Fund, such as Leonard Lewisohn and Henry.[38]

Although the mortgage terms were considered fair by the sponsors, they represented tremendous burdens to the immigrants, many of whom had large families to support. During the first years, the farmers could not earn sufficient income from their plots. Clearing the land was slow. To supplement their incomes, the colonists worked picking berries for local farmers. Children worked alongside their parents, picking strawberries and cranberries. It was, as one historian notes, "hard work at low wages . . . and a far cry from the ideal of an independent yeomanry." As additional immigrants arrived, sent to the colonies by HEAS, the population grew in the second year to 650, "some of whom were temporarily housed in the Alliance Colony with no intention of settling them on the land."[39] HEAS, on the brink of dissolution and lacking money to support the new arrivals, appealed to the Alliance Israélite Universelle, which contributed three thousand dollars toward the establishment of a factory. By late 1884, the original Castle Garden building was transformed into a sewing factory and a cigar factory.[40]

Despite the aid of HEAS, AIU, and other Jewish philanthropic organizations, such as the London Mansion House Committee, the Alliance colonists were still struggling in late 1884, when colony leader Moses Bayuk appealed on their behalf to the AIU. Bayuk reported that most farmers had prepared only four to six acres and planted fruit trees on two. He explained that some had not harvested the crops because they lacked the money to buy or lease the necessary work animals. Bayuk's report also complained of the exploitation of workers at the factory, and the lack of employment elsewhere. He detailed the desperate situation of the settlers:

> During the summer they feed themselves one way or another, but during the winter, nobody would envy their condition. Young and old people suffer from hunger and cold, and even the American adage, "help yourself," doesn't help here. . . . The men were healthy during the whole time. . . . However most women suffered. . . . The doctors find the reason for that in the poorly built houses which don't protect from cold temperature and strong winds, and which are, during the summer, too hot.[41]

Bayuk was not exaggerating the harsh conditions. His report included the news that during the first year forty-nine babies had become sick and nineteen had died. Deaths for the first two years totaled thirty-three. Although he acknowledged the extensive aid to the Alliance families—including nine months' allowance in the first year of eight to nine dollars per month, a hundred dollars for seeds in the first year and thirty dollars in the second, supplies of furniture, agricultural implements, and household goods, various sums for farm buildings, and forty sewing machines—Bayuk claimed that only five of the farmers had brought in enough of a harvest to pay the interest due on their mortgages. In addition, he reported, "we don't have any work animals, any agricultural machines, any money to lease those for next spring, and, what's even worse, at the present time we don't find any work and we lack all basic necessities."[42] Bayuk's appeal echoed that of Henry S. Henry, president of HEAS, who had written to the AIU in February 1884,

> Our European brethren lose sight of the fact that the Colonization thrust upon us of these Russian Refugees demands funds far in excess of what would be required if only single men had been sent as originally demanded— but here we have men with large families of small children requiring daily rations, clothes, which it is impossible for them to provide, however industrious, out of the soil during the early years of their emigration. There are over 500 souls at Alliance, all mainly dependent on 67 heads of families who are generally industrious and good colonists, but the result of their labor at present is entirely inadequate to their support.

Henry suggested that the Paris Alliance contribute seven to ten thousand dollars for improvements and seeds, "unless they want these people back again in Europe."[43]

Henry's appeal to his European counterparts implies sympathy and understanding for the struggling colonists, but his dealings with the colonists themselves appear to have been based more on practicality than sympathy. In response to a plea from Bayuk in late 1884, Henry explained the desire of the sponsors that the colonists be independent. Although he agreed to try to ease the terms of the colonists' mortgages, Henry reprimanded them: "None of you yet have ever paid anything, either interest or taxes, on the land, and if you choose to leave it you are welcome to do so; but you cannot possibly expect us to support you any longer, and if you cannot make a living for yourselves and [your] families and see no prospect of doing so, you must go elsewhere but it must be at your expent [*sic*]."[44]

Aid from such philanthropic organizations as AIU and HEAS led to important changes in the developing colony. For example, the addition of the AIU-funded factory at Alliance was a significant break from the concept of agricultural colonization. Although Bayuk's report demonstrates that the colonists themselves looked upon factory work as a possible means of saving the struggling colony by providing a supplement to agricultural income, the sponsors focused instead on the potential of rural factories to provide incentive for nonagricultural immigrants to relocate to the countryside.[45] The effort to draw industrial workers out of urban centers and into the country became a consistent policy of the sponsoring agencies throughout the 1890s and early 1900s, when incentives to industry were given as low-interest factory mortgages and cash reimbursements to manufacturers establishing factories in the colonies.[46]

These policies significantly altered the colony's economy. In 1889, the 529 residents of Alliance colony were primarily farmers; only sixteen families lived in the colony without owning land. These sixteen worked as farm laborers in the summer and earned their living by sewing in the winter—as did most of the farm owners.[47] Yet by the early 1890s, sponsor policies led to the development of flourishing industrial villages in Norma and Brotmanville, at either end of the Alliance settlement. There were farmers in Norma and Brotmanville, but both were dominated by industrial workers in the 1890s and they increasingly developed separate identities from Alliance proper.[48]

Besides promoting industrial growth in the colonies, sponsors shaped the settlement by exerting control over recruitment. In many cases, the sponsors attempted to control the quality of the settlers, through screening new applicants, and, on occasion, purging those deemed unacceptable. As early as 1881, the AIU decided to aid migration and "sent a committee to Russia for the purpose of making a judicious selection so that only the strong and healthy, those able and willing to perform hard work, or who possessed a knowledge of some handicraft would be chosen."[49] Sponsors of agricultural colonies repeatedly expressed confidence that immigrants with farming experience could be found and easily placed, although opponents of colonization claimed that the immigrants were misrepresenting their agricultural experience.[50]

Although efforts to discourage immigration by persons unfit for manual labor were used to sort the mass of potential migrants, colony sponsors frequently aided or excluded persons based on personal factors as well. For example, when Hirsch Coltun requested aid from the AIU to bring over his brother from Russia in 1885, AIU's American agent reported that "Mr. Coltun is doing fairly and can provide for his brother," and the request was granted. However, when several Alliance parents requested that their children, who had studied agriculture in schools in Vienna and Jaffa be brought over, their request was denied. Despite the fact that children with agricultural training would be an asset to the settlement as a whole, and to their families, Isidore Loeb of HEAS recommended denial of the request because the families "are entirely dependent on the charity of this Society."[51]

A harsher means of controlling the colony's population was through the expulsion of "undesirables." In the early years, this method was used primarily to rid the settlement of "troublemakers" and "complainers." This control by the sponsors over the composition of the settler population was asserted from the earliest days of the colony; the first documented case of such a conflict was in the winter of 1883.

On February 6, 1883, less than one year after the settlement of the colony, the *South Jerseyman* reported that "several months" before seventeen families "belonging to the Jewish settlement in Pittsgrove township [Alliance] . . . were sent to Estelville [a colony founded by land developers in an unfertile area near Mays Landing], because they were too lazy to work, and thus were a disadvantage to the Alliance Colony." Fifteen of the seventeen had, according to the report, returned to Alliance "nearly naked and almost starved." In the conflict that followed, "these wanderers took forcible possession of the old quarters in the barracks [Castle Garden]." When HEAS secretary S. H. Mildenberg arrived to settle the dispute, "he was kept imprisoned in the barracks by the refractory Jews 'just to hear the children cry for bread'. The Secretary, rather than sleep in a room with 60 people all night was allowed to go free upon his paying 50 dollars." The dispute was settled when HEAS agreed to pay a hundred dollars to each family (except those who had extorted the fifty dollars from Mildenberg) on condition that they "leave the colony immediately and seek new pastures." The three 'ringleaders', who had taken the fifty dollars, protested, and were arrested on February 3, 1883, and jailed. The saga continued as the wives of the three men arrived at the jail, with their children, "half famished and crying for bread." Ultimately all three were found innocent of assault and released. They were defended by Augustus Seeman, New Jersey commissioner of immigration, who "denied to the reporter that the Estelville party were lazy, but said they were willing and anxious to work. Mr. Seeman says the refugees have been treated cruelly and he will leave nothing undone to punish those who have treated his countrymen so unjustly."[52]

Not all settlers who were asked to leave the colony had participated in such overt revolts against the sponsors' authority. In an article printed in the *Philadelphia Ledger* in early August 1884, Cyrus Adler, a member of the New York Committee, reported on an inspection tour of Alliance. Adler wrote that twelve families had not succeeded as farmers and "were advised by the Society to leave the colony as the latter would no longer be responsible for them, particularly since this group continued to multiply complaints, and stir up quarrels and dissension amongst the colonists." Some of these families failed to meet mortgage payments, were tried in Salem County Court House, and evicted from the colony. Adler noted that these men (after the trial) were "the ones who caused the scandal in the city of Salem and were arrested, put in jail, and thus besmirched the name of the colony." He further justified the eviction by reporting that other colonists told him that the evicted farmers "were always complaining and lazy and could not be compared to the rest of the farmers." Although colony sponsors did not tolerate nonpayment of debt, neither did they want former farmers to leave the area and return to the large urban ghettos. Rather, Adler reported, "for such complainers who want to leave the colony, there was established a factory to manufacture cigars."[53] Thus foreclosures and evictions in the agricultural sector of the colony economy bolstered its nonagricultural population.

As the sponsoring agencies developed, tighter policies for screening potential colonists were gradually implemented. The control of Alliance mortgages was passed from HEAS to the New York branch of United Hebrew

Charities in 1884, and then on to the Alliance Land Trust in 1885. The Alliance Land Trust, established by the London Mansion House (the English version of the AIU), issued new mortgages with thirty-three-year contracts at 3 percent interest to the colonists after interviewing each. Interviews were conducted personally by the trustees, including such prominent American Jewish leaders as William Strauss, Henry S. Henry, Isaac Eppinger, and Leonard Lewisohn. The Land Trust issued new mortgages to the colonists in March 1885, except in the case of three who were "found unfit for farming." In these cases "arrangements were made for them to leave."[54]

Besides increasing the proportion of industrial workers at Alliance, sponsor efforts to exercise control over the composition of the colony's population undoubtedly contributed to the departure of many of the Am Olam members who had arrived in these early years. Although the names of those evicted from the colony are not known, and the records of the Land Trust interviews have been lost, it is reasonable to assume that Am Olam members would be likely targets of these purges. The experience of a number of Am Olam members in radical politics and the orientation of many toward communal living arrangements meant that they did not fit the profile that the sponsors sought for the colony. Dissatisfaction among idealistic Am Olam members with the direction the colony was taking might lie behind the sponsors' many references to "troublemakers" and "complainers." Sponsor-screening procedures, along with the realization of the committed idealists among the colonists that Alliance was not evolving along the lines they had envisioned, probably contributed to the high attrition rate among the Am Olam colonists.

Disputes between colonists and sponsors that led to foreclosures or court cases helped breed an atmosphere of distrust.[55] Colonists found the mortgage terms difficult to comprehend, and in some cases failed to understand that the money, land, equipment, and houses provided to them were loans and not gifts. As word spread among the Jewish migrants that colonies were being established with the aid of the AIU, some migrants believed that farms were being provided free of charge. Thus in 1885, the Hebrew Emigrant Aid Society of Philadelphia provided lodging to a family of nine who "were persuaded in Russia to come to this country where they will receive farms for nothing."[56] When the Alliance Land Trust issued new mortgages in 1888, many colonists expressed suspicion about the Land Trust's motives. In later years, Alliance farmers accused the managers and agents of the sponsors of having "mismanaged [money granted to the farmers] to such an extent that the farmer derived very little benefit from the money."[57]

These misunderstandings regarding the intentions of the sponsors can be attributed to the contrasting assumptions of the colonists and their patrons concerning philanthropy. The sponsors placed their faith in businesslike transactions, such as loans, accepting the popular American belief that charity bred indolence and dependence. In contrast, the colonists came from a society that upheld "the right to charity as a birthright of a member of the community."[58] Jewish communities in eastern Europe had long been held responsible for their own poor. In small communities these obligations, particularly on the Sabbath or holidays, were generally met by families who would take in poor guests to share a meal. In addition, taxes were collected within the Jewish community to provide for the poor on a more formal basis.[59] This giving rested on the belief "that the affluent need charity for the salvation of their immortal souls and that the needy, providing them with such opportunities, thus participate in an equivalent exchange."[60] Considering this background, it is not surprising that many colonists assumed that the aid granted to them was a gift.

✳✳✳

The importance of the sponsors' policies to colonial development is made apparent by comparing Alliance with neighboring Jewish colonies in New Jersey. Although Alliance gained the support of a number of Jewish aid organizations even before the settlement of the colony, neighboring colonies were largely neglected by the established financial sponsors in the early 1880s, and this neglect retarded their development.

Rosenhayn, several miles southwest of Alliance in Cumberland County, was, like Alliance, established by the Hebrew Emigrant Aid Society of New York in 1882. Land in Rosenhayn was originally purchased to create an outlet for population overflow from Alliance, and six families were established there in 1882. Yet, unlike Alliance, Rosenhayn did not benefit from continued aid. Unable to face the hardships of clearing the land and establishing a settlement without aid, the colonists abandoned the place within a short time.[61] This fate was shared by other South Jersey colonies, many of which were initiated by land developers who brought the settlers in but gave them no support. Colonies such as The Seventeen, Mizpah, Reega, Malaga, Ziontown, Halberton, Estelville, and Hebron all vanished within a short period, because of inadequate support.[62] The extreme deprivation at Estelville, which led to the 1883 riots in Alliance, indicates the impossibility of unaided settlement in South Jersey. Very little is known about these projects, or about the first attempt at Rosenhayn, and it is not clear whether these early colonists were connected to the Am Olam movement.

In 1887, as conditions at neighboring Alliance began to improve, new families resettled Rosenhayn. Settling after the demise of HEAS, during a period when American-Jewish relief organizations had turned away from colonization plans, the colony failed to attract support from the organized Jewish community. This lack of support meant that many had to work in the city—

often as far away as Philadelphia—until they could pay for the land themselves. One such colonist was Harris Venezky, who migrated from Odessa in 1882 and worked in New York as a butcher for several years before buying land in Rosenhayn in the late 1880s. Venezky, whose brother-in-law was one of the early Am Olam Alliance settlers, did not move to his farm until crops had been planted.[63] Other Rosenhayn settlers took in home work from factories in neighboring cities until a shirt factory was established at the site. Because the lack of sponsorship forced them to work in industry, the Rosenhayn settlers could never devote themselves to agriculture to the extent that their neighbors in Alliance did.[64] In addition, because settlers arrived and established themselves individually, the colony was not exclusively Jewish, as was Alliance. The lack of support in the early years slowed development at Rosenhayn, so that in 1889 it included only sixty-seven families with a population of 294— about half the population of Alliance.[65]

Although many sources emphasize the industrial nature of the Rosenhayn colony, the effort of the settlers to concentrate as much energy as possible on their farms is demonstrated in the 1889 statistics, which show that only two years after the resettlement of the colony, 261 acres were under cultivation.[66] Little is known about the regional origin or ideological background of the Rosenhayn settlers, but it is clear that some had experience as farmers. In his 1889 report on the colonies, Moses Klein noted that "15 of the settlers were employed in farming in Russia."[67] This number, representing 22.4 percent of all the heads of household in Rosenhayn at that time, belies the oft-reported supposition that Jewish colonists had no farming experience. Because most Russian-Jewish farmers were concentrated in the South Pale, it is likely that these Rosenhayn farmers were of South Pale origin.

Despite their assiduous efforts both in industry and in farming, insufficient support caused the Rosenhayn colonists to suffer extreme financial hardship. Many were forced to abandon the project. Lacking the opportunity to acquire low-interest loans and aid through the Jewish philanthropic societies, Rosenhayn colonists turned to private financial markets. Only when they were threatened with foreclosure in the early 1890s did the newly established Baron de Hirsch Fund step in to issue new mortgages on more favorable terms.[68] Under the care of its new sponsor, Rosenhayn's development in the 1890s became more closely parallel to that of Alliance.

A second Cumberland County colony, Carmel, also developed during its early years with little help from the established German-American Jewish aid societies. Gaining support from Michael Heilprin's Montefiore Agricultural Aid Society, the same organization that supported many of the western Am Olam settlements, Carmel's early development contrasted with that of Alliance, by remaining closer to its ideological roots in the Am Olam. Carmel was first settled by Jewish colonists in 1882, on a site owned by a land developer with an interest in colonization. W. H. Miller had previously brought German immigrant farmers to work his land, and upon their departure, he joined efforts with Michael Heilprin to bring Jews to South Jersey to form a colony.[69]

Heilprin, the patron of the Carmel colonists, was not typical of the Jewish philanthropic establishment discussed in chapter 3. Born in Russian Poland to a family of Hebrew scholars, he shared an East European background with the settlers. Like many of the idealistic and intellectual colonists whom he aided, he was well educated both in Jewish and in secular subjects.[70] This background made him a more empathetic sponsor than his German-Jewish counterparts, who viewed the immigrants as alien.

Heilprin had been involved in various democratic causes throughout his life—first, as an advocate of Hungarian liberty in the early 1840s. There he became the literary secretary of the Department of the Interior in Kossuth's revolutionary government in 1848. He spent time in Paris and England, and briefly returned to Hungary, before arriving in the United States in 1856. Heilprin then moved to Philadelphia and became deeply involved in the anti-slavery movement. In the United States, Heilprin pursued a career as a scholar and writer, contributing to the *Evening Post* and *The Nation,* and publishing a two-volume work, *The Historical Poetry of the Ancient Hebrews.* His scholarly orientation also set him apart from the leaders of the major Jewish philanthropic organizations, who were almost exclusively businessmen.[71]

Heilprin's empathy for the Russian-Jewish immigrant and his belief in agricultural colonization as a solution to the "Jewish problem" led him to work tirelessly for that cause, first as an agent for HEAS, and, after its dissolution in 1883, as the founder of the MAAS, devoted exclusively to aiding agricultural colonization. Heilprin's MAAS, operating out of a basement in Philadelphia, was dwarfed by the established Jewish aid societies, many of which boasted prestigious New York City addresses. Heilprin personally dealt with the immigrants in their language and identified strongly with them. Once, at a meeting of prominent aid officials, Heilprin, responding to "inconsiderate talk" about the East European Jews, rose and said, "I am a Polish Jew, I belong to that despised race." His regard for and understanding of the immigrants led his organization to establish policies that contrasted sharply with those of the major aid societies. For example, Heilprin opposed liens on property given to settlers, favoring instead "a reliance on their personal honor."[72] In a report on Jewish colonies published in 1887, Heilprin was critical of the Alliance colony sponsors, writing that "ignorance and reciprocal mistrust—between protected and protectors—have made this undertaking very costly," but, as a perpetual supporter of agricultural colonization, he added that "success has not been purchased too dearly."[73]

Despite his personal belief in the merits of capitalism, Heilprin did not fear cooperative economic arrangements as did the wealthier philanthropists. He advocated the provision of agricultural equipment to be held communally by the group, and was the primary source of support for some of the communal western settlements, such as Sicily Island and Cremieux, South Dakota.[74] His ability to speak to the immigrants in their language, his tireless work on their behalf, and his defense of the experiments despite the many setbacks in the West, "made him beloved by the immigrants of all groups and of every shade of opinion; they felt themselves understood by him as by no other in the community. He became their interpreter to the older Jewish groups."[75]

Heilprin was enthusiastic in his support, but his funds were far more limited than those of the larger sponsoring organizations. As a result, the colonists whom he supported at Carmel faced a difficult struggle in the early years. The original seventeen families were reduced to only ten within the first two years, because of the difficult circumstances. Despite Heilprin's aid, Carmel settlers faced severe difficulties in this period, and even felt compelled to appeal directly to the AIU for support in July 1885. With Heilprin's support, a new influx of settlers replenished Carmel in the mid-1880s.[76]

In contrast to Alliance, where colonists were required to purchase family farms and single-family houses, many Carmel colonists rented houses from Mr. Miller and worked as tenants for the first few years. Like the colonists in Rosenhayn, Carmel farmers found it impossible to survive through farming alone in the early years, and many worked as farm laborers for gentiles or performed home work for shirt manufacturers. The Montefiore Agricultural Aid Society did not finance mortgages, so the settlers turned to private financial markets to build their homes.[77]

After Heilprin's death in May of 1888, the colonists were forced to turn elsewhere for help. Under the threat of foreclosure, they appealed to Baron de Hirsch of the AIU through Philadelphia rabbi Sabato Morais.[78] The baron's decision to take on sponsorship of the Carmel colony ultimately resulted in its inclusion under the Baron de Hirsch Fund, and Jewish Agricultural and Industrial Aid Society umbrella in the 1890s and beyond.

Little is known about the first group of settlers in Carmel, but one family that moved to Carmel during the initial period of settlement in 1882 was the Sobelman family. Although it is unclear whether the Sobelmans were members of the Am Olam, they did fit that organization's profile. The family originated in South Russia, near Kishinev in Bessarabia, and spoke Russian and Hebrew as well as Yiddish. The son had a secular Russian education to the gymnasium level.[79] There is little information concerning the Sobelman's contemporaries, but it is known that many Am Olam members arrived in Carmel in the mid-1880s, including Moses Herder and Mordechai Woskoboynikoff, founding members of Odessa Am Olam.

Despite its financial difficulties, Carmel became a haven for Am Olam radicals during the mid-1880s. Although many such persons left Alliance in this period, Carmel attracted a number of veteran Am Olam colonists. After playing a key role in the founding of Am Olam in Odessa and participating in the unsuccessful colonization attempt in Arkansas, Moses Herder joined with several of the Arkansas colonists and set out for Carmel.[80] In his 1889 report, Moses Klein refers to these Arkansas colonists, writing that the seven early Carmel colonists who left were "replaced by Western Russian Jewish farmers who, owing to the extremely hot climate, had to quit those regions and were settled by Mr. Heilprin on hired soil at Carmel."[81] Besides the Arkansas contingent, Herder's friend, Mordechai Woskoboynikoff, who had traveled to America with Herder, joined the Carmel settlement.[82]

The influx of this Am Olam group, coupled with Heilprin's more trusting attitude toward his protégés, led to economic cooperation among Carmel colonists that would have been impossible under the more stringent supervision at Alliance. Although plots were sold only to single families at Alliance, Herder, Woskoboynikoff, and three other Carmel settlers bought their land jointly in March 1887.[83] Similarly, a cooperative farm was established in Carmel in 1889 by eight Russian-Jewish families. In their cooperative, each member was to give one dollar per week to the cooperative for twenty weeks to supply the down payment on 185 acres. The members of the cooperative worked in Philadelphia to earn this money, traveling to Carmel in their free time to clear the land.[84]

In February of the same year, an "Industrial Co-operation in Combination with Consumer-Patrons" was organized in Carmel, "for the purpose of conducting farm-work on co-operative principles, combining with it other manufacturing industries that are more or less connected with farming, such as dairy, canneries, manufacture of jellies, etc." The statement issued by the cooperative listed the following conditions:

> 1. Those of us who at present hold in private ownership farms do hereby lease our lands—amount of acres set opposite our respective names—to the said Industrial Co-operation for as long a term of years as it be required, in the same time pledging ourselves to cultivate the same by collective efforts and labor under the direction and superintendency of the functionaries elected and authorized by us from our own midst as stated below.
>
> 2. Those of us who have no farms of their own, or though they do have, prefer co-operative ownership to private ownership, agree to establish and cultivate by united efforts and labor a farm which shall be their common property, held in possession on the co-operative plan.
>
> 3. All the enterprises of the said Industrial Co-operation are to be the concern of all the members; every working member, laborer or officer, shall

be paid regular wages or salary from the income of the Co-operation, and shall besides share in the profits thereof in proportion to their wages or salary in accordance with the by-laws of the Co-operation.

4. Members are free to withdraw from the Co-operation but once a year only, namely: every first of January, giving three months notice to the authorities of the Co-operation, and all their wages and shares of profits due to them shall then be paid out to them in full to the last day of their connection with the Co-operation.[85]

Charles Woskoff (formerly Woskoboynikoff), who grew up at Carmel, described the establishment of the cooperative as follows.

A town meeting was called in which all the elders of the village participated, to discuss how to live a better and fuller life. First, it was decided that the economic basis must be fixed, and it was agreed that the cooperative plan would be best. The work could not belong to a private individual or group to profit at the expense of the rest. The work was parcelled out in accordance with ability to produce, but not so as to deprive the needs of slower workers, and was paid for at the prevailing rate for that particular kind of work.[86]

The co-operation, which at first divided sewing work among member-workers to do at home, ultimately decided to consolidate operations in a factory, financed by Mr. Miller, and mortgaged to the co-operation.[87]

The cooperative arrangement at Carmel extended beyond economic structure and into cultural and social life. The co-operation, besides providing economic benefits to its member-workers and consumer-patrons, planned to establish schools for children and adults, a library, weekly lectures, health care, and social activities.[88] Lectures were among the most popular activities at Carmel, and the intellectuals of the settlement frequently served as speakers. Community celebrations included May Day, as Charles Woskoff recalled:

Everyone had stopped work for the day, and joined in line in front of the factory. About 150 men, women, and children, holding aloft slogans printed in English and Jewish [Yiddish], paraded down the main road, led by a small band of musicians (local talent). They were led by a fiddler who, although he had the conventional four strings to his fiddle, could seem to evoke only one tune out of them, which he kept repeating over and over; a small drum; a tin fife, and a flute, which emitted anything but flute-like sounds. Their combined efforts resulted in such a cacophony of inharmonious sounds that no one could tell just what they were playing. It didn't matter; the marchers trudged along the dusty road, their heads high, trying to proclaim to the world that they were now free.[89]

6. Fred Herder working his Carmel farm toward the end of the depression. Son of Moses and Rachel Herder, Herder became a leader of the Carmel colony and served as the community's justice of the peace. Herder was one of Carmel's leading farmers. *Courtesy Faith Klein.*

Fred Herder, Moses' son and a successful Carmel farmer and longtime justice of the peace, held such reverence for May Day that he apparently altered his daughter's birthday so that it could be celebrated on that day.[90]

Am Olam members who settled in Carmel tended, like their counterparts elsewhere, to be nonreligious. Like the other Am Olam founders, Moses Herder had a religious upbringing and was descended from a rabbinic family, but neither he nor his son was observant.[91] Although other members of the community who were more observant established an informal synagogue during this early period, there apparently was no friction between the religious and the nonobservant. Woskoff recalled that all attended the lectures and "although the lecturer was often a non-believer, the villagers listened with rapt attention, for they were proud to belong to the same community with such intelligent men."[92]

Carmel gained a reputation during these early years as the most radical and intellectual of the South Jersey colonies. Some colonists in Alliance viewed it with suspicion. Arthur Goldhaft, son of Alliance settlers, recalled that Carmel was the liveliest of the colonies: "The new group [at Carmel] was

7. Members of the Woskoboynikoff family in Carmel. Mor-
dechai Woskoboynikoff was a founding member of Odessa Am
Olam and an early settler at Carmel colony. *Courtesy Mildred
Gay.*

strictly composed of intellectuals, even atheists, anarchists and the like. It was
actually whispered that certain couples among them were unmarried and were
practicing free love."[93] Historian Joseph Brandes reports that in Carmel, the
colonists "developed a reputation as intellectuals imbued with the ideas of
Russian nihilism, atheism, and even—some said—free love. Bold individuals
among them tried to deliver inflammatory socialist lectures in an imperfect
English on the main street of Bridgeton [county seat of Cumberland
County]." Carmel colonists, like their western Am Olam counterparts, were
criticized in the Jewish press of Philadelphia for their lack of concern for
religious education. In Carmel, the first synagogue was not dedicated until
1908, twenty-five years after the founding of the colony.[94]

✳✳✳

By comparing Alliance with Carmel, Rosenhayn, and the failed attempts
at colonization in South Jersey, the tremendous impact of the sponsors on the

8. A young woman from Carmel colony
reading outside her home. *Courtesy Mildred
Gay.*

development of each community becomes clear. In Rosenhayn and the other
colonies where no sponsorship was forthcoming, colonization proved extremely difficult, resulting in failure. Only when colonists with enough money
to establish themselves on the land settled at Rosenhayn, and then only when
they turned to factory work, did a lasting settlement shakily emerge. Even
then, the colony would have again failed had Baron de Hirsch not stepped in
to save it from foreclosure.

In the colonies that did receive the attentions of sponsors, the type of aid
and the goals of the sponsors were crucial in determining the shape of the
colony. In Alliance, the goals of the sponsors combined with the effects of a
heterogeneous settler population during the early period of settlement worked
to shape the colony as a mixed agricultural-industrial settlement based on
private ownership. The sponsors' belief in the benefits of private ownership
and reverence for the yeoman farmer as the model citizen led them to pattern
the agricultural sector of the colony's economy after the independent family
farm and to offer farms only to single-family units. Their acceptance of con-

temporary notions of charity and dependence led them to emphasize individual financial responsibility and to aid the settlers through loans. Their business orientation and their desire to create incentives for more immigrants to leave the city led them to encourage investment in factories. Finally, their expectation that the immigrants would be grateful and submissive, and their general conservative bias and fear of "mischief" led them to screen out, or purge, immigrants considered disruptive. All these beliefs precluded arrangements that might otherwise have emerged. For example, the focus on the family farmer precluded multifamily or community-operated production.

In contrast, Carmel was sponsored by Heilprin, who was much more sympathetic to the Am Olam goals. Heilprin did not exhibit the suspicion of cooperative economic organization expressed by Alliance's more conservative sponsors. Under Heilprin's patronage, Carmel developed during its early years as a colony in which cooperation played a large role both in production and in consumption. In addition, it attracted radicals, both as settlers and as visitors, and became known as the most radical of the colonies. Yet Heilprin's inability to adequately aid the farmers led to the development of industry in the settlement, as in Alliance. Although the development of Carmel, Alliance, and Rosenhayn became increasingly similar after the late-1880s, Carmel retained its radical reputation throughout its existence.

The role of the sponsors was one key factor shaping the early development of the colonies, but the background of the settlers was equally important. In the early period of settlement, institutional patterns were developed that would leave an imprint on the colonies for decades to follow. Understanding the background of the early settlers is crucial to tracing this development.

Many observers of the Jewish agricultural colonization movement have assumed that the colonists shared a uniform background with the mass of Jewish immigrants. It has been thought that, like most Jewish immigrants, they were urban in background, often employed in the garment industry in eastern Europe, and that they lacked agricultural experience.[95] For example, Samuel Joseph, historian of the Baron de Hirsch Fund, writes, "The effort of the immigrant Jews to engage in farming has been usually referred to as a 'back to the land' movement. It was rather a 'going to the land,' an attempt on the part of a people completely divorced from the soil to venture into a new and untried field."[96] Most historians of the movement, though recognizing the intellectual component in the Am Olam colonies, fail to make any distinctions concerning variations in social, economic, or religious structures within the premigration community from which the colonists and other immigrants came.[97]

In reality, the immigrants who chose to join the agricultural colonies during the early period of settlement differed in several important respects from the mass of immigrants. First, as noted above, the colonies included a good number of Am Olam intellectuals. Second, during the first years of settlement at Carmel and Alliance, 1882 to 1885, immigrants from the South Pale dominated the colonies. Third, limited data on the premigration occupational background of the earliest immigrants indicates that these settlements included more merchants and farmers, and fewer tailors and other preindustrial craft workers than might be expected from the statistics on Jewish immigrants at large. These three factors were closely related.[98]

The 34 immigrants from the South Pale made up fully 59.6 percent of the 1882 to 1885 arrivals to the colonies for whom a regional origin is known. During this same period, the origins of the remaining colonists were evenly divided: five colonists from Galicia (8.8%), five from Russian Poland (8.8%), six from the North and Northwest Pale (10.5%), and seven from other parts of eastern Europe (12.3%), most notably Hungary and Romania.[99]

These findings are confirmed by several early observers. In his 1912 *American Jewish Yearbook* account of Jewish agricultural activity, Leonard Robinson noted that the earliest Alliance settlers "hailed from southern Russia, mainly from Odessa, Kiev, and Elizabetgrad."[100] Similarly, in his 1889 report on Alliance, Moses Klein wrote, "The 43 families that formed the settlement in the spring of 1882, hailed from almost as many cities, principally of Southern Russia—such as Odessa, Kief [*sic*], Elizabethgrad, etc." In *The Russian Jew in the United States* (1905), Charles Bernheimer also emphasizes the South Pale as the region of origin for most South Jersey colonists.[101]

Although the concentration of pogroms in the southern region of the Pale might imply that the dominance of settlers from the South Pale was typical of Jewish migration in the early 1880s, this was not the case. As discussed in chapter 1, Jewish immigration figures for the period of mass migration indicate that most were from the North or Northwest Pale—those areas hit most strongly by economic hardship.[102] Even during the earliest period of mass migration, there are indications that the proportion of South Pale Jews, though greater than in later periods, never constituted the majority. George Price, a Russian-Jewish newspaper correspondent, analyzed the figures for the 1881 to 1891 migration for a study published in the Russian-Jewish periodical *Voskhod* in 1898. Using annual reports of the United Hebrew Charities, reports of the commissioner of labor, and his own observations as inspector of the Sanitary Aid Society of the Tenth Ward of New York City, Price concluded, "We may safely assume that a major part of the immigrants stemmed from the western,—mostly from the Lithuanian,—provinces (here the Northwest). During the early years of immigration, the immigrants from the southern and southwestern provinces constituted about 40 percent of the total

(200,000) . . . but during the past several years their number did not exceed 20 percent of the total."[103] Similarly, in his 1907 report, "Economic Condition of the Jews in Russia," Isaac Rubinow reported that "the Lithuanian Jews have until recently constituted the vast majority of the Russian-Jewish immigrants to the United States."[104] Thus the percentage (59.6) of settlers during the first three years who were from the South Pale is disproportionately high—even when using Price's higher figure of 40 percent as the basis for comparison.

The predominance of immigrants from the South Pale is important in assessing the background of the colonists because of the contrasts between that region and those regions of the Pale from which most Russian-Jewish immigrants to the United States originated. As discussed in chapter 1, Jews from the South Pale were more integrated with secular society and less religiously traditional than were Jews of other regions. In addition, South Pale Jewry differed from its northwestern counterpart economically, because there Jews were concentrated in the commercial sector and a greater proportion were in agricultural and agriculture-related occupations. These regional characteristics shaped the immigrants that the South Pale produced, and therefore helped shape the New Jersey colonies.

The disproportionate number of colonists from the South Pale is tied to the large number of Am Olam members in this early group. The Am Olam emerged as a direct response by populist-oriented Russified Jewish intellectuals to their betrayal by the peasant masses and Russian populists in the pogroms.[105] Because the Am Olam took hold among Russified intelligentsia, who were located disproportionately in the South Pale, and because it was a response to the pogroms that raged primarily in the South Pale, the Am Olam centered in this region. Thus the Am Olam, which began in Odessa, was most widespread in the South, where it had groups in Elisavetgrad, Kiev, Balta, and Kremenchug. Indeed, of the colonists from the South Pale who arrived in this period, almost all hailed from either Kiev or Odessa, the homes of the two largest Am Olam chapters.[106]

Limited data on the occupational background of settlers during this period reflects the South Pale profile. In his plea to the AIU in 1884, Bayuk reported that nearly all the settlers were merchants, the most common occupation for South Pale Jews.[107] Although previous occupations could be established for relatively few of the colonists (twenty-three for the 1882 to 1885 period), this limited data does suggest dominance of the intellectual professions typical of the Am Olam and of the South Pale in general. Of the twenty-three, six were either students/scholars or had professional occupations (one lawyer/ tax collector and one bookkeeper). An additional five were merchants, three of these known to be in agricultural-related trade (a tobacco dealer, a livestock dealer, and a grain merchant). Two more had professions that would entail a degree of interaction with Russian peasant populations: an innkeeper and a railroad worker. Five were farmers, including one from Poland and four from the South Pale. Finally, five were craftsmen, including a baker, a cabinetmaker, a tailor, a carpenter, and a mason.[108] This distribution contrasts sharply with the occupational profile of Jewish immigrants at large, where manufacturing occupations dominated and merchants were severely underrepresented.[109] It is noteworthy that only one of the twenty-three colonists in this group was employed as a tailor before migrating—by far the most common occupation of Jewish immigrants in this period.

The presence of five farmers and three merchants in agriculture-related trade again belies assumptions that the colonists had no agricultural experience. Although the occupational data presented here is limited, it is confirmed by contemporaneous reports on the occupational backgrounds of settlers in other colonies. For example, the evidence of agricultural experience among the colonists is supplemented by Klein and Price's reports of the presence of fifteen farmers among the sixty-seven heads of household at Rosenhayn.[110] Similarly, the Sicily Island, Louisiana, colony reportedly included eleven farmers in a group of fifty-one men.[111] Although the percentage of farmers in the early population of the colonies was not large—between 21.7 in the small sample here and nearly 23.0 reported by Klein and Price for Rosenhayn—it was significantly greater than the percentage of Jewish farmers among Jewish immigrants in general—2.3.[112] The high percentage of farmers also reflects the South Pale background—only 2.3 percent of all Jews in the Pale were farmers, but 7.0 percent of the Jews from the South Pale region of Kherson, which included Odessa, were so employed.[113]

Indeed, sponsor records confirm the trends suggested by data on Alliance and Carmel, and the reports of observers, by frequently noting that a number of colonists had been farmers in Russia. For example, in his 1912 history of Jews in agriculture in America, Leonard G. Robinson, general manager of the Jewish Agricultural and Industrial Aid Society, stated that in the early period "a number of the immigrants came from agricultural districts, and it was only natural that 'back to the soil' should have become their motto as well as that of their well-wishers."[114]

The degree to which potential colonists did have agricultural experience became a controversial issue among the sponsors; supporters of agricultural colonization tended to emphasize this experience while detractors argued that few Jews had been agriculturalists. For example, Baron de Hirsch, the major supporter of Jewish agricultural colonization in the Americas, sent his agent to visit the South Pale, including the Jewish agricultural colonies there, to evaluate the fitness of the Jews for agricultural colonization. The report was very favorable.[115] In contrast, Dropsie, the AIU representative in Philadelphia and opponent of colonization, argued that claims of farming experience were often fraudulent: "When, to our surprise after a strict investigation, we discov-

Table 4.1

Occupational Distribution by Regional Origin

	Agriculture	Manufacturing	Commerce	Craft	Other
South					
Number	42	9	3	1	1
Percent	48.3%	27.3%	25.0%	14.3%	50.0%
Galicia					
Number	6	5	3	0	0
Percent	6.9%	15.1%	25.0%	—	—
North/Northwest					
Number	8	5	3	0	1
Percent	9.2%	15.1%	25.0%	—	50.0%
Poland					
Number	23	6	1	5	0
Percent	26.4%	18.2%	8.3%	71.4%	—
Other					
Number	8	8	2	1	0
Percent	9.2%	24.2%	16.7%	14.3%	—
Total	87	33	12	7	2

ered that of the 40 families [to be settled in a proposed colony in 1882] who alleged that they were agriculturalists, there was but one male who had been a farmer, and one other who had some knowledge of farming . . . this project was abandoned."[116]

The popular notion among both historians and descendants that the colonists had no farming experience whatsoever may result from an effort to explain the failure of so many agricultural colonies. In addition, the differences in farming techniques and crops between Russia and New Jersey often made such experience useless, even where it did exist. Although the Jersey colonists were primarily engaged in growing fruits and vegetables in this period, Russian-Jewish farmers planted cereals, which required different methods and implements.[117]

Once settled in the colony, South Pale origin was important in determining the likelihood of a settler becoming employed in agriculture. The percentage of immigrants from the South Pale in the colony shrank in later years (they represented 40 percent of the total population for the entire period 1882 to 1920), but they dominated the agricultural sector throughout the life of the colonies. Fully 48.3 percent of the farmers in the colonies were of South Pale origin, and 75 percent of the settlers from the South Pale were employed in the agricultural sector throughout the life of the colonies (see table 4.1).

The strong connection between South Pale origin and occupation in the colonies' agricultural sector is tied to factors discussed above, such as the tim-

Table 4.2

Occupational Distribution of Settlers, by Arrival Date, 1882–1890

	Agriculture	Manufacturing	Commerce	Craft	Other
1882–1885					
Number	93	9	9	0	3
Percent	81.6%	7.9%	7.9%	—	2.6%
1886–1890					
Number	39	38	17	6	6
Percent	36.8%	35.8%	16.0%	5.7%	5.7%

ing of migration, the conditions of settlement in the first few years, and affiliation with the Am Olam. In the earliest years of the colonies, 1882 to 1885, immigration from the South Pale to the United States was at its peak, because of the concentration of pogroms in that region. These years also include the period of migration for Am Olam members, mostly of South Pale origin, intending to farm. In addition, during these years, the colonies offered few nonagricultural activities. Because the first factory was not established until 1884, those who settled in the 1882 to 1885 period concentrated heavily in the agricultural sector. The work distribution among the colonists for this period is as follows: 93 colonists in agriculture (81.6%), 9 in manufacturing (7.9%), 9 in commerce (7.9%), and 3 in other areas (2.6%). Thus, a group of mutually reinforcing factors led to the concentration of settlers from the South Pale in the colonies' agricultural sector.

Sponsor policies and shifting migration patterns, as early as the late 1880s, began to alter social and economic patterns in the colonies. The sponsors' policies were a major factor shaping the composition of subsequent cohorts of settlers. First, by aiding the colonists consistently, the sponsors kept the colony afloat and made it a viable alternative for new migrants. Second, by encouraging the establishment of an industrial sector, the sponsors attracted nonagricultural workers who differed in goals and background from the earlier settlers. Finally, by precluding developments toward communalism, and by purging settlers considered outspoken, they discouraged continued settlement by radicals.

Similarly, changes in the pool of potential immigrants shaped the composition of later groups of settlers. The dissolution of the Am Olam and the increasing involvement of the Russian-Jewish intelligentsia in the emerging socialist and labor movements in American urban centers, reduced the pool of radical intellectuals interested in settling in agricultural colonies.[118] The increased crowding in the urban ghettos of cities, such as New York, led other, nonidealistic and nonagricultural immigrants to look to the colonies as an escape from harsh employment and residential conditions. In a number

9. The Alliance cemetery gate dedicated to the founders of the colony. *Courtesy Ellen Eisenberg.*

of cases, religious Jews were attracted to the colonies because they believed there would be fewer impediments to religious observance in an all Jewish settlement.[119]

By the late 1880s, all the South Jersey colonists were indebted to sponsoring organizations, primarily the Alliance Land Trust. The need to earn cash to pay off these mortgages led the colonists to welcome the addition of factories to the colonies. However, in aiding the development of factories, sponsors not only provided supplemental work for farmers but also intended to make South Jersey attractive to nonagricultural workers. By the end of the decade, the colonies not only boasted factories in Alliance and Carmel, but two new communities were growing at either end of Alliance—the nuclei of the settlements that were to become the primarily industrial colonies of Norma and Brotmanville were in place. The development of the industrial sector in the colonies resulted in an occupational distribution for settlers arriving in the 1886 to 1890 period that contrasted sharply with that of the earlier period. Although 81.6 percent of settlers arriving in the first half of the 1880s worked in the agricultural sector, and only 7.9 percent in manufacturing, the manufacturing

10. Inscription on the cemetery gate. *Courtesy Ellen Eisenberg.*

sector employed 35.8 percent of the later group and stood on an equal footing with agriculture (see table 4.2).

The influx of nonagricultural settlers and the waning of the Am Olam influence can be seen in the changing statistics on settler origins. In contrast to the 1882 to 1885 period, when settlers from the South Pale clearly dominated migration to the colonies, in the 1885 to 1890 period, no one region was dominant. In this period, settlers from the South Pale dropped as a percentage of total arrivals from 59.6 percent to 20.0 percent. The increasing share of settlers from the Northwest Pale (from 10.5 percent to 23.3 percent), the region that supplied the most Jewish immigrants to industrial centers, such as New York, corresponds to the expansion of the colonies' industrial sector (see table 4.3).

The movement away from purely agricultural colonies, the influx of increasing numbers of settlers with backgrounds contrasting with those of the earlier settlers, and the consolidation of sponsorship in the late 1880s set the stage for changes in the colonies in the 1890s and beyond. During the first few years, a good part of the settler population shared Am Olam ideology, South

Table 4.3

Regional Origin of Settlers, 1882–1890

	South	Galicia	North/Northwest	Poland	Other
1882–1885					
Number	34	5	6	5	7
Percent	59.6%	8.8%	10.5%	8.8%	12.3%
1886–1890					
Number	6	6	7	4	7
Percent	20.0%	20.0%	23.3%	13.3%	23.3%

Pale origin, and a nonindustrial occupational profile. This shared premigration background set a tone that seemed to echo that of the western agrarian colonies, though modified by active sponsor supervision and by the greater heterogeneity of the settlements. As sponsors extended and consolidated their control in the 1890s, development of the New Jersey colonies diverged even more from the western pattern. In the next chapter, the continuation of the movement away from agrarian communalism toward mixed agricultural and industrial economies is traced. The impact of these changes on the social, religious, and economic life of the colonies are analyzed as a function of sponsor policies and changing settler constituencies.

5

The Middle Years

Settlers and Sponsors, 1890–1910

THE TREND toward industrialization and private ownership that began in the colonies in the late 1880s was strengthened in succeeding decades. As the weak, short-lived philanthropic agencies of the 1880s passed out of existence, they were replaced in the 1890s with more permanent organizations, which used their policies to further their goals of Americanization, immigrant removal from urban areas, and "productivization." At the same time, new immigrants, who did not share the communal, agrarian goals of the early Am Olam settlers, arrived in the colonies. These newcomers, whose backgrounds contrasted sharply with those of their predecessors, helped transform the colonies socially, religiously, culturally, and economically.

In chapter 4, the origins of the colonies' economic transformation from agrarian communalism to a mixed agricultural-industrial economy, based on private ownership, were traced. In this chapter, the continuation of this pattern is analyzed. The changes in sponsorship and in the composition of settler population that contributed to this transformation, and the impact of these changes on the colonies' social, religious, and cultural life are explored.

After the demise of the Hebrew Emigrant Aid Society, the loans of the financially strapped colonists were passed first to the United Hebrew Charities, then to the Alliance Land Trust. In the 1890s, the loans were again transferred to the newly founded Baron de Hirsch Fund. This transfer, and the consolidation of sponsorship under the auspices of the fund, an organization that had not yet defined its position on the colonies, combined with a faltering national economy and increased anti-Semitism to make the 1890s a decade of uncertainty for the colonists. Only the resolution of the fund to take forceful steps toward aiding the colonies in the late 1890s, and to create the Jewish Agricultural and Industrial Aid Society (JAIAS) in 1900, provided some assurance of increased growth in the colonies. The fund's conclusion that industry was necessary to make rural colonies viable, coupled with its continued emphasis on the goals of Americanization, productivization, and removal from urban areas, set the tone for the twentieth century.

At the time of Moses Klein's 1889 report, Alliance colony had a total farming population of 529, including 282 males and 247 females. This population included 84 children ten years and under, 91 teenagers, and 38 persons over fifty years of age. Only sixteen additional families lived in the colony without owning land. Rosenhayn had, at the same time, sixty-seven families, including 194 people; Carmel's population was 286.[1]

In the ten years after the report, the colonies grew substantially. In the 1900 federal census, Alliance colony was composed of about 150 households. Many of these households included single boarders, relatives not part of the nuclear family, and, in a few cases, servants. The population in the 1900 census for these households was 877.[2] Carmel and Rosenhayn also experienced much growth in this period. By 1900, these two settlements had 204 households with a population of 1,154.[3]

The healthy population increase between the 1889 report and the 1900 census masks the severity of conditions in the colonies in the early and mid-1890s. During the 1890s, the colonies suffered through general economic instability and repeated depression. In addition, there was a marked growth in local anti-Semitism.

Although the Jewish farmers were aided by natives of the region and enjoyed a generally harmonious relationship with them in the initial years of settlement, tensions grew during the early 1890s because increasing numbers of Jewish industrial workers in the area entered the job market just as the area's manufacturing sector was feeling financial strain. The resentment of native-born workers for their Jewish counterparts erupted in September of 1891, when workers in nearby Millville's Whitall, Tatem and Company glass factory struck, refusing to work with Jews. The five hundred strikers, armed with clubs, chased Jewish workers through the streets. As the company locked out the strikers, they "paraded through the streets singing, 'we don't care whether we work or not', or 'we won't work with Jews.'" When the strike spread to the Cumberland Furnace Glass factory in Bridgeton, the company accepted the strikers' demands and fired the Jews "declaring that they were unfit to work."[4]

This venting of nativism reflected the increasing antiimmigrant sentiment that spread through the American labor movement in the 1890s—both the American Federation of Labor and the Knights of Labor advocated restriction of immigration in the early 1890s.[5] In Salem and Cumberland counties, this nativism spread beyond the workplace during this unsettled decade. The temperance issue was used to attack Jews in this period, and several colonists were arrested for distilling alcohol. The strong temperance stand of the Vineland community, which had been dry since its founding, led this issue to become a source of tension for decades.[6]

Difficult financial times, coupled with new mortgage agreements with the Alliance Land Trust, also contributed to the woes of the colonies' farmers. The Alliance colonists were presented with deeds for their properties during the July 1888 dedication ceremony of the synagogue, Eben ha'Ezer. The mortgages on these deeds represented a community indebtedness of ten thousand dollars, to be paid over ten years. The issuance of the deeds enabled the settlers to qualify for loans on the private market, to finance household repairs, the digging of wells, and the construction of barns and community buildings.[7] When colonists began taking on these additional debts, their weight combined with both severe weather and a poor regional economy, proved too difficult for many colonists to bear.

In 1894, a committee of Alliance farmers appealed directly to Baron Maurice de Hirsch. They wrote to Hirsch of their indebtedness both to their sponsors and to the Franklin Loan and Building Association of Salem (for a community debt of fifty-seven thousand dollars), claiming that early frosts since 1891 combined with the lack of manufacturing jobs in winter, the lack of a canning factory, and low depression prices, made them unable to pay. "Interests, fines, and assessments are accumulating every month," they reported, emphasizing that foreclosures were imminent.[8]

The Alliance settlers' report on the dismal situation was confirmed by an 1897 report by Arthur Reichow of the Agriculture Department of the Baron de Hirsch Fund. After visiting Alliance, Carmel, and Rosenhayn, Reichow reported that the condition was "serious" and that "only immediate and substantial aid can save its settlers from economic ruin." Reichow reported that the number of farmers had dropped from two hundred in 1894 to seventy-six, leaving 130 abandoned homesteads where "100,000 hard earned dollars of our people has been invested." Reichow blamed the farmers' situation on the lack of local markets, suggesting that the establishment of factories to create such markets was the only solution. He believed that twenty-six thousand dollars was needed to establish "needle industries," as well as twenty-five thousand dollars to settle with the Building Association, twenty thousand dollars for private mortgages, and fifteen thousand dollars to successful colonists for loans for "productive purposes"—namely, investment in clothing manufacturing businesses.[9]

The need for local markets was not a new idea. For years before Reichow's report, both sponsors and colonists had argued that farmers could not survive without a local market for their produce. In the early 1890s, colonist George Seldes wrote to Adolphus Solomons of the Baron de Hirsch Fund, reporting on the desperate situation in the colonies and recommending the creation of "a home market for the disposal of our produce."[10] In 1891, a Board of Trade was established by Alliance colonists "to diffuse information concerning the trade, manufacturing of Alliance, to promote intercourse between business men [sic], to protect all the business interest of said Alliance from impostors, to co-operate with similar societies in other places, to attract capital, incourage [sic] the establishment of manufacturing industries, and to aid in the development of Alliance's resources and advantages generally."[11] The Board of Trade also hoped to establish a factory of its own, financed through the sale of ten-dollar shares. Yet attempts by the colonists to expand local markets were insufficient. The colonies were saved only by the decision of the Baron de Hirsch Fund to support the colonies.

The consolidation of loans under the Baron de Hirsch Fund, and that organization's decision to create local markets through the support of industry in the colonies, was the single most important factor shaping the colonies after 1890. The policy of aiding industry and supporting growth in the rural settlements grew directly out of the fund's established goals. Like the earlier sponsoring organizations, the fund focused on Americanization, productivization, and removal of immigrants from the crowded urban ghettos.

The fund's support for these goals is evident throughout its records and those of its subsidiary, the JAIAS. Baron de Hirsch himself believed that the assimilation of Jews into the American populace was the key to preventing the growth of anti-Semitism in the United States. In a letter to Judge Myer Isaacs and Jacob Schiff of the New York Committee, Hirsch wrote,

> My opinion always has been and will always continue, that it is proper that Jewish workmen, agriculturalists, and merchants should mingle as much as possible with the people among whom they live, who are of other religious faiths; that is, in my judgement the only means of amalgamating the Jewish element with the native element, to dissipate the prejudice which has already lasted too long, and to remove from anti-Semitism one of its chief weapons, one of its favorite arguments.[12]

Adolphus Solomons, a trustee of the fund, expressed the same goal in an 1891 *New York Times* interview: "One of the objects we have in view is to Americanize the immigrants, and to assimilate them with the masses, and thoroughly imbue them with the American Constitution and American institutions."[13]

For the American trustees of the fund, all successful bankers or businessmen, Americanization meant not only ability to speak English (the fund did sponsor an English school) or adoption of American dress but also acceptance of the values of American economic life. Such values included economic independence, home ownership, and respect for private property. Thus, like

HEAS, the fund and the JAIAS structured their aid to reinforce these values by prohibiting charity, funding mortgages on business principles for home and farm ownership, and discouraging radicalism. The connection of these values to Americanization in the minds of the sponsors was clear. In his *Times* interview, Solomons not only advocated adherence to the U.S. Constitution but also warned, "None of the Nihilists, Socialists, or anarchist elements will be tolerated."[14]

Both the effort to make the immigrants productive, through manual training and loans to craftsmen for tools, and the attempt to "remove" them from urban ghettos supported the goal of Americanization. By giving the immigrants the skills and tools they needed to earn an independent living, they would be freed from dependence and allowed to establish themselves as productive citizens. Similarly, moving them out of an unhealthy, immigrant-populated ghetto would allow them to settle among the native-born American population and begin to assimilate. Thus the Provisional Plan of Organization of the fund specified several areas of activity, including removal of new immigrants to areas outside the major cities, training in various trades, furnishing craftsmen with tools and other necessities for earning a living, and, only in "exceptional" cases, providing loans that would enable the borrower to earn a living.[15] It is significant that sponsorship of colonization was not even mentioned.

Although the fund did ultimately support the New Jersey colonies, both by taking over the colonists' debts and by creating incentives for industrial employers to establish factories, only after negotiations was colony support included in the fund's goals. Despite the connection of the Hirsch name with Jewish colonization projects, most notably in Argentina in the 1890s, the American leadership of the fund emphasized removal, education, and training, over colonization. In a 1906 directory of New York charities, the Baron de Hirsch Fund's stated goals were: "To Americanize and assimilate the immigrants with the masses by teaching them to become good citizens; and to prevent by all proper means, their congregation in large cities."[16] Their activities accurately reflected these goals, the expenditures for removals accounting for most activity.[17]

Indeed, when Hirsch made it known to the American Jewish philanthropic leadership in New York and Philadelphia that he intended to create a fund to aid immigrants, sponsorship of colonization was expressly opposed by the Philadelphia group, led by William Hackenburg and Moses Dropsie. The Philadelphia group's proximity to the New Jersey colonies and their familiarity with the difficulties there underlay their skepticism. As Hackenburg explained to the New Yorkers, "I should think the experience with Alliance Colony's early history, if you knew it as well as we Philadelphians do, will teach you that you err." The Philadelphia group acknowledged that Hirsch wanted "to assist those who are willing to become farmers by loans and gifts," but they voiced their opposition "to any part of the Baron's benefaction being spent to colonize." The dispute between the New York group, which ultimately gained control of the fund, and the Philadelphians raged for several months in the spring and summer of 1889.[18]

Although the Philadelphians tried to convince the New Yorkers that Hirsch did not have "any such intention as your letter suggests to invest a large amount of money in land near New Jersey or elsewhere,"[19] it is clear from his actions in Argentina beginning in the early 1890s that Hirsch was supportive of colonization. In a letter to the New York group in July of 1889, he urged the two factions to work together, claiming, "I have positively no wish to advance my personal judgement since I am less informed than you are." Yet, though expressing reservations about the merits of establishing exclusively Jewish enclaves as detrimental to his assimilationist goals, he did endorse the idea of buying lands "some distance from New York" on which immigrants could be settled. In a later letter to Jacob Schiff, Hirsch's true enthusiasm for colonization emerged. Suggesting that a hundred thousand immigrants could be established in large-scale colonies in the United States with an investment of 20 million dollars, he enthusiastically claimed, "Every co-religionist will gladly be willing to give his money on good interest without market risk and at the same time being conscious of having lent aid to a good work."[20]

The baron's belief in agricultural colonization forced the American trustees to include it as one area of fund activity. Yet the support given the colonies did not emphasize the agricultural sector. Rather, it was accepted by the fund leadership that mixed agricultural-industrial settlements in rural areas could better aid their goal of removal. In the fund's deed of trust, which took shape through lengthy negotiations between Hirsch, the New Yorkers, and the Philadelphians, agricultural training and loans were the only forms of aid for farmers mentioned. Only one of the four committees established was concerned at all with agriculture, and that committee was given dual responsibility for "industrial and agricultural training."[21] Myer Isaacs, a trustee of the fund from its inception until his death in 1904, argued in a letter to Schiff in October 1889: "I am of the opinion that farming will always be a failure if adopted by people who are not accustomed to it, but [I] am certain that Industrial Colonies will be a great success." Isaacs suggested that the fund should focus on four goals: "to abolish pauperism and to disencourage [sic] the petty traders among the Russian Jews"; to remove them from the ghetto; to "scatter them all over the United States"; and to "educate them to become good American citizens." Isaacs called for the establishment of colonies near railroads, consisting of fifteen families, each with a "cheap dwelling," a workshop, a general store, and a schoolhouse that would double as a synagogue and lecture hall. These settlements would be supervised by a salaried superintendent, and would require a twenty thousand-dollar investment per colony, to be repaid by each colonist with a hundred dollars down and five dollars per month.[22]

Although Isaacs's plan was not adopted, Hirsch's support for colonization, coupled with the idea that mixed agricultural-industrial colonies might facilitate the desired removal of immigrants from ghettos to rural locations, left the door open to aiding the existing colonies and to sponsoring new ones. Indeed, the baron's enthusiasm for colonization and his belief that productivization through agricultural labor was the solution to the "Jewish problem," led the fund to include support for agricultural projects, and ultimately to create the Jewish Agricultural and Industrial Aid Society to concentrate specifically on such projects.[23] Most immediately, the decision of the baron to earmark 240,000 dollars for colonization made the founding of the Woodbine colony in Cape May County, New Jersey, one of the first activities of the fund.[24] Yet the belief of the trustees that exclusively agricultural settlements were not viable, and that the establishment of industry in rural areas would provide an opportunity for removals, led to Woodbine's development as a mixed agricultural-industrial town, rather than as a farming settlement.

Established under the auspices of the Baron de Hirsch Fund in 1891, Woodbine was planned as an agricultural and industrial colony. Beginning with a population of fifty families, Woodbine became the largest of the colonies by the turn of the century, with a population of twenty-five hundred. In 1894, Woodbine became the home of the Baron de Hirsch Agricultural School, designed to carry out the baron's goal of agricultural training for Jewish children. Rapid development in the first years by the Woodbine Land and Improvement Company gave the colony factory buildings, a modern power plant, a public bath, and wide avenues. In 1903, Woodbine was incorporated as a borough, making it the first American town in which all official posts were held by Jews.[25] Woodbine was unique among the Jewish colonies because it was intended from its inception to be both an industrial town and a farming center; and because it was created at the initiative of the sponsors, not of the settlers themselves. Although these circumstances create sharp contrasts between Woodbine and the earlier New Jersey colonies, it is important to understand Woodbine's development, because the fund used lessons learned there to develop policies for the other colonies.

Woodbine's successful growth was not without cost to the fund. An effort had been made to include Russians in the Woodbine leadership, but the differences between eastern colonists and western sponsors surfaced violently in Woodbine within the first few years. Despite the installation of a Russian Jew,

Prof. H. L. Sabsovich, who was both a former Am Olam member and an expert agronomist, as superintendent at Woodbine, the financial sponsors retained much control. The sponsors enforced their policies, designed to create independence and discourage charity, to the fullest degree. Woodbine Land and Improvement Company directors were all fund trustees; Julius Goldman served as president. Mortgages were issued for the thirty-acre farm plots, in a remote area of southern New Jersey rather than in a suburban location, to discourage return migration to New York.[26] Colonists were selected by the directors, who favored south Russians, "for it was believed they would make the best farmers." The baron's investigation of the south Russian colonies undoubtedly contributed to this decision. In addition, twelve settlers who had left the Argentine colonies were selected.[27]

Agricultural experience was not the only criterion used in selecting colonists. To insure that recruits were hardworking and productive persons, only those who could afford the two hundred-dollar down payment were accepted, a method of screening which became standard under both the fund and the JAIAS.[28] In 1898, Isaacs, both a fund trustee and a director of the Woodbine Land and Improvement Company, wrote to Hirsch's Paris-based Jewish Colonization Association that only potential farmers with two to four thousand rubles to invest would be aided "as only such a self-relying element can be expected to accomplish satisfactory results and encourage others with even smaller means to follow their good example."[29] Settlers were expected to make prompt and regular payments on their mortgages of approximately eleven hundred dollars per family. After less than two years, with the establishment of the cloak factory, subsidies were cut off because most of the trustees felt that the colony should be self-supporting.[30]

The determination of the fund to wean the Woodbine colonists from subsidies early, and thus avoid the continued dependence that so disturbed them at Alliance, led to demoralization among the colonists and ultimately to outright revolt. The farmers, who had settled on virgin land, were not yet capable of self-sufficiency, and in 1892, several work stoppages threatened the progress of town building. Sponsors warned the colonists to desist from such actions, posting a notice stating that wise settlers "will continue to labor industriously for the benefit of themselves and their families." The notice went on to warn that the trustees would not tolerate disorder and that dissatisfied settlers should leave, admonishing them: "Be men. Be true to yourselves, to your brethren who have sought an asylum in this great country and whose cause you are damaging by your conduct."[31]

Despite such warnings, early in 1893, the colonists rebelled against the fund, refusing to make payments on their loans. Sabsovich, caught between the colonists and the sponsors, tried to mediate, but was seen by the colonists as a traitor, vilified as "the man ruling Woodbine like the Czar of Russia." Colonists telegraphed the fund in April of 1893: "Sabsovich keeps Pinkertons who keep shooting every night. Yesterday they nearly killed one of us. Come at once, if not there be murder [*sic*]." Colonists argued that Baron de Hirsch, who died just before the dispute, had intended the farms to be gifts. After months of conflict, during which the farmers refused to plant, the colonists filed suit in Cape May against the fund in September 1893. When the court found their claims groundless, compromise terms were offered to most of the colonists and several of the "mischief-makers" were forced to leave, ending the dispute.[32]

The sponsors blamed the trouble at Woodbine on "agitators who wished no good to Woodbine or its settlers,"[33] and expelled such persons as an example to the community, but the conflicts called into question the wisdom of establishing new colonies. As the young Baron de Hirsch Fund defined its policies in the 1890s, the shadow of the Woodbine experience reinforced the doubts of many trustees about colonization projects.[34]

The difficulties at Woodbine fueled the arguments of those who had long opposed colonization, and persuaded others to join their ranks. Goldman, who had been a supporter of the Woodbine project, reversed his views as a result of the experience. By the mid-1890s, Goldman joined Isaacs, whose disapproval of large-scale colonization had been consistent. Isaacs had warned before the establishment of Woodbine, "I do not think we should repeat the experiment of sending a certain number of families, whose capacity and history are unknown, to an uncleared tract of land and to be held responsible by them or in our own minds for their failure to become successful farmers."[35] The fact that the Woodbine colonists had been selected on the basis of agricultural experience and proven industriousness (as represented by their ability to invest their own money), and that they shared no ideological or educational background that might predispose them to rebelliousness, made the Woodbine revolt even more shattering to colonization plans.

Within the settlement, disillusionment marked by a high turnover among the colonists followed the resolution of the conflict.[36] Criticism of the fund for its harshness in dealing with the colonists resulted in negative publicity both within the Jewish community and outside. Fund officials were aware of the danger of bad publicity during the conflict, as when Superintendent Sabsovich wrote to Reichow of a reporter who "does not care to find out the truth; he only wants to arouse public opinion favorable to the agitating farmers. I know that their case will be lost when brought before a court . . . but I see disaster for Woodbine if legal proceedings are not taken up."[37] The concern about publicity was warranted: in 1893 several articles favorable to the colonists were published in the New York newspapers.[38] Sabsovich was disheartened by the conflict, writing, "I am trying to bury my feelings, trying to be calm, but it costs me my health. I feel so uneasy every time I have to leave Woodbine on business that I shall have heart failure. I begin to lose courage. I am afraid I am becoming quixotic. Threats are being made openly, and I am warned by several outsiders to be cautious."[39] Amid the struggle, Sabsovich collapsed in the street, seriously ill, and required several months to regain his health.[40]

The trustees' concern about publicity was not due solely to a desire to protect the image of the fund. Rather, trustees worried that negative publicity might fan anti-Semitic feelings toward Russian Jews as a group. These fears reinforced the sentiments expressed before the founding of Woodbine by opponents of colonization. For example, Dropsie of Philadelphia had written in 1889 that aid from the fund should be for persons "not concentrated in one area" and not for large-scale enterprises, industrial or agricultural, because such aid would result in anti-Semitism.[41]

The experience at Woodbine was a major factor shaping the subsequent fund decision to emphasize aid to farmers in scattered sites as the primary method of supporting agricultural development among immigrants. In surveying agricultural ventures, Goldman argued in an 1896 letter that the most positive results had been achieved not in the Jersey colonies, but among "industrial farmers" in New England. These farmers, who invested their own money in their farms, had achieved a success rate of 75 percent and required little assistance from the fund. In advocating aid to farmers who had their own money to invest, Goldman argued that colonies made up of settlers without their own money were doomed to failure. Such settlers, he claimed, had nothing to lose and were likely "to lose their energy and self-reliance to become permanent charges upon those who have started them in life. The slow progress that they make, the many years that are consequently required to enable them to see a future before them, and the general characteristics of human nature seem to be such that settlers of this kind are a failure." Goldman concluded that "agricultural settlement upon any extended scale among the Russian Jews is not feasible," explaining the fund's decision to abandon this type of colonization in favor of aid to farmers "on strict business principles" in amounts corresponding to the settler's own investment.[42] Similar support for the single-family model was expressed by Isaacs, writing that, in the United States, agriculture should be "undertaken by families for the sole purpose of establishing an agricultural homestead, which must be worked by the owner, with the assistance of the members of his family alone." When the JAIAS took over responsibility for the agricultural aid in 1900, their bylaws specified that agricultural loans were to be made to qualified applicants who "also show that they have acquired or are about to acquire with their own means, the title of the farm."[43]

The cautious attitude of the fund's trustees regarding investment in agricultural loans led them not only to mandate that settlers invest their own money, but also to institute strict screening procedures to determine an applicant's aptitude for farming. The trustees had long recognized that many Russian farmers were unfit for American farming. Thus many failures were blamed on "primitive" farming methods in Russia.[44] The more suspicious Philadelphians warned that "you will find plenty of shiftless people coming to this country who want to become farmers without any idea of what farming means." Hackenburg of Philadelphia warned, "In my experience with our Russian immigrants I have heard of many who call themselves farmers but when placed in that position knew nothing at all about agricultural pursuits."[45] In dealing with this problem of screening, trustees advocated agricultural training, both through schools, such as that established at Woodbine, and through practical experience under capable farmers.

Although the Woodbine school was established as the primary training ground for children of immigrants already in the United States, the best means of training adults and new arrivals was a subject of much debate. Sponsors, hoping for a return on their investment, attempted to avoid plans deemed financially risky. Thus just as with the agricultural loans themselves, sponsors decided to make agricultural training available only to those willing to invest their own money. In 1898, Isaacs proposed such a plan for training the children of "intending emigrants from Russia." A group of twenty such children would be enrolled at Woodbine Agricultural School "to come here as 'avant-coureurs' of their respective families, to acquire such knowledge as is absolutely necessary for any agricultural enterprises in which the parents might engage after their arrival." To insure the investment in such a plan, the children were to be "twenty carefully selected sons of families from different parts of Russia, who are possessed of at least from 2000 to 4000 rubles, to enable them to buy farms in this country without any charitable aid."[46]

Practical training and testing of adult applicants was more problematic for the trustees. This was to prove a continual difficulty in the fund's agricultural program. In 1910, the JAIAS Annual Report noted that "our most difficult task does not lie so much in finding material for the farm, as in keeping from the farm those who, for various reasons, are not fit for it." In the early 1900s, when placement of trainees under experienced farmers proved too limiting for a large-scale training program, members of the JAIAS began discussing the idea of a "test farm."[47] In April of 1902, the Special Executive Committee of the JAIAS met to discuss the options for testing the farming ability of agricultural applicants.

The meeting focused on how best to test the farmers, in Loeb's words, "to see if the man has the experience which he claims or if he will make a

good farmer." Although Sabsovich focused on training people through placement with established farmers in upstate New York, many of the trustees
expressed concern that this plan would make supervision difficult. Nearly all
those present agreed with Loeb that supervision "in the house as well as the
land" was crucial to the success of the experiment. As one trustee explained,
"We are simply doing what you would do with children. You don't throw an
inexperienced child on the world." Only Sabsovich, the sole Russian on the
committee, argued against such paternalism, claiming, "Those farmers who
have succeeded best have never been supported by us. In those Jersey farming
localities they have done the best work who have not been assisted. . . . In
spite of all our paternalism there are farmers in Massachusetts who have never
heard about us and who are successes."[48]

Although a consensus emerged that the necessary supervision could most
easily be undertaken in the New Jersey colonies, Loeb and others expressed
concern: "I fear the environment there, there are so many there who are
Russian Jews; I want to take a fresh locality and start away from influences that
might be harmful." Besides worries about the potential influence of the Jersey
colonists, who had been so troublesome to the sponsors in the past, and about
the possible ill effects of increasing the concentration of Russian Jews in that
area, the committee argued that trainees would be unwilling to work on a
farm that they could never purchase. The recognition of the need to provide
an incentive to the trainee, combined with an unwillingness to risk financing
mortgages to untested farmers, led to the emergence of a plan under which
the fund itself would own the land. Thus, if the farmer did not succeed, the
loss would not be as great as with a loan. In addition, holding the land in the
society's name would allow the sponsors to run the operation and closely
supervise the trainees.[49]

A key advocate of the test farm idea was Loeb, who compared the program to the running of English classes: both provided the immigrant with a
skill so that he could support himself. To Loeb, the combination of training
and testing was essential: "Our proposition is to put them in a place where
they can learn those [American farming] methods and where they may remain
until we are satisfied that they know enough and then we send them out."
Thus Loeb's test farm would have tenant laborers who received wages for their
work on the main farm, as well as land for their own use. Observation
by supervisors would show whether a person was "worth something" or "a
failure."[50]

Ultimately Loeb's plan was adopted by the JAIAS, and a farm was purchased during the summer of 1904 in northern New Jersey. To insure a high
level of trainees and to guarantee that graduates had the means to meet farm
loan requirements upon completion of their training, applicants had to possess

two hundred dollars. Upon graduation, they would be required to pay a 10 percent deposit on their own farms. By the summer of 1906, seven test farm graduates had become farmers in Woodbine.[51]

✳✳✳

Although the Woodbine experiment led the sponsors to abandon the idea of establishing new agricultural colonies and to emphasize instead agricultural training and loans for farmers able to invest in their own farms, the old settlements were not abandoned. Sponsors felt that these colonies could be valuable as an outlet for the effort to remove Jews from urban ghettos. Even those opposing the establishment of new colonies felt that too much had already been invested in the existing colonies to abandon them. Learning from the Woodbine experience, sponsors argued that the Salem and Cumberland County colonies could be revivified through wise investment, careful screening, and supervision.

Several lessons from the Woodbine experiment shaped fund policy toward the Salem County and Cumberland County settlements in the 1890s and beyond. The emergence of Woodbine as a successful town after the "troubles" reinforced the belief that industry was essential to the success of any such settlement, both because it created a local market and because it made the settlements viable destinations for the relocation of industrial workers. Reichow, whose reports in the late 1890s led directly to the policy of supporting industrial development in the colonies, conducted extensive correspondence with the fund's trustees in this period, attempting to convince them of the centrality of industry to the success of the colonies. In June of 1897, Reichow reported to Dr. Julius Goldman that the difficulties at Alliance, Carmel, and Rosenhayn were a result of "the entire absence of industrial activity, which appears indispensable for the building up of local markets for agricultural products."[52] Only the new colony of Woodbine was prosperous, reported Reichow, because of the "strength and stability of industry" in that colony.

In his report, Reichow was preaching to the converted—Goldman had already expressed a similar confidence in the power of industrial development to salvage the colonies. In 1896, Goldman had reported to the Jewish Colonization Association on behalf of the fund that the primary reason for Alliance's difficulties was that "the industries that, in our opinion, are necessary to enable any settlement of this kind to prosper have always been wanting." Goldman's views were colored by the Woodbine experience. He noted that, though successful as a town, Woodbine's development as an agricultural center had been thwarted by several factors, including "agitation among them by socialistically inclined persons about three years ago, at a time when all of their energies should have been devoted to the cultivation of the soil."[53] Thus even before Reichow's report, Goldman recommended the support of industry in Alliance, Carmel, and Rosenhayn.

Although the trustees had soured on the idea of creating new settlements, they became convinced that, through the introduction of industry, unsuccessful agricultural colonies could be made useful. The key to support for industry in the colonies was the fund's stated goal to remove immigrants from the crowded ghettos. This motive was made clear by the fund's advocates of industrial development. In his 1896 letter, Goldman wrote that the primary need was "to clean out the ghetto," and suggested that aid to immigrants be made conditional on agreement to leave the city. Those leaving the cities, he wrote, should be placed in manufacturing centers nationwide.[54] Similarly, though Reichow repeatedly cited the benefits that the establishment of industry would bring to agricultural sectors through expansion of local markets, the opportunity to remove workers from crowded ghettos to work in the rural factories was also a constant theme.[55]

On Reichow's recommendation, the fund set out to reorganize affairs at Alliance, Carmel, and Rosenhayn, with aid from the fund's parent organization, the Jewish Colonization Association.[56] The JCA made an appropriation that enabled the fund to complete the takeover of both Alliance Land Trust and private mortgages in 1898, including 10,571 dollars in Franklin Loan and Building Association mortgages and 3,170 dollars in Alliance Land Trust loans to Alliance colonists; and 10,246 dollars and 9,665 dollars in mortgages held by the Merchants and Mechanics Building Association for colonists of Carmel and Rosenhayn respectively.[57]

Along with the restructuring of loans, the fund embarked on a policy in the late 1890s to bolster industry in the colonies, a policy that continued after 1900 under the JAIAS, and resulted directly in the expansion of the colonies' industrial population by 1900. Reichow's consolidation plan included loans to industries in the colonies, totaling more than fifteen thousand dollars.[58] Besides loans, industries were entitled to cash subsidies. Thus the JAIAS minutes for October 8, 1903, reflected that a subsidy agreement had been made with Abraham Brotman "some time ago." Under the agreement, Brotman received the use of two floors of the Brotmanville factory rent free, a ten-dollar subsidy per week, and a credit on his mortgage debt equal to 7½ percent of his payroll. In addition, Brotman was not required to pay interest on his mortgage. Brotman received an additional ten dollars per week subsidy and free use of the third floor of the factory as a contractor for the Carlton Manufacturing Company. Finally, as owner of the factory building, the JAIAS was responsible for repairs, which in 1903 totaled 223 dollars, paid to local contractors (29 dollars for window repair, 5 dollars for step repair, 14 dollars for pipe repair, 37 dollars for roof repair, and 165 dollars for exterior painting). To qualify for these benefits, Brotman was required to pay at least 6,000 dollars per year in wages, including nine months at 400 dollars per month.[59]

JAIAS records show that Brotman's arrangements were not unique. Factory owners and contractors in all the South Jersey colonies received various subsidies, favorable loan terms, and cheap or rent-free facilities in exchange for running their businesses in the colonies. In the same October 8, 1903, meeting of the JAIAS, manufacturers in Carmel, Rosenhayn, and Norma were also voted various forms of aid. In Carmel, I. Rosen was allowed to use the Columbia Hall (a JAIAS property) as a temporary shop and was supplied with money to purchase machinery and equipment. The construction of Carmel's Factory Number Two was authorized at the same meeting, an expense of up to fifteen thousand dollars, that would include the building of houses for ten workers. The cost of this construction was mortgaged to the factory owner at 4 percent interest, with the provision that an 8 percent payroll subsidy would be credited to the account. At the same time, expenses for two Rosenhayn factories were authorized: first, a subsidy of 300 dollars per year was granted along with 290 dollars in repairs to L. Rezneck, on the condition that he pay a 500-dollar payroll per month; second, H. Feinberg was granted the same subsidy agreement as Rezneck, along with nearly 1,000 dollars for a combination of factory repairs, machinery and engine purchases, and machinery repairs. Finally, in Norma, an authorization for just under 34 dollars in factory repairs was approved, as well as an agreement with Eskin for a 200-dollar per year subsidy and the use of a house and lot, on the condition of a 7,000-dollar annual payroll, for three years.[60]

Similar agreements can be found throughout the JAIAS records in the first five years of the century, when virtually all the industrial enterprises in the colonies were aided in some way by the JAIAS. Even after 1905, when the society concluded that further industrial growth in the colonies could not be sustained, the existing factories continued to receive support.[61]

The decision of the Baron de Hirsch Fund to come to the aid of the struggling colonies led directly to the recovery of the colonies in the late 1890s. The growth in population by the time of the 1900 census was accompanied by increased financial security. A report published by the Bureau of Statistics of New Jersey in 1901 remarked on the successful farms in Alliance: "The visitor will observe good houses, improved and thoroughly up-to-date outbuildings, healthy, well-conditioned stock, and crops growing that are admirably adapted to the character of the soil." Similarly, the report called Rosenhayn a "well developed town," remarking on its wide avenues, sidewalks, railroad, and telegraph and telephone offices, as well as on its "excellent farming." Carmel's farmers were also praised by the report, which singled out one Isaac Rosen as an outstanding example.[62]

Several of the intellectually oriented leaders of the early period of settlement led the way to successful farming. Sidney Baily's linguistic ability made him a logical leader, and he brought agricultural knowledge to the colony by corresponding with the office of the United States secretary of agriculture, which sent him advice on what to plant. Baily led the way in planting unusual luxury crops, such as asparagus, which would bring high prices. Similarly, Raphael Crystal, another of the early farmers to plant asparagus, taught himself to farm by reading agricultural publications.[63] Clearly, the improvement in the agricultural sector resulted in part from the rapid expansion in colony population brought by the growth in the industrial sector.

Although the farming sector became increasingly stable after the fund's takeover of the mortgages, the policy of developing local industry led the growth in the colonies to be felt disproportionately in the nonagricultural sector. In 1889, the colonies were primarily agricultural. In Alliance, where all but sixteen families owned farms, 1,400 acres were owned by Jews, with 889 acres cultivated, an average of 9.7 acres per farm. Average farm income was 280 dollars in 1889, but Klein reported that this average was half of the normal income, because of heavy summer rains. The Alliance farmers focused on fruit and vegetable production, as evidenced by Klein's report on Dr. Kallman's farm earnings (357 dollars), based on strawberries, blueberries, raspberries, grapes for wine, corn, sweet potatoes, and peaches. Virtually all of the Alliance colony's farmers supplemented their income with second occupations, primarily factory work. While twenty-two supplemented their farm work with craft, professional, or ritual occupations, fully 150 worked as machine operators.[64]

In Rosenhayn, which had grown from thirty-seven to sixty-seven families between 1888 and 1889, a smaller proportion of colonists were established on the land. Farm income in Rosenhayn averaged only 150 dollars in 1889, because many of the new arrivals had yet to clear their land. Some Rosenhayn residents, not yet able to afford to build on their land, earned their living by sewing while living nearby in "the hotel" (a boardinghouse). Similarly, in Carmel, of 848 acres only 124 were cleared and 123 cultivated. Klein reported that the colonists were surviving on sewing, as the fruit trees and vines were not yet mature.[65]

The contrast between 1889 and 1900 was stark. Only 16 families in Alliance had not owned farms in 1889; by 1900, only 95 of the 150 families lived on farms (63.3 percent). In Alliance, the average number of cultivated acres per household dropped from 9.7 in 1889 to 9.36 in 1901; average holdings dropped from 15.2 acres to 14.3 acres. The distribution of land among the residents had become far less uniform. In the 1880s, virtually all the Alliance families had farms of roughly 15 acres; by 1901, 34 families held 20 or more acres, with 8 holding 40 or more. At the other end of the scale, 42 families cultivated 2 acres or fewer. In the Cumberland County colonies of Carmel and Rosenhayn, the proportion of settlers living on farms was less than a quarter; only 50 of 204 households resided on farms.[66]

The declining importance of the agricultural sector and the rise of industry was noted by visitors to the colonies. The New Jersey Bureau of Statistics report mentioned the newly developed village of Brotmanville, just north of Alliance, noting that its one large factory, operated by Alliance Cloak and Suit Company under Abraham Brotman, employed 35 workers. At Rosenhayn, the report noted that the population was equally divided between agriculture and industry, with nine manufacturing firms in the colony. These included clothing firms, employing 160; a brickyard, employing 17; a hosiery, employing 5; a foundry, employing 4; and a tinware, employing 2. Half the operatives, whose average salary was ten dollars per week, owned their own homes. Carmel had three factories at the time, two producing ladies wrappers and one manufacturing men's and boys' clothing. This colony, where operatives earned eight to ten dollars per week, was the most independent of sponsor support, according to the report.[67]

Even the most successful farmers turned to manufacturing to supplement their incomes. Thus Sidney Baily took in home work, finishing garments for New York contractors and distributing the work to other farmer-workers through a cooperative based on his farm. Meanwhile Esther Baily worked several seasons in New York as an assistant to a pharmacist, to supplement her family's farm income.[68] Many farm families took in home work or sent members of the family to work in factories year-round, but virtually all did some form of manufacturing work during the winter months.

The major growth in industry was due, however, not to the seasonal and supplemental employment of farmers but to the establishment of a full-time industrial work force in the colonies. In Alliance, the nonagricultural population was concentrated in the two villages, Norma and Brotmanville, which developed at either end of the colony. Norma was a squalid and undeveloped village in the early 1890s, with "a reputation among Vineland's natives as the dirtiest of 'Jew towns'." Yet later, the aid of Philadelphia philanthropist Maurice Fels paid for a model farm and a canning factory (1901), which provided both employment opportunities and a market for farm produce. At the same time, Norma gained the support of the newly formed JAIAS, further spurring its growth.[69]

Similarly, Brotmanville, at the northeast end of Alliance, grew from a nonentity into a bustling industrial village by the early 1900s. A factory surrounded by small plots for homes was established through the efforts of Abraham Brotman, an Austrian Jew, in the 1890s. Brotman, according to his descendants, was patriotic and hoped to help his fellow immigrants by establishing a community centered in his factory.[70] He arrived in Philadelphia from Austria-Hungary in 1885, and went on to establish in New York the factory that he subsequently moved to Brotmanville. Yet he apparently had earlier connections with the colonies, for the records of HEAS in Philadelphia show that on April 25, 1885, Abraham Brotman, then thirty-five years old, was given two nights of lodging and five meals, for which he could not pay. Brotman then "returned from the farm for having no clothes" on April 29, and was given an additional night of lodging and two free meals.[71] It is not clear how Brotman found the means to establish a factory in New York, but by the time that he moved the factory to Brotmanville, it employed forty to sixty workers, who relocated with him.[72]

In the 1890s, as noted above, Brotman benefited from the Baron de Hirsch Fund's subsidies aimed at developing manufacturing firms to create local markets. In his 1897 recommendations to the fund, Reichow advocated a three thousand-dollar loan to "A. Broadman [sic], cloak manufacturer at Alliance." This loan was granted the following year.[73] By the turn of the century, Brotmanville was home to about forty families; the factories employed additional workers from the Alliance farm population. For example, several Levinsons, sons of one of the original Alliance colonists, worked in Brotman's clothing factory because their farmland was poor and the family could not support itself through farming alone.[74]

Rosenhayn and Carmel experienced similar expansion in their industrial sectors. The establishment of the Carmel factory (1893), financed by Mr. Miller and under the auspices of the Carmel Industrial Co-operation, led sewing to become the town's principal industry. This power-driven factory freed the Carmel home workers from pedaling their foot-powered sewing machines and gave the village a new lease on life: "Not only was there a release from the day long foot pedaling, aching muscles and ragged nerves were relieved; and when night came, less attention was paid to sleep and the social amenities sprang to the fore."[75] This development was the key factor in the tremendous increase in Carmel's industrial population between 1889 and 1900. In subsequent years, an additional five factories were built and they became the primary source of income for the Carmel colonists until the shortage of cloth and high cost of transportation during World War I forced several closures.[76]

Support for the development of industry had immediate results, and was a major factor in the recovery of the colonies' population by 1900. As early as January 1899, Reichow could report that the fund's new policy of aiding industry in the colonies was successful.[77] Besides the mortgage takeovers,

Reichow reported success in inducing "the removal to Rosenhayn . . . [and] Alliance, six small manufacturers and contractors . . . taking along with them about 40 families."[78] The result of these actions, according to Reichow's 1899 report and subsequent correspondence, was "economic prosperity" and "satisfactory development of the colonies."[79]

Reichow's assessment of the improvements in the colonies was not shared by all the Baron de Hirsch Fund officials. General secretary of the fund, A. S. Solomons, expressed his doubts in notes written after a visit to the colonies by the top fund leadership in April of 1900. Solomons, accompanied by Judge Isaacs, Isaac Eppinger, Leonard Lewisohn, Reichow, Elkan Adler, Joseph Jacobs, and Professor Sabsovich, visited all the South Jersey colonies and gave the colonies negative reviews. He was particularly critical of Alliance, where he reported on decaying houses, poor roads, and a synagogue in need of repair. He did praise the Brotmanville factory and saw enough positive in the colony to recommend "helping them out of the mire," but he saw supervision by the fund and an extension of the fund's power as the key to such assistance.[80]

The discrepancy in assessments of colony conditions might be attributed to Solomons's unfamiliarity with actual immigrant conditions—he was, according to George Price, a critic of the established Jewish American philanthropies, "unfamiliar with the needs of the immigrants. He neither understands Yiddish nor German. He very seldom sees the Russian Jews."[81] Yet it is more likely that Solomons's view was colored by his concern with the bottom line. His comments on Alliance follow praise of Woodbine, where his more positive assessment seems to stem from the fact that in that colony, few were making financial requests of the fund. It is in comparing a financially dependent Alliance with Woodbine that "the contrast was painful in the extreme."[82] In contrast, the New Jersey Bureau of Statistics, which had no financial interest in the colonies, was far more positive in its assessment.[83]

The colonists' repayment schedule to the fund was one of the primary factors used in evaluating colony success under the Baron de Hirsch Fund and the JAIAS, which took over the fund's supervisory role after 1900. In the 1902 JAIAS annual report, "success in obtaining regular payments upon our advances at the time when they fall due" is listed as one key test of farmer success. However, this method of evaluation posed a problem in the South Jersey colony where "much of the dissatisfaction expressed by old beneficiaries at being obliged to fulfill their obligations would never have entered their minds, if they had not been allowed, in the earlier years of their farming, to consider as gifts what were intended as loans."[84] Given their frustration with the Jersey colonists' reluctance to repay, it is not surprising that, though mentioning improvements in the colonies, sponsors reported that "the only agricultural colony that does not appear to thrive is the one located in the South Jersey settlements."[85]

The JAIAS report for 1903 again demonstrates the frustration of the sponsors with the South Jersey farmers. Reporting that the South Jersey farmers' situation was unfavorable compared with individually settled farmers in other regions, the link between the negative assessment and the poor record of loan repayment becomes explicit. The report compared the Jersey farmers, who were denominated as "debtors," with their counterparts in Connecticut, where "installments and interest are paid much more promptly." After reporting on improvements in conditions in South Jersey, the JAIAS admitted that

> the financial relations between this Society and its South Jersey debtors cannot be taken as a measure of their prosperity; from a variety of circumstances familiar to our members, the South Jersey farmers have been remiss in the observance of their obligations and many of them resent bitterly any attempt to enforce payment even of interest. Personal visits to the region give ocular demonstration of a greater degree of financial ease; houses are kept in good repair, extensive additions have been made in some cases, and we also learn with satisfaction that local banks are willing to extend credit on better terms than heretofore. . . . While such statements may be exaggerated, they at least indicate that the farmers can gradually be made to rely on their own resources, if they are not treated as objects of charity, but upon a business basis.[86]

Despite this admission, loan repayment continued to be a major criterion for measuring colony success.

When the fund established policies tightening control on aid to new farmers by requiring investment by the settler, and by testing the ability of applicants through training and supervision, they also moved to tighten control over those who had already been granted loans. In assuming the mortgages of the established settlers, the fund screened the farmers individually, only taking on the loans "after a careful investigation."[87] For example, in 1894, Charles (George) Seldes, an early Am Olam settler, was investigated by a local lawyer at the request of Julius Goldman. The investigation of Seldes not only focused on his farming ability (which was highly praised) but also delved into more personal matters. For example, the report mentioned the rumored infidelity of one of Seldes's sons.[88]

Similarly, investigations probed the character of settlers negligent in repaying fund loans. In 1905, one such case, again conducted by the fund's lawyer in nearby Bridgeton, investigated Barman Spirt. Despite several positive recommendations, the JAIAS general manager, William Kahn, wrote, "It is evident that there is no excuse for his failure to pay you the interest accrued on the Morais mortgage, since he entered into a written agreement to regularly pay such interest." Although Kahn admitted that Spirt was a diligent farmer and had made improvements to his farm, he continued, "It may be that I would recommend to make him pay also the interest accrued prior to that date if he continues to disregard his obligations."[89]

Many examples of such investigations appear throughout the JAIAS records. Several of the cases extended over years, as with a Carmel farmer, P. Schlossberg. After falling behind in his payments, Schlossberg entered negotiations with the fund, claiming that, because his land was virgin, he had not been able to repay the principal (he was making interest payments). In the correspondence that follows, Schlossberg seems mystified over a fire insurance agreement that the fund insists he sign. The fund's Bridgeton lawyer, calling Sclossberg "ignorant" and "pigheaded," suggested that "a letter threatening to foreclose in case he does not [sign] it might bring him to terms."[90]

Under the tough policies of the fund, foreclosures were not uncommon.[91] One particularly controversial case was that of Solomon Luberoff, one of the original Alliance settlers. In a conflict that dragged on for several years, Luberoff was accused of failing to pay off an Alliance Land Trust loan in 1904. As notice of sheriff's sale was posted in August of 1914, Luberoff's wife protested that he had paid, and wrote to trustee Eppinger, "I beg you to please save my home." The legal battle between the Alliance Land Trust (by then a subsidiary of the fund) and the Luberoffs raged for several months, the defendant claiming that the statute of limitations had already elapsed. Finally the case was tried in Salem County Court in August of 1914, the fund prevailing and the Luberoffs evicted. This case caused internal dissension within the fund. Gabriel Davidson of the Jewish Agricultural Society (formerly the JAIAS) wrote that, while he did not believe the Luberoffs' story and agreed with the fund's negative view of Luberoff, "I think that the Alliance Land Trust dealt with Luberoff in as unbusinesslike a manner as he dealt with them." Davidson concluded that this foreclosure was "an uncharitable act."[92]

Whatever Davidson's expectations, it was not the purpose of the fund to provide charity. Set up as an investment company, the fund was not designed to dispense alms. The fund operated on proceeds from investments made primarily in New York real estate.[93] Hirsch had hoped that his cosponsors would receive interest on monies invested in the fund. Similarly, the JAIAS annual report for 1902 noted that although agricultural placement of immigrants requires a greater initial expense than placement of industrial workers, "most of the capital placed in the hand of farmers will return to the Society."[94] Baron de Hirsch himself had once advised Schiff to investigate new programs for aiding immigrants "from a financial point of view, from a business and not from a philanthropic standpoint, just as if it were a question of a new railroad or any other project destined to repay the capital invested."[95] The emphasis on business principles in the operation of the fund and the JAIAS led not only to stringent screening of loan applicants but also to a resistance to charity.

The fund's opposition to charity, based on the belief that charity bred a dependence antithetical to the goal of adapting immigrants to the American economic system, was clearly articulated from the time of the fund's establishment. As early as 1889, the New York and Philadelphia groups outlining the organization and policies of the new fund wrote in a letter to Hirsch that charity should be ruled out: "Alms to persons who will never be able to help themselves, is deemed foreign to the object of the Fund."[96] Many examples of the fund's reluctance to be seen as a charity can be found in both the minutes and annual reports of the fund and the JAIAS. For example, when Fischel Stavitsky, one of the original Alliance farmers, died in an epidemic leaving a widow, five young children, and elderly parents, the fund agreed to support the widow and children for one year at ten dollars per month, on the condition "that the distribution be made by someone not connected with this Society." The following year, when the residents of Alliance petitioned the JAIAS for continued support for Mrs. Stavitsky, aid was refused because "it was the sense of the meeting that this was no case for this Society." Because of the termination of aid, Mrs. Stavitsky was forced to place three of her young sons in a Philadelphia orphanage.[97]

The sponsors were quite willing to aid industrial enterprises, but their reluctance to provide charitable relief to persons extended to industrial workers. In the 1920s, the fund received a letter from an A. Steiner, who had lost four of his fingers in the Baron de Hirsch Fund trade school printing department. Hoping to marry, Steiner requested aid from the fund. His request was refused by a fund representative who responded, "We do not extend any pecuniary aid, particularly for the purpose you request. The only thing I can say is if you cannot support a wife, it would be inadvisable for you to get married."[98]

The desire to discourage any form of charity extended beyond cases of direct appeals to the fund, to include an insistence on businesslike policies by industrial enterprises aided by the fund. Although it was well within the scope of fund activity to provide incentives, including cash subsidies to industrialists, charity by these industries to their workers was expressly discouraged. For example, when Philadelphia industrialist and philanthropist Maurice Fels, recognizing the difficulties presented by high transportation costs, fees paid to brokers, and unstable markets for produce, decided to help the Jersey farmers by constructing a canning factory in Norma,[99] the sponsors expressed concern that it be run on business principles. For example, Hackenburg wrote to Sabsovich, "The canning establishment is to be conducted on strictly business principals, [that] the products of the farms will be bought at a reasonable and fair market price, the employees of the canning factory will get fair and good wages, and there will be no charity in the matter at all." The purpose of the factory, Hackenburg emphasized, was "only for the express purpose of improving the condition of the people by their work." Similarly, Hackenburg assured Solomons in New York that the canning factory "is to be conducted strictly on business principles, no charity to anyone." The factory, subsequently augmented by the addition of the experimental Allivine Farm, was repeatedly hailed for the tremendous boost it provided to farmers in the region and to the town of Norma.[100]

The dislike of charity and dependence was indicative not only of the sponsors' desire to aid the immigrants' adaptation to the American economic system but also of a concern for the moral improvement of their wards. The disdain for the eastern Europeans as "uncivilized" and concern that this lack of culture might spark an anti-Semitic backlash was coupled with a recognition that, without the provision of cultural and social activities, the colonies would lose their best residents.

In the early years of the colonies, aid for cultural and social activity was on an ad hoc basis. The colonists often received aid for such activities from individual sponsors. For example, in an 1892 letter from the Carmel colonists to Fels, they mentioned his provision of English books for their library and the assistance given by Philadelphia rabbi Sabato Morais to the Hebrew school and English night school.

By the early 1890s, the colonists began increasingly to turn to sponsoring organizations rather than to individuals for such aid. Thus the 1892 Carmel letter asked that Fels present their request to the Baron de Hirsch Fund to keep the night school open. Demonstrating a keen understanding of the fund's attitudes, the Carmel colonists wrote that "there is not any better place to aducate the Russian Jewish emigrants than it is in Carmel [*sic*]," and emphasized that "the vast majority of the young and old are good and hard-working people, willing to learn they would do all possibilities to advance themselve to know the costum, style and language of the country [*sic*]."[101]

With the reorganization of activities in the colonies under Baron de Hirsch Fund auspices, support of activities dedicated to intellectual and cultural improvement became formalized by the turn of the century. Much of this activity was inspired by the recognition of a need to increase supervision in the colonies, not only of economic enterprise but also of moral conditions. Thus Solomons's 1900 report on the colonies emphasizes the need to extend fund power and appoint a superintendent to improve the settlements.[102]

Under the JAIAS, cultural and educational activities became a primary goal both because of the sponsors' concern for moral conditions in the colonies and because of their belief that such activities were necessary if the colonies were to attract and keep residents. In its second annual report, in 1902, the JAIAS deemed such moral improvements a central concern, arguing that "before . . . any other expenditure would be justified, it seems necessary to raise the morale of the settlers, arouse them from their indifference to self-improvement and inspire them with a feeling of enterprise." The report focused on attrition among the colonists, particularly among "the more intelligent farmers," who were sending their children to the cities. This phenomenon was attributed in the report to "the utter lack of social and educational advantages" in the colonies. The report warned, "There can be no doubt that the more intelligent population will gradually withdraw from districts where their children cannot obtain proper instruction, leaving only the less desirable element to vegetate in these places."[103]

To improve the situation, the JAIAS placed its faith in a non-Jewish Frenchman, Louis Mournier, who was entrusted in 1901 with the supervision of the night schools and all other social and educational work in the colonies. Mournier and his wife were to devote themselves "first, to lectures and social work . . . second, to individual musical instruction given by them; third, to the betterment of the libraries and social facilities in the settlements; fourth to the supervision of the . . . night schools." Mournier's devotion to his task was admirable: in 1902 he made 245 official visits to the colonies, for a total of a thousand hours. Under Mournier's guidance, the libraries were expanded, social halls built, and extensive programs of lectures and music were implemented.

Although such aid was not invested in a formally interest-yielding activity, it was justified as "the sole means of saving that district from apathy and decay, which would soon lead to the loss of all the money, time, and labor heretofore spent in that direction." Clearly concerned about appearing to violate the fund's anticharity policy, the JAIAS distinguished this social and educational aid from charity, going to great lengths to justify these actions, and expressing confidence that it would lead not to dependence but to the building of a self-reliant community:

> We do not propose to institute a paternalism, which shall supply these people with all their material wants, we do not wish to pauperize them: but we wish to stimulate them to proper endeavor. It must be remembered, too, that the original settlers in South Jersey were the only ones, now under our care, who occupied land which they had not chosen for themselves: if they settled in an unlovely region, it must be our business to provide compensation. Having promoted a communal spirit, fostered better methods of agriculture and settled the industrial question, we may leave them to their own devices with the hope that they may ultimately succeed.[104]

Optimism that the Jersey colonies would soon be weaned from the aid of the society was unwarranted. Aid for social, educational, and cultural activities continued throughout the early 1900s. In 1904, for example, the JAIAS board of directors authorized 150 dollars to aid libraries in the colonies. Yet the continued ambivalence of the sponsors toward this type of aid was clear. Occasionally aid was provided on the condition that the colonists themselves provide a matching contribution, as when the JAIAS executive committee agreed to provide four hundred dollars toward the salary of a doctor for Carmel if the colonists there would contribute a like sum. Such conditional aid reinforced the sponsors' belief in self-help. On at least one occasion, the society helped finance the activities of the Jewish Chautauqua, under the condition "that our Society's connection in the matter should not be known." The ambivalent attitude of the sponsors toward such aid is also demonstrated in the inconsistency of aid decisions. Similar requests were granted in one instance and refused in another. For example, the Rosenhayn colonists' request for four hundred dollars for a doctor, to be matched by the contribution of residents, was refused only five months after the approval of the Carmel doctor. At times, previous support for funded activities was ended, with only a vague explanation. Thus in 1909, the JAIAS board recommended discontinuing subsidies for music lessons because of the "unsatisfactory condition of educational activity in the colonies." Denials of requests were as frequent as approvals. Although much of this aid was granted as gifts, in some instances loans were issued to finance a community project, particularly in cases of synagogue construction, as in Carmel.[105]

✳✳✳

The emergence of the Baron de Hirsch Fund and its subsidiary, the Jewish Agricultural and Industrial Aid Society, in the transitional decade between 1890 and 1900 had a profound effect on the development of the colonies through the 1920s. The support of industry, insistence upon business principles in aiding the colonies, and support of cultural activities all furthered the sponsors' goals of making the colonies both a viable destination for immigrants and an effective training ground for Americanization of those immigrants.

Although never absorbing a large number of immigrants, the colonies seemed by the 1910s to be fulfilling many of the sponsors' goals. The increase in population between 1889 and 1900 had been maintained, and by 1909, there were 43 more families in the colonies than there had been in 1900. Alliance, including Norma and Brotmanville, had grown from 150 to 177 families; Carmel and Rosenhayn increased from 204 to 220 families. The United States Immigration Commission reported in 1911 that the progress of the colonies since 1900 had been considerable, with farmers enjoying expanded local markets and with new industries established in all the colonies. The commission also reported on the active social life in the colonies, including dances, picnics, plays, athletic clubs, as well as a flourishing educational program under Mournier.[106]

Indeed, residents of the colonies recalled these years as the "golden age." Accounts from the period are filled with recollections of heated baseball rivalries between the various athletic associations, educational programs sponsored by the Jewish Chautauqua Society, theatrical productions, and celebrations of American holidays, such as the Fourth of July.[107]

The Americanization the sponsors hoped for appeared to be taking place. Jewish holidays were still central in community life, and a few boys studied in a traditional *heder*-style school under Isaac Krassenstein, but many practices had been Americanized. By 1910, the modern Hebrew school sponsored by the Jewish Chautauqua Society (and secretly underwritten by the sponsors) was increasingly popular.[108] At the Chautauqua Hebrew school, in marked contrast to the traditional *heder*, instruction was in English and was "in accord with the latest pedagogical methods."[109] Saturdays were marked by afternoon baseball games and shopping trips to Vineland, indicating laxness in Sabbath observance. Religious events frequently took on an American flavor, as when the Carmel synagogue was dedicated in 1908. The celebration of this event was marked by the decoration of houses with American flags and bunting, and speeches by various sponsors. In these speeches, "American opportunity and freedom" were stressed, as the settlers were urged "to break away from their dependence on external subsidies."[110]

Further evidence of successful adjustment could be found in the public schools, where, according to the Immigration Commission report, the colonies' children "advance more rapidly than those of American parentage."[111] By 1909, the number of Alliance children attending high school in Vineland had grown so large that school officials contracted for a wagon to transport them.[112] Public school education was supplemented through the efforts of both Mournier and Fels, who provided manual-training classes for boys, domestic training for girls, and a demonstration garden program, besides public lectures and music lessons.[113] The JAIAS praised the efforts of Mournier and his wife, whose joint influence was credited for "much of the local patriotism, which is certainly being displayed at the present time."[114] Residents of the colonies held elected local offices by the turn of the century; Moses Bayuk and Fred Herder (son of Moses Herder) served long terms as justices of the peace in the Alliance and Carmel areas.

By the middle of the decade, the JAIAS was finally reporting success in the economic adaptation of the South Jersey colonists. After years of frustra-

tion with delinquent loans and frequent appeals for aid, the JAIAS reported in
1905 that "all obligations are being met fully and promptly." Success was reported both in the industrial sector and in agriculture, where "after so many
years of rather hopeless struggle with adverse conditions, the farmers have at
last learnt how to make their farms productive." In general, the report stated,
"the Vineland section, to which we had been obliged to refer rather regretfully
in our earlier reports, is now in a highly encouraging condition." The optimistic report on farming led the society to once again advocate growth in the
colonies' agricultural sectors.[115] Despite occasional setbacks caused by unfavorable weather conditions, the reports on agricultural development remained
generally positive in this decade.[116]

During this "golden age," radical and communal activities that had so
disturbed the sponsors during the first decade of settlement were muted. Although Carmel retained its reputation for radicalism, hosting noted radicals,
such as Eugene Debs and Emma Goldman, as lecturers, and with a small
group experimenting briefly with communal living,[117] the trend in the colonies was away from such activities. The United States Immigration Commission reported in 1911 that no cooperatives existed in Alliance because of
"poor leadership, suspicion, and lack of confidence," among the colonists. In
Carmel and Rosenhayn, farmers' associations sponsored educational and social
activities, as well as limited cooperative buying of supplies, but no cooperative
selling had been attempted.[118] Even cooperative efforts were directed at helping
members achieve such sponsor-approved goals as purchasing family houses and
establishing private businesses. One such organization was the Workingmen's
Cooperative Business and Loan Company, based in Alliance, which aided its
members through the method most favored by the sponsors: the issuance of
loans to persons or single families.[119]

The exception to this low level of cooperative activity occurred not
among idealist farmers but among the new industrial workers, many of whom
had been exposed to unionism and strike activity in urban America before
migration to the colonies. As the industrial population in the colonies grew,
strike activity became an increasingly prominent part of colony life. In Carmel, long the hotbed of radicalism among the colonies, one settler recalled, "It
was easier to call a strike . . . than to get ten men to make a *minyan*."[120] Yet
strike activity did not reach a high level until the close of this period, and it
was insignificant enough during the first ten years of the century to be largely
discounted by the sponsors.

The lack of cooperative economic activity in the colonies is striking,
considering the communal roots of the settlements. Even as late as the 1890s
there had been in Carmel a socialist atmosphere, and "on the street there
were frequently groups discussing socialism, anarchism, and religion."[121] In

1894, Carmel residents welcomed a contingent of Coxey's Army of unemployed, marching to Washington to plead for relief. As one resident proudly recalled, "Many towns through which they passed just shooed them on their way. Not so the Carmelites. . . . Never in the course of their march were they treated with such hospitality as shown by the Carmelites."[122] Yet after the turn of the century, Carmel settlers, such as Charles Waskoff, bemoaned the decline in communalism: "A few of the Carmelites may have achieved a few more comforts of life, but the esprit de corps is lacking. No more can one hear the gay laughter and happy singing of groups as they strolled the country roads in the moonlight. Yes, there has been a marked change in the lives of the people in Carmel. Materially, perhaps, somewhat better than before, but spiritually far worse. The collective spirit has declined, while the ego has become predominant."[123]

Along with dwindling communalism, changes in gender roles also indicated the decline in radicalism from the 1880s. Although not all the colonists had been Am Olam members in the 1880s, and not even all of the Am Olam members held what can be considered radical views of the role of women, there had been a contingent of colonists in the early period who had insisted on equality for women. The views of women such as Esther Baily, an educated woman and a member of Am Olam before marrying her husband, had an impact on other early settlers. For example, Baily's determination to give her daughter a high school education, when grammar school had previously been deemed sufficient for girls, led to a trend of secondary school education for the colony girls. As Elizabeth Rudnick Levin recalled, Esther Baily "accompanied her daughter Margaret and me as we walked the two and a half miles to the Norma station, for she found it necessary to establish a store in Vineland, in order to send her daughter through high school."[124] After Margaret Baily and Elizabeth Rudnick entered high school, it became common for the girls of the colony to do so, even though it required a good commute—to Vineland from Alliance, Norma, and Brotmanville, or to Millville from Carmel and Rosenhayn.

Although it continued to be common for girls to attend high school in later years, other expectations about women's roles changed as colony populations changed. This change was particularly true in work. In the early years, it was common for women to work alongside their husbands in the fields. As Elizabeth Rudnick Levin writes, "I can well recall those prematurely old women, plodding along, day after day, through the hot summer, doing the work of man and beast. Clearly can I picture women like Mrs. Rothman, Mrs. Bakerman, Mrs. Helig and my mother . . . bending low to the ground, slowly following their husbands along the long rows of corn or sweet potatoes."[125] It was common for women not only to work their own farms in the early years but also to be hired as pickers at local cranberry and strawberry farms. In later years, however, while women often worked on family farms, and children worked as pickers for others, women apparently ceased hiring themselves out as pickers. Clearly, part of this change was because of the greater availability of alternate forms of employment for women, such as factory work, but the change was so complete that it seems to indicate a change in community attitudes about women's work.[126]

For sponsors who had earlier participated in purges of radicals, the changes in women's roles, as well as the decrease in communalism and radicalism, were taken as signs of successful Americanization. Such progress led the JAIAS to conclude in 1910 that Americanization could be achieved in group settlements. In their report for that year, the JAIAS reversed its view that Americanization is best achieved through isolated settlement of immigrants: "While the segregation of the immigrant may in theory be the most effective plan for his early Americanization, its impracticability is now generally conceded. The belief that the Jewish farmer is making better progress when isolated is no longer tenable. For every successful isolated Jewish farmer, there are scores living in groups who are equally successful."[127] The sponsors proudly expressed their satisfaction with their progress in Americanizing the Jewish farmer, both in the colonies and elsewhere, by quoting extensively from the United States Immigration Commission report in their own annual report of 1912. Although the Immigration Commission was less than enthusiastic about the agricultural ability of the Jewish immigrants, their praise for their successful Americanization was effusive:

> In general, the Russian Hebrew has proved more apt in civic relations and in commerce than in agriculture. He is likely to become a citizen sooner than most east European immigrants and to take a more intelligent interest in politics; few are illiterate, and practically all of the American born or the minors who have been in the United States ten years can speak, read and write English with more or less fluency. The ownership of the land and the proprietorship of a farm enterprise have developed independence, self-reliance, and self-respect. The objection of the Hebrew to rural life lies in the meager returns for labor expended, the isolation and the absence of social conveniences. The social position of the farmer is satisfactory.
>
> Whatever may be said of his agriculture, the Hebrew farmer is a thinking, protesting citizen. Assimilation or fusion with other races is retarded by religious tradition and rural segregation. Americanization in the sense of desire for representative government, democratic institutions, an educated electorate, equality of opportunity, and the free agency of the individual is developed rapidly in the land-owning Hebrew. The Hebrew on the land is peaceable and law-abiding, but he does not tamely submit to what he

believes to be oppression, and he has a highly developed sense of personal rights, civil, and economic. The rural Hebrew has shown his capacity for self-government and no colonies were visited whose members voted less as a unit than those where rural Hebrews made up a material part of the electorate.

The Hebrews have demanded better schools nearly everywhere they have settled. Where they are segregated with sufficient compactness, their leaders have originated social, educational and recreative enterprises for the benefit of the community. The few who are really interested in farming realize the need of knowledge and training, along agricultural lines; the others want their children to have at least a good commercial education and some are striving to send their children to college.[128]

Although a social transformation had clearly taken place in the settlements, it can be argued that the Americanization of the colonies was achieved as much through changes in the composition of colony population as through sponsor-backed Americanization programs or the transformation of individual immigrants. Indeed, the greatest change caused by the sponsor policies between 1890 and 1910 was not the alteration of the character of individual colonists but the transformation of the composition of new groups of settlers arriving in the colonies. Sponsor policies interacted with changes in the potential migrant pool to cause a dramatic shift in origins of the newcomers to the colonies. Thus, many of the changes in the community were caused by a shift in the makeup of the settlements' population.

As discussed in chapter 4, by the late 1880s, the composition of new cohorts of settlers arriving in the colonies shifted away from the idealistic Am Olam members of South Pale origin. The disintegration of the Am Olam in the mid-1880s, coupled with the growth of a community of radical, Jewish intellectuals in the urban labor and socialist movements, all but eliminated further influx of such persons into the South Jersey communities. At the same time, a continued high level of migration increased crowding in urban industrial and residential sectors. This crowding made relocation to the country attractive to nonidealistic industrial workers and potential farmers.

By supporting the growth of industry in the colonies, the Baron de Hirsch Fund, and later the JAIAS, hoped to attract immigrants from industrial, urban centers to rural New Jersey. In this effort, the sponsors supported the establishment of Brotmanville and Norma as industrial villages, and bolstered the industrial populations of Alliance, Carmel, and Rosenhayn. Between 1900 and 1910, the industrial population of the colonies consistently surpassed the agricultural population.[129] In the Salem County colonies of Norma, Brotmanville, and Alliance, the percentage of families engaged in farming shrank from 63.3 in 1900 to 38.98 in 1909.

Table 5.1

Occupational Distribution of Settlers, by Arrival Date, 1882–1900

	Agriculture	Manufacturing	Commerce	Craft	Other
1882–1885					
Number	93	9	9	0	3
Percent	81.6%	7.9%	7.9%	0%	2.6%
1886–1890					
Number	39	38	17	6	6
Percent	36.8%	35.8%	16.0%	5.7%	5.7%
Total, 1882–1890					
Number	132	47	28	6	9
Percent	60.0%	21.4%	11.8%	2.7%	4.1%
1891–1900					
Number	22	39	9	2	3
Percent	29.3%	52.0%	12.0%	2.7%	4.0%

From the formation of the Baron de Hirsch Fund in 1891 to the decision of the JAIAS in 1905 that further industrial growth in the colonies was impractical and that agriculture should be encouraged instead, almost all newcomers to the colony joined the nonagricultural work force. Although 60.0 percent of the settlers who arrived from 1882 to 1890 had worked in the agricultural sector, only 29.3 percent of new settlers from 1891 to 1900, when the combination of agricultural depression and fund support for industry made this trend most marked, did so. The proportion of merchants and craftsmen in the two cohorts was unchanged, but the percentage of settlers entering the manufacturing sector grew from 21.4 for the 1882 to 1890 settlers to 52.0 for the 1891 to 1900 settlers (see table 5.1).

The increasing influence of industrial workers gave rise to changes in the social, cultural, and religious life in the colonies. Established farmers greeted the opportunities presented by the factories with enthusiasm, but many were less pleased by the new industrial labor force that accompanied them. According to several descendants, the idealistic farmers looked down on the factory workers and tailors.[130] A descendant of an Am Olam pioneer notes that her family kept a social distance from those in Norma, where most residents were factory workers, emphasizing that the Norma factory workers were not highly regarded by the Alliance farmers, who were the intellectuals of the community.[131] In Brotmanville, where more than two hundred people lived by 1908 in homes owned by JAIAS,

> Lighted by electricity generated on the premises and powered by steam, the modern factory seemed to symbolize Brotmanville's betrayal of the agrarian

ideal, or at least so it appeared to the farmers of Alliance. The *schneiders* [tailors] and the farmers looked upon each other with contempt, their objectives pinned on differing values. In effect, Brotmanville's operators lived always in a kind of company town (though a benevolent one), lacking the idealism of the Am Olam, the dream of tilling one's own soil, the spirit of communal development.[132]

The Brotmanville workers were so far removed from the purpose of the original Alliance settlers that their descendants, in contrast to descendants of the early Am Olam settlers, frequently refer to Alliance, Norma, and Brotmanville as "Jewish towns," failing to recognize the *colony* aspect of the settlements.[133]

The differences between the established farmers and the new industrial population were rooted not only in their contrasting occupational profiles but also in the divergent backgrounds of the two groups. Although agricultural families, particularly those who settled in the colonies earliest, were primarily of South Pale origin, those in the manufacturing sector were disproportionately of Galician, Northwest Pale, and non-Russian (Hungarian, etc.) origin. Although Galician, Northwestern, and non-Russian Jews accounted only for 9.9, 12.1 and 13.5 percent of the population for whom regional origin could be determined, they represented 15.1, 15.1 and 24.2 percent of the manufacturing population (see table 4.2).

Contrasting backgrounds can be found not only between industrial and agricultural workers but also between the farmers who had arrived early and those who came to the settlements later. One reason for this dissimilarity can be found in the waning of agricultural idealism among South Pale intellectuals. In addition, the screening policies of the sponsors led to a shift in the background of the farmers. Because of the stipulation by the sponsors that new farmers must be able to invest their own capital in their farms, the Immigration Commission reported in 1911,

> Those who are now taking up lands or have been coming since 1900 differ financially and spiritually from the earlier settlers; they are men who have some money, often a considerable sum. They buy for investment with the idea of making a good home and a fair profit at the same time on the land. They do not wish to clear wild land; they want cleared fields ready for the plow and the first spring's seeding. As a matter of fact, while the Aid Society buys farms, builds houses and barns, and sells at cost to the newcomer, it is almost essential that the prospective farmer have at least 700 or 800 dollars to start with.[134]

Thus in general, the new farmers were not refugees fleeing pogroms but persons of some means looking to farming as an economic opportunity, rather than as a means to spiritual and cultural rejuvenation.

Table 5.2

Regional Origin of Settlers, by Time of Arrival

	South	Galicia	North/Northwest	Poland	Other	Total
1882–1885						
Number	34	5	6	5	7	57
Percent	59.6%	8.8%	10.5%	8.8%	12.3%	
1886–1890						
Number	6	6	7	4	7	30
Percent	20%	20%	23.3%	13.3%	23.3%	
1891–1895						
Number	5	1	1	7	3	17
Percent	29.4%	5.9%	5.9%	41.2%	17.6%	
Post-1896						
Number	15	1	3	17	4	40
Percent	37.5%	2.5%	7.5%	42.5%	10.0%	

Besides the spiritual and financial differences between the old and new farmers, they stemmed from dissimilar regional backgrounds. In contrast to the early settlers who hailed disproportionately from the South Pale, later settlers migrated from other regions, most notably Russian Poland. Between 1891 and 1895, the percentage of newcomers from the South Pale shrank to 29.4 while the percentage from Poland grew to 41.2. This trend continued throughout the later period, Polish Jews comprising 42.5 percent of the post-1896 arriving settlers, while South Palers represented 37.5 percent. The percentage of new settlers from the North and Northwest Pale, the group that dominated among Jewish immigrants to America, shrank after 1890, to less than 10 percent (see table 5.2).

These general trends in regional origin affected the regional background of farmers as well, as the percentage of agriculturalists who were of South Pale origin shrank from 56.1 for pre-1890 settlers to only 31.0 for post-1890 settlers. Almost all agriculturalists settling after 1890 were of Polish origin: 65.5 percent. Among those agriculturalists of known origin, there were no Galician or Northwest Pale farmers who settled after 1890 (see table 5.3).

Polish Jews, who joined both the farming and the manufacturing sectors, brought with them a cultural and religious outlook that differed from that of the South Pale, Am Olam group and that greatly affected community life. These Polish Jews brought with them Yiddishkeit, or Yiddish culture.[135] Whereas early accounts of cultural life in the colonies, written by members of the Am Olam contingent, tell of heated philosophical debates in a mixture of Russian, German, and Yiddish,[136] later memoirs stress an increasingly Yiddish and traditional orientation. One such account is by Mollie Greenblatt Kravitz, the daughter of a Polish settler who arrived in Brotmanville in the early 1890s.

Table 5.3

Regional Origins of Farmers, Pre- and Post-1890

	South	Galicia	North/Northwest	Poland	Other	Total
Pre-1890						
Number	32	6	8	4	7	57
Percent	56.1%	10.5%	14.0%	7.0%	12.3%	
Post-1890						
Number	9	0	0	19	1	29
Percent	31.0%	—	—	65.5%	3.4%	

Kravitz stresses the extreme religious orthodoxy of her family.[137] In fact, the colonies were attractive destinations for such families because in an exclusively Jewish town there was no compulsion to work on Shabbat.[138] Yiddish was the sole language in such households until English was learned, in contrast to many of the Am Olam households where Russian and German were also spoken. In the Brotmanville and Norma districts, which contained the largest proportion of newcomers, these trends were most pronounced. Joseph Greenblatt, born in Brotmanville in 1896, recalled that Yiddish was the primary language in Brotmanville during his childhood. It was, he remembered, "as if they took a village from Poland and brought it right here to Brotmanville."[139]

The Yiddish culture of these newcomers increasingly took center stage in community activities. Yiddish theater became a popular activity; plays were presented at the community halls, housed in the synagogues. The libraries established in the colonies, though still reflective of the liberal tastes of community leaders in content, became primarily English and Yiddish in language.[140] In Carmel, still considered the most radical of the colonies in the early 1900s, one library organizer reported: "Most of the books and periodicals read, though ever of the better class, were in the Yiddish language. Only the classics in that jargon were patronized. If they did not assimilate they broadened our minds, extended our sphere of circumspection, deepened the scope of our vision. Readings and discussions on political economy, socialism, history, natural science and many other topics were held pell-mell."[141]

Religious differences among the colonists had led to the development of two separate synagogues in Alliance by 1889, but these differences were accentuated in subsequent years as Am Olam-style intellectuals ceased arriving and the more traditional groups were greatly augmented by newcomers. The first of the two synagogues, Eben ha'Ezer (also known as Emanu-El), was founded in 1888 and was the more progressive of the two. In his 1889 report, Moses Klein characterized this synagogue as one of the "reformers," in contrast to the 1889 Tiphereth Israel (also known as Shearith Israel).[142] Although both were traditional in design and ritual, Eben ha'Ezer was associated with many of the intellectual leaders and early farmers. The modern Hebrew school was conducted there, and it became a community center as well as a religious institution. Alliance Hall, the community center in the Eben ha'Ezer basement, was the site for cultural and social activities. Housing the community's theatrical productions, lectures, library, weddings, and an array of community gatherings, Alliance Hall fulfilled far more roles than a traditional synagogue's study and prayer, much like the Reform temple/community center that was emerging in many American-Jewish communities in this period.[143]

Tiphereth Israel, with its more traditional stance, was associated primarily with the more religious settlers, most notably Isaac Krassenstein, "the *hasid*," and Solomon Salunsky, who had some rabbinical training in Russia.[144] This faction dominated the Chevrah Kadisha (burial society), Krassenstein serving as sexton from its founding until 1924. Tiphereth Israel came to be identified by many as more of a Brotmanville synagogue. Yet this institution eventually became known as the "Bayuk synagogue" because of both of Bayuk's leadership and its location across the street from his house.[145] How Bayuk's ambivalence toward religion was reconciled with Tiphereth Israel's more traditional approach is unclear, although it is possible that the "Bayuk synagogue" appellation occurred in Bayuk's later years, when he became more observant.[146]

Ultimately the Norma and Brotmanville villages established their own synagogues and religious schools. In contrast to the modern religious education available first through Sidney Baily's Sabbath school in Alliance (where, according to his account, poetry, current events, postbiblical history, and ethics were stressed) and later through the efforts of the Jewish Chautauqua Society financed by the sponsors, the Brotmanville religious school was modeled more on the traditional *heder*. A longtime Brotmanville resident, Mollie Greenblatt Kravitz, recalled that Brotmanville boys generally attended *heder*.[147] Her reference to the school as a *heder* and the fact that girls did not attend this school indicate its more traditional nature. The curriculum in this school, as in an Alliance *heder*, taught by Isaac Krassenstein of Tiphereth Israel, stressed education in Hebrew and Yiddish by a *melamed*, a traditional Hebrew teacher.[148]

Both modern and traditional forms of religious education in the colonies indicates the extent of the cultural and religious shift in their population. The traditional *heder*, taught by the *melamed*, was scorned both by *maskilim* in eastern Europe and by western philanthropists. Ridiculed for their primitive conditions and lack of concern for practical education, *hederim* had been lambasted by reformers throughout the nineteenth century. The productivization movement, which stressed the rehabilitation of Jews through labor in craft or agriculture, and which was a primary factor in the establishment of agricultural colonies, targeted the *heder* as uncivilized and backward. The development of several religious schools in the colonies based on this model indicates the increasing deviation from the earlier cultural pattern as the population expanded.[149]

✳✳✳

The changes in the colonies after 1890 can be traced both to sponsor policies and to the changing profile of new settlers. As sponsorship was consolidated, screening procedures were implemented that helped shape new cohorts of settlers. In addition, sponsor policies supporting industry made the colonies a viable destination for industrial workers. Yet the changes in the type of migrant arriving in the colonies was equally influenced by preferences among individual migrants. Only when the desire to relocate to a rural community came together with the opportunities presented by the sponsor could this migration take place. Clearly, this coincidence of push and pull came together most often for Polish Jews, rather than the Jews of the Northwest Pale who dominated mass migration.

The impact of these changes was to transform an agrarian community with distinctly intellectual and idealistic roots into a settlement less distinct from the American-Jewish community as a whole. Although the colonies' rural location and small size, as well as the regional origin of their settlers —now disproportionately from Poland as well as the South Pale—provided many contrasts with the immigrant Jewish community at large, these distinctions gradually became less striking. Where there was once a community of farmers, the occupational profile of the community after the turn of the century became more like Jewish communities elsewhere (although still containing a large contingent of farmers). Where communal and agrarian ideologies had dominated, diversity increased, "American" ideologies of individualism gained strength, and social and economic life based on single-family life dominated. Cooperative efforts were no longer based on communistic models but were more like the mutual aid organizations and labor unions common in larger Jewish communities. Where immigrants from the South Pale had once held sway, new groups came to challenge their leadership, bringing with them more traditional views of religion and respect for Yiddish culture.

Although this infusion of newcomers, and the expansion of Yiddish culture that they brought, temporarily retarded Americanization in the sense of cultural adjustment and language acquisition, it was clear to the sponsors that the tendency toward communalism, which they perceived as so threatening, had been all but extinguished. The mesh between the goals of the new colonists—home ownership, economic advancement, citizenship—and the goals of the sponsors for an economically independent, hardworking population with a respect for private property so pleased the sponsors that they apparently overlooked the newcomers' emphasis on Yiddish language and culture.

Although irreversibly altering the character of the colonies, these changes also allowed for their continued survival. At the most basic, economic level, it is clear that the settlements would not have survived without intervention and investment by the sponsors. In addition, the pool of immigrants like the early settlers had disappeared, because of the demise of the Am Olam and the waning of agrarian ideologies among Jewish immigrants to America. The population growth in this period, achieved through sponsor investment, expansion of industry, and an influx of nonagricultural and nonidealistic settlers, led to the "golden years" between 1900 and World War I, when the settlements thrived economically and socially. Yet after the first decade of the twentieth century, cracks began to appear in the facade, as migration to the settlements diminished and attrition increased. These trends, which are analyzed in chapter 6, led to the demise of the colonies in succeeding decades.

6

Dissolution of the Colonies

I N CHAPTER 5, the changes in the type of settlers arriving in the colonies, the policies of sponsoring organizations, and the resulting transformation of the character of the colonies from 1890 to 1910 were explored. As sponsors encouraged growth in the settlements' industrial sector, the number of non-agricultural settlers who did not share the idealism of earlier groups increased greatly. Even the agriculturalists who migrated to the colonies in these years were of different regional and ideological origin than the early Am Olam colonists.

The expansion in the nonagricultural sector of the colonies led to the "golden years," when the colonies' economy stabilized and opportunities for cultural, social, educational, and athletic activities multiplied. This period of growth continued in the years leading up to World War I, when reports on the colonies were increasingly favorable. Sponsors, colonists, and outsiders all commented on the progress in the South Jersey colonies.[1] Yet even during these "golden years," there were signs of weakening, as attrition began to take a heavy toll on the colonies. During the war years, and in the following decade, these negative trends were amplified, with increasing industrial strife and a reduction in support by the colony sponsors. In this chapter these trends, which led to a gradual fading away of the colonies as distinct settlements, are explored.

Despite the optimism expressed in the early 1910s, the pattern of growth from 1900 to 1910 demonstrated that there were cracks in the facade. Although the number of families increased by 27 in Alliance (including Norma and Brotmanville) and by 16 in Carmel and Rosenhayn between the 1900 census and the 1909 United States Immigration Commission survey, the total population remained stable. Despite the increase in the number of families, the population for the Salem County colonies increased only from 877 to 903; Rosenhayn and Carmel decreased in population, from 1154 to 1138.[2] This stability in total population in a community where average family size was 5.7

in 1900 reveals a high level of attrition, particularly among the American-born offspring of the colonists.

Attrition among the second generation had been of concern for more than a decade. In the early 1900s, as the newly formed Jewish Agricultural and Industrial Aid Society (JAIAS) began to grapple with the colony question, they expressed concern about this issue. The 1902 JAIAS report noted that attrition was particularly high among the children of the more "intelligent" farmers, and recommended the institution of social, cultural, and educational programs to encourage young people to remain in the colonies.[3]

Because of both encouragement by the JAIAS and desire from the settlers themselves, clubs and organizations proliferated in the colonies in the first decade of the century. In the Salem County colonies alone, deeds were issued to mark the founding of the Norma Athletic Association (1904), the Norma Social Club (1908), and the Brotmanville Social Club (1910). These clubs joined an existing network of mutual aid organizations, such as the Women's Society of Somech Noflim (1903), the Chevrah Bikur Holim (Society for Visiting the Sick, 1892), and the Burial Society.[4] In addition, many activities, from English classes and music lessons to concerts, plays, and lectures had been added to the colonies' cultural calendar by Louis Mounier. During the 1910s, popular activities for the youth included Mounier's educational programs, Fels's manual-training classes, the athletic associations and social clubs, theatrical productions, the Boy Scouts, the Seeds of Zion (a club for students in the Jewish Chautauqua Society religious classes), and frequent dances.[5] These activities were recalled fondly by the young people who came of age in this period, such as Herman Eisenberg, who wrote: "The hub around which all of the local activities centered was the Norma Athletic Association. . . . The baseball team was the major activity of the association. That more than anything else, gripped our youthful imagination, which showed that we were really Americans."[6]

Despite the development of this extensive network of programs and activities to enrich life in the colonies and prevent attrition, the attrition problem continued during the 1910s. By 1919, the population of the Salem County colonies dropped to 115 families; the number of families in Carmel and Rosenhayn decreased from 220 in 1909 to 156. Population also declined absolutely, from 903 to 560 in Alliance, Brotmanville and Norma, and from 1,138 to 709 in Rosenhayn and Carmel, an overall decrease of more than one-third.[7]

Contemporary observers placed much of the blame for the high level of attrition on a distaste of Jewish youth for farm life. One such observer, Philip Goldstein, a Jewish Chautauqua worker who wrote a dissertation on the colonies, reported: "Most of the Jewish adolescents, caring not at all for farm-life, hankering after change, after new, different companions, lured by the city—go to the city at the first opportunity." Although his report also discussed the difficulties of farming, Goldstein argued that the negative attitude toward agriculture was a primary cause of attrition: "So long as the Jewish public is not enthusiastic about farming but considers farm-life a drudgery and misfortune rather than an honorable and wholesome means to a livelihood, then it must be said that the outlook for Jewish farming is not very bright."[8] Similarly, the Immigration Commission had reported nearly one decade earlier that the colonies' children were particularly prone to attrition. The JAIAS belief that an expansion in social and cultural activities would thwart attrition indicates its acceptance of the idea that the root of the problem was cultural.

Despite the emphasis placed by observers and sponsors on cultural and attitudinal factors, it is apparent that much of the blame for this high level of attrition can be traced to poor economic conditions in agriculture *relative to other fields.* For the colonies' farmers, economic conditions improved somewhat by the early 1910s, but, as always, the work was difficult and constant, while markets and natural conditions were unreliable. Although Goldstein's 1919 report indicated that the farmers' "earnings today and their margin of profit are higher than they were ever before—their prospects brighter,"[9] many farmers compared their earnings not with farmers in previous years but with their nonfarming counterparts. Here farmers found themselves lacking, their net incomes lagging significantly behind those of the colonies' nonfarmers. Thus, although the average net income of farmers in Alliance and Brotmanville was thirteen hundred dollars, nonfarmers in those colonies earned an average of fifteen hundred dollars. In the other colonies the disparities were even greater: in Carmel, farmers averaged nine hundred dollars, while nonfarmers earned sixteen hundred dollars; in Rosenhayn, farmers earned twelve hundred dollars to the nonfarmers' eighteen hundred dollars; and in Norma farmers earned twelve hundred dollars while nonfarmers earned two thousand dollars. These discrepancies existed despite the fact that most colony farmers had *increased* their holdings: in 1919, Goldstein reported that "most farmers own about thirty acres and some have more than twice that number."[10]

Even those observers stressing cultural factors to explain the declining colony population acknowledged the poor return on farming relative to other opportunities. The Jewish farmer, noted the Immigration Commission in explaining the causes of attrition, "wants his children to be educated and to enjoy the comforts of life; he wants to receive some surplus return from the toil of his hands, and to exercise the prerogatives of a citizen of his country."[11] Similarly, Goldstein included economic as well as cultural factors in analyzing the high attrition rates:

It is difficult to expect men and women to work on a farm at low wages, to put up with primitive conditions, with little if any social intercourse, with comparatively little opportunity for intellectual development, at a time when superior alternatives are offered to them in the city. No matter what the trade or industry, however skilled or unskilled, wages are higher [in the city]. If expenses, too, are higher in the city,—people are willing to spend more, if they earn more.[12]

Despite improvements in the market, conditions for farmers continued to be difficult after World War I. Thus, observers found that even on farms that appeared prosperous, colonists were struggling. One *Saturday Evening Post* reporter who visited the colonies in the early 1920s was impressed by the apparent productivity of a farm she visited. Yet the second-generation farmer that worked the farm

> had the classic story of hardships to tell—high cost of labor, machinery and fertilizer; early drought; bad markets. Sometimes he sold his crop to the commission man for less than the actual cost of putting it into the ground. And then there were taxes, interest and payments on the mortgage—altogether a tough strain on a family man. He had a farm of 32 acres, and he was forced to do outside work for ready cash, so he had taken a side job as a shipping clerk.[13]

A second apparently prosperous farmer encountered by the reporter emphasized the constant work of farming and, despite his apparent success, was frustrated by the comparison of his progress to that of his brother in the city: "Look at my oldest brother. He pulled out and went to New York and inside of three years he's made more than we've made here in seventeen. What I say is, farming as a business doesn't pay. You can make more money in town, spend less energy and have more of a life." Although the reporter was told that plots of fewer than forty acres were too small to succeed, a shortage of hired farm labor made it "practically impossible" for a small family to work a forty-acre farm.[14]

Even the most dedicated colonists found themselves frustrated by the difficulties of farming. Sidney Baily, one of the Am Olam founders and an Alliance farmer since the 1880s, led the colony's agriculturalists in experimenting with new crops and methods. Yet even as late as the early 1920s, Baily was still struggling. Despite the fact that he had expanded his farm to thirty-two acres, Baily reported, "I'm poor. I'm still often behind with my taxes. I get up at dawn and work far into the night in order to take an hour or so off at lunch to read." Baily found that the demands of farming precluded the activities that he so enjoyed, including "theater, opera, contact with brilliant minds." The three Baily children had all entered the urban professions; one was a doctor, one a government worker, and one a chemist. Ironically, Baily, who had earlier scorned "careers" and dreamt of reviving his people through dependence "upon the elements of Father Sun and Mother Earth instead of depending upon the whims of others," by the early 1920s regarded his children's professional success as the end for which "we have slaved."[15]

The difficulties of farming and the perception that an easier life could be found in the cities was not unique to the Jewish farmers. Even observers who emphasized the disdain of the Jew for farming as the cause of attrition had to admit that the attrition among Jewish farmers reflected a national trend. After stressing the dissatisfaction of the Hebrew with the returns of farming, the Immigration Commission admitted that "it may be doubted whether they are more inclined to leave agricultural pursuits than are the children of American parents." Similarly, Goldstein, while emphasizing cultural factors that dissuaded Jewish farmers, noted that an increasing proportion of all Americans were residing in urban areas, and conceded, "The problem of the Jewish farmer is but a part of the larger problem embracing farming in general throughout the country."[16]

The hardships of farming led many families to turn to the boarding business. Goldstein reported in 1919:

> After laboring under difficulties for years, some farmers have neglected, if not entirely abandoned, their farming and have become boarding-house keepers. Their farms are utilized only to the extent of gardens to supply the vegetables needed for their clientele. Most of these men have succeeded financially better than they did at farming, and consequently they hesitate to return to general farming, even now that farmers are enjoying greater prosperity than ever before. And it is quite impossible to apply oneself to both occupations with equal energy, because the boarding and the farming seasons are more or less coincident: one must be neglected for the other.[17]

In this period, boardinghouses sprang up throughout the colonies to serve vacationing city dwellers. The boarders brought both an important source of income and a contribution to the social life of the colonies. As the Immigration Commission reported, "These city dwellers not only bring in an urban atmosphere, but add much to the gaiety and social enterprise and recreations afforded."[18] Yet the boarding business was also a difficult one. Bea Harrison, granddaughter of Alliance founding colonists Levin and Coltun, recalled that she and the other members of her family had to give up their beds and sleep in the barn or out of doors during the summer boarding season, an experience common among the boardinghouse families.[19] A 1910 report emphasized these hardships:

> It is hard to imagine the martyrdom of the wife and family of the farmer who has boarders for the season. . . . Getting up at three o'clock in the

morning, going to bed at eleven o'clock at night, the whole family works like convicts to take care of the 10, 15, or 20 boarders, 30 sometimes, that are crowded two and three in one room. . . . The family sleep where they can, in the kitchen, the stable, and out of doors. The boarders ruin the fruit trees, trample the vegetable garden, grumble and criticize all the more as they pay less, and it all has to be borne in silence.[20]

Interaction with relatively well-off urbanites who vacationed in the colonies helped reinforce the perception that life in the city was easier than country life.

The comparison between difficult life on the farm and a perceived easy existence in the city led many longtime residents to abandon the colonies in the 1910s and 1920s. Thus Harrison explained that people left the colonies because it became apparent that life was much easier in the city.[21] Moey Lihn, who was born in the colonies at the turn of the century, explained that it was because farming was such a hard life that he never wanted to farm. Jack Helig, one of the few farmers of the generation that came of age during this period—and the last of the colony farmers in Alliance by the 1970s—recalled that when he informed his father that he wanted to farm, his father wept because farming was such a hard life.[22]

Although the level of attrition among the colonies' farmers was high, it could not alone account for the population decline in the 1910s. In the colonies' industrial sector, decreasing sponsor support and increasing labor strife, coupled with expanding opportunities in nearby cities and other urban areas, led many nonagricultural workers to relocate away from the settlements.

From the beginning, JAIAS support for the colonies had been somewhat reluctant. Although enthusiastically aiding Jewish agriculturalists throughout the country, including some who settled in the Jersey colonies, the idea of supporting an expansion of the colonization movement had never been a part of JAIAS program.[23] Although JAIAS reports in the first few years of the century revealed increasing satisfaction with the stability brought to the colonies through society support, society trustees were discouraged by the continued dependence of the colonies' industries on subsidies, and began to abandon projects that had proven particularly troublesome. As early as 1905, the JAIAS began to withdraw from colony support in the form of industrial aid. The 1905 annual report noted that "no attempt has been made to increase the number of industries or the number of industrial workers." By 1906, the JAIAS concluded, "The Colonies are not favorably situated for the establishment of new business activities, and therefore any effort that is made to encourage factories will only be successful as long as subsidized."[24]

Despite their resolution not to aid the expansion of industrial activity in the colonies, the JAIAS continued to issue subsidies to existing factories.[25] In its effort to wean the colonists from support, the JAIAS made some of these subsidies conditional on the contribution of matching amounts by the colonists. Thus in 1908, a Philadelphia manufacturer was granted a subsidy of five hundred dollars to set up shop in Carmel's Factory Number One, on condition that the Carmel residents themselves contribute half of the subsidy. A similar arrangement was made in 1909, when Rosenhayn residents were required to raise a thousand dollars for a two-year subsidy for that colony's Factory Number Two.[26]

Besides their disappointment with the colonies' continuing need for industrial subsidies, JAIAS officials were also dismayed by increasing industrial strife in the colonies. Thus in 1905, the JAIAS discontinued aid to Rosenhayn's Factory Number Two, where "there have been so many quarrels between the different managers whom we have brought to this factory, and the employes [sic]."[27] Factories in the colonies had been subject to strikes from the earliest days of industrial activity, particularly in Woodbine, where industrial development was most extensive. In Rosenhayn, a strike in 1900 led to the founding of a local of the United Garment Workers.[28] Both the link of the colonies' workers with national labor unions and the fact that most factory operators in the colonies were Philadelphia or New York manufacturers, tied the colonies' industrial workers to major strikes in larger cities. Thus in 1913, the strike of workers from Kramer and Sons in Philadelphia spread to the firm's Brotmanville factory, where riots broke out between union and nonunion workers.[29] Local newspapers blamed the strikes on outside agitators, claiming that "the Brotmanville workers are receiving good wages and are satisfied to remain at work." However, the participation of longtime colonists, such as Nathan and Samuel Barish, Morris Eisenberg, Aaron Ruvinsky, John Levin, Samuel Glassman, Isaac Bleznak, and John Lihn in the riots against nonunion workers, and the refusal of other colonists to perform their duties as constables, indicates that at least a portion of the colonists agreed with union demands and casts doubt on newspaper allegations of agitation by outsiders.[30]

The war boom eased industrial tensions in mid-decade, but the hiatus was neither total nor long-lasting. In 1917, the manufacturing firm of Mendelson brothers, which had branches in Norma, Rosenhayn, and Brotmanville, was struck amid fulfilling a government contract. In the same year, the Norma and Vineland branches of the Eskin manufacturing firm were struck "partly out of sympathy with the great wave of strikes in New York's clothing industry and partly to prevent strike-breaking subcontracts in the rural factories." Both during and after the war, strikes raged in the Rosenthal-Dias and Roschkin factories in Rosenhayn and Carmel, where both firms resisted unionization of their workers.[31]

The strike activity in the colonies resulted in an exodus of manufacturing plants to Vineland, where manufacturers believed that the larger industrial work force and better facilities would improve their situation. Before the war, a number of factories, including M. Joseph and Son of Rosenhayn, M. Cooper Company of Brotmanville, and even Brotman and Sons, relocated to Vineland. The Eskin factory, which moved later in the decade, was accused of leaving Norma in a direct effort to avoid unionization.[32]

By 1919, observer Philip Goldstein indicated that a number of the colonies' factories were standing vacant. In Rosenhayn, he reported, one factory had been closed for years, and another, which had opened and closed sporadically, had finally been vacated when the firm relocated to Vineland. In Carmel, Goldstein noted that the Henry Dix factory had closed several years before, and another large factory "has been idle for many years." In Norma, one of the three factories was closed, and the other two were unstable. Alliance completely lacked factories; in Brotmanville only one of the three factories was functioning.[33]

As factories relocated to Vineland, the colonies' workers followed. Although several factories left the colonies because of strike activity, they found no shelter from such actions in Vineland, and frequently were forced to pay higher wages. Because of this wage differential, reported Goldstein, "many of the colonists . . . prefer to travel each day to work in the neighboring urban centers."[34] Even during the war, when many of the colony factories secured government contracts, workers often chose to pursue more lucrative options in Vineland, Philadelphia, or New York. Thus Molly Greenblatt left her job as a teacher in the colonies to take a position as a secretary in Philadelphia, because it paid more than double her teaching salary. When she married two years later, Molly Greenblatt Kravitz set up house in Philadelphia.[35]

Even after it became clear that the exodus of manufacturers from the colonies was having a severe impact, sponsors continued their policy of refusing to encourage industrial expansion. For example, in 1928, when Norma settlers, organized as the Norma Improvement Association, appealed to the JAS ("industrial" had been dropped from the organization's name) for aid to construct a factory to stem attrition, they received a negative reply. Eugene Benjamin of the JAS wrote that such aid would be "a very foolish investment." He continued, "I could not conscientiously recommend an investment of any of the funds of the Jewish Agricultural Society in a movement which I am convinced would be unsuccessful."[36] When a Norma factory burned down in the same year, Benjamin was reluctant to allow the colonists to use the insurance money to rebuild. Benjamin clearly stated that, in his opinion, the project was unwise, writing, "Why the people of Norma should have been so stupid as to put their money into this building passes my understanding." In the same letter, Benjamin outlined the JAS experience with funding industry in the colonies:

> I have not changed my opinion that the erection of this building was a most stupid and unwarranted proceeding in view of the past history of all similar buildings in that section. The Mendel [factory] Building never was instrumental in aiding the community except for short and uncertain periods and the manufacturers only stayed there because the Society kept feeding them with funds. The Brotman Factory erected for similar purposes had a similar experience. The various small factories started in Rosenhayn and Carmel were only maintained just as long as we subsidized the contractors and the large factory in Carmel met the same fate eventually as all the others.

Grudgingly authorizing the use of the insurance money to rebuild the factory, Benjamin stipulated that the directors of the JAS "must put ourselves definitely in writing to the effect that we have disapproved the erection of this building and that we will not help in or subsidize its operations."[37]

The contrast between the growth in Vineland and the attrition in the colonies led merchants and the increasing number of second-generation professionals, as well as manufacturers, farmers, and industrial workers, to relocate to that city. By the 1920s, the pattern of Jewish colonists purchasing Vineland property became so marked that the *Vineland Evening Journal* took note of it.[38] As second-generation colonists attained higher educational levels and entered the professions, some, such as veterinarian Arthur Goldhaft, dentist Gilbert Greenblatt, and lawyer Joe Greenblatt, set up practices in Vineland.[39] Although such professionals felt that Vineland offered greater opportunities than the colonies, others felt confined even in Vineland and chose to move to larger cities, such as Philadelphia and New York. Thus Bluma Bayuk, daughter of colony leader Moses Bayuk, decided to move to Philadelphia to pursue her career as a nurse—even after Maurice Fels offered to pay for her studies if she returned to practice in Alliance. Similarly, Gilbert Greenblatt later moved from Vineland to Philadelphia. As one Carmel descendant remarked, "Young people left to get an education, to succeed in the American way, and only older people stayed. Many of the Jewish families of Carmel, Rosenhayn, and Alliance moved to Bridgeton and Vineland and stayed there as merchants, professionals, and entrepreneurs. Others left the area entirely."[40]

The high level of attrition in the 1910s and 1920s, combined with the resolve of the JAS not to aid new industrial growth in the colonies, led to a dissolution of colonial life by the 1930s. While *individual* farmers, many of them refugees from Germany and Poland, continued to settle on the land with the aid of the JAS in the 1930s, 1940s, and 1950s, the settlements were gradually reduced from independent colonies to virtual suburbs of the Vineland Jewish community.[41]

The German and Polish refugees who joined the farming community both before and after World War II were aided by the JAS. However, consistent with JAS policy over the previous thirty years, these farmers were settled as individuals—not as members of a colony or even of a partnership. Gabriel Davidson, managing director of the JAS, explained:

> Refugees see in partnership a social advantage, the comfort of sharing responsibility, financial and otherwise. They see, too, in the pooling of resources the opportunity of operating on a larger scale. Compelling as this may appear, the Society opposes, as it always did, farm partnerships. Long experience has proven that these so-called advantages are more than nullified by the weaknesses inherent in a venture which is not only a business carried on by the heads, but a mode of living in which all members of the families are thrown into close contact; where, therefore, clashes of temperament are sooner of later bound to occur.[42]

Thus the JAS settled refugees throughout the United States on independent farms. Most of the refugees were settled on poultry farms, the form of agriculture considered best suited for the refugees, who generally had little money to invest and were middle-aged.[43] JAS records demonstrate that a large cluster of refugees—140 families by 1941—were settled in the area of the colonies, but their reports no longer referred to the colonies as such, calling the region instead "the Vineland district." By the early 1950s, roughly 1,000 families settled in the Vineland area, making this the largest wave of Jewish settlers to the region.[44]

The insistence of the JAS that the new farmers settle as individuals, rather than as colonists, was not resisted by the refugees themselves. Although many of the refugees were interested in forming partnerships,[45] the ideological commitment to agrarianism and communalism possessed by the earliest settlers was clearly missing from their farmward movement. Arthur Goldhaft, whose parents had been part of the Am Olam movement, contrasted the World War II refugees with the earlier settlers. Commenting on the new refugees, Goldhaft wrote, "Suppose we dropped 'back-to-the-soil' as a slogan, or as a moral idea. Let the Jews of Palestine carry that out as a noble issue; we didn't have to prove that point. All we had to do was find the best practical solution for absorbing the refugees." Thus Goldhaft endorsed the JAS perspective that such farm settlement was a practical solution to the refugee crisis, rather than an ideological response to "the Jewish problem": "Wasn't the small poultry farm still a good idea? First of all, it would keep these people off the labor market that was still so touchy in the thirties, with relief and WPA and unemployment still widespread. It would keep the newcomers from competing in the professions. And it would give them a healthy life, where they had the least amount of social adjustment to make—out on small farms, in their own groups."[46]

As the older settlers—farmers, merchants, and workers—left the colonies and the newly settled farmers arrived, community life became less independent, and more tied to the Vineland Jewish community. Attrition, combined with decreasing religiosity among the offspring of the more traditional second wave of immigrants, who had arrived at the turn of the century, led to deterioration of the settlements' religious institutions. As synagogue attendance declined, so did the youth groups and other organizations linked to these institutions. Although religious stalwarts among the older residents desperately tried to maintain the synagogues, it became increasingly difficult to find the *minyan* necessary for services. This decline in synagogue attendance revealed the dwindling community spirit in colonies where, previously, even non-religious residents had participated in religious services out of a sense of solidarity with the community. The venerable Alliance synagogue, Eben ha-Ezer, while briefly revived by German refugees in the 1930s, did not survive the 1940s.[47]

The relocation of the center of Jewish life in the area of Vineland was apparent in the proliferation of Jewish activities in that city. The increased ease of transportation provided by the automobile allowed young residents of the colony area to attend services in the Conservative Vineland synagogue, Beth Israel. As Beth Israel grew in the 1920s and 1930s, it added social, educational, community service, and Zionist organizations, many of which served the population of the colony districts. As cultural activity in the colonies declined after World War I, it increased in Vineland. Thus Yiddish theater, once popular in the colonies' social halls, was increasingly centered in Vineland.[48]

In the colonies themselves, though some cultural and social activity persisted—and there was growth in organizations catering specifically to the new Germans, Austrians, and Poles—the most vibrant organizations were those specifically targeted to agriculturalists. In this area, the JAS provided educational support and other extension services to poultry farmers' organizations. In addition, surviving farmers banded together during the depression for mutual support through organizations such as the Rosenhayn Farmers' Cooperative Marketing Association and the Alliance–Norma Farmers' Protective Association of New Jersey, which advocated government relief and mutual aid. Poultry farmers from the colonies were active in the New Jersey Poultry Association, which concentrated on education and advertising. Some farmers resided in Vineland, as did expert poultry veterinarian Arthur Goldhaft, but most of these organizations, which focused on the economics of agriculture, were based in the rural districts, rather than in Vineland. Despite this tendency, the JAS, reinforcing its bias against the colonies, established its branch office in Vineland, rather than in one of the rural settlements.[49]

The emergence of Vineland as the center of the Jewish community led observers and surviving settlers to consider the colonization project over. Although the Jewish population in the colony area increased in the 1930s and 1940s, the collective spirit and sense of purpose that characterizes a *colony* diminished. One Carmel descendant noted, "By the middle 1930s Carmel had become largely empty, devitalized; the sewing industry was gone, and only a few families continued farming."[50] When the descendants and surviving settlers of Alliance, Brotmanville, and Norma gathered in 1932 to commemorate the fiftieth anniversary of the founding of Alliance, they published a memory book that clearly demonstrated that they considered the colony a completed chapter. In the book, the essay by Herman Eisenberg, son of a Norma farm family and by 1932 a Philadelphia lawyer, served as a eulogy for the colonization project:

> Today, in 1932, as we "Old Timers" return to celebrate the "Golden Jubilee," the landscape presents a vast change. The old factories are gone. Brotmanville has practically disappeared. Many of the old farmsteads are no more. In their places have sprung up many small poultry farms. The type of farming has undergone radical changes. . . . Living conditions have greatly improved. The homes are modern in every sense of the word. . . . A majority of the residents own automobiles, and are perhaps as much urban-minded as those of the later generations who migrated to the cities. This migration is neither difficult to explain or should it be a cause for sorrow. If greater numbers have migrated than have remained, they have merely been carried along by the relentless tide of the Cityward movement.[51]

Although a few of the old colony families remained in the area through the 1930s, the colonies were generally referred to in the past tense. Thus when Arthur Goldhaft, son of Alliance settlers and a Vineland veterinarian, referred in his autobiography to the colonies in the 1930s, he wrote: "Those old little farms around Norma, where the Alliance colony had been, and that famous place Carmel, where the free-thinkers had thrived, and where people had even whispered of free love and socialism and all kinds of wild things. Carmel was just a tangle of neglected old farms now, with a few summer resorts."[52]

In less than fifty years, the colonization projects in southern New Jersey had ended. In less than five decades, the colonies completed their transformation from agrarian communal settlements into communities of families, differing little from mainstream Jewish communities. The community, now centered in Vineland, was dominated by second-generation merchants and professionals, and their community networks and institutions, including the

Conservative Vineland synagogue and its social and fraternal organizations, were like those in Jewish communities elsewhere in the United States. Although the community included more farmers than the typical American-Jewish community, and a particularly large number of refugee Jewish poultry farmers, these farmers were independent entrepreneurs—not idealistic rebels. Neither they, nor their colony predecessors, looked upon the community in the 1930s and afterward as part of the *colony* experience.

The disappearance of the Jewish agricultural colony from the American scene has often been considered confirmation of the idea that Jews were unfit for farming. One historian of the Baron de Hirsch–sponsored Argentine colonies has observed that "long after Israeli farmers have made the desert bloom, almost all observers accept the notion that Argentine Jewish agricultural settlements failed because Jews do not make good farmers."[53] This comment applies equally well to observers of the American colonies. Even the colonists' descendants look to the dissolution of the colonies as evidence of a lack of either technical or cultural aptitude of the Jew for farming. Arthur Goldhaft recalls, "We used to argue to each other, the experiment didn't really work—the Jews didn't stay on the land—they're not farmers. . . . The fact is, the first Jewish groups that came here, a couple of hundred families, made a big campaign, a moral issue about going back to the soil, but that didn't mean that every one of them was suited for it. Mostly the opposite was true."[54]

Yet despite the failure of the colonies to survive as such, Jewish farming continued in America long after the colonies' demise. Just as the colonies faded away in the 1910s, 1920s, and 1930s, the Jewish farm population was *expanding* rapidly. Although the number of Jewish farm families was only four thousand in 1910 (for a total Jewish farm population of nearly thirty thousand), the number grew to about sixteen thousand families (about eighty thousand individuals) by the early 1930s. As the Jewish population in the United States quadrupled during the first three decades of this century, the Jewish farm population increased by forty times. Even as the colonies declined, Jewish farmers in New Jersey continued to increase in number in the 1940s, and New Jersey remained one of the strongholds of Jewish farming after World War II.[55]

The expansion in Jewish farming during the first half of the twentieth century indicates that assertions of Jewish urban proclivities cannot account for the dissolution of the colony movement. Rather, internal factors, including sponsor policies and changes in the composition of the settler population can explain developments in the colonies that led to their ultimate demise. Thus sponsor policies that increasingly channeled agricultural aid to independent farmers at the expense of the colonies were a key factor in the deterioration of the colonies' economic life, as was the sponsor decision to cease aid to colony industries. In addition, as subsequent waves of migration replaced the early idealists, the settlers' goals changed. New settlers, who were not a part of the Am Olam movement and who were selected under sponsor policies that encouraged individual entrepreneurship, embraced the opportunity for family ownership and did not share the commitment to the colony ideal with those who preceded them.

Even if the dissolution of the Jewish colonies does not indicate a failing of the Jews as farmers, it might indicate a failure of the colonization ideology and movement. Indeed, the dissolution of the colonies in South Jersey, despite the persistence of Jewish farmers in the area, has been taken by many historians to indicate an essential failing in the colony movement.[56] Yet rather than focusing simply on colony persistence as a meter of success, assessment of the success or failure of the colony experiment in New Jersey is best judged against the varied goals of the settlers and sponsors who advocated colonization.

For the first group of colony settlers, those who shared the Am Olam ideology, the dissolution of the colonies appears to indicate a fundamental failure of their plans. Although the Am Olam ideology was somewhat diffuse, its plans called for the establishment of a network of colonies that would be agricultural. In addition, many members advocated the creation of colonies that would be communal, and identified their project with an international socialist movement.[57]

For most of these Am Olam idealists, the colony experience in the United States proved an unequivocal failure. Many abandoned the plan before ever setting foot on a farm. Others participated in short-lived projects in the West. For those who did settle in the New Jersey colonies, disappointment was often bitter. Some, such as George Seldes, found the Jersey colonies insufficiently radical, and left to join other experiments or, more often, the Jewish labor movement in New York.[58] Others, such as Am Olam cofounder Moses Herder, found farming difficult and unsatisfying. Although he was dedicated to the Am Olam ideal of agrarianism in principle, he preferred sitting under a tree, thinking and reading, to performing farm labor.[59] Even those who lived out their lives in the colonies met with disillusion. Founders Baily and Bayuk compromised their early ideals in the face of the realities of colony life—and both saw their children leave the farm for the cities that they had abandoned.[60] Baily expressed doubts about the project to a reporter in 1923: "I wonder! Years of atrocious toil! Years of spiritual loss! I often wonder that very thing— has it been worthwhile?"[61] The colonies that developed in Salem and Cumberland counties fulfilled neither the dream of agrarianism nor that of communalism, as they became increasingly industrial and single-family oriented, even within the first decade of settlement.

Similarly, the deterioration of the colonies seems to indicate a failure to meet sponsor goals of establishing rural agricultural-industrial centers that would absorb Jewish immigrants. Sponsor goals varied, but one of the primary aims shared by the philanthropists was to divert migration from the major immigrant centers in large cities, such as New York. Thus sponsors aided industrial projects that they believed would enable the expansion of the rural settlements.[62] The colonies fell short of these goals, as demonstrated by the closure of the colony factories in the 1910s and 1920s and the high level of return migration to the cities in these and subsequent years.

Yet though the colonies failed to thrive as either the Am Olam's agrarian, socialist settlements or the sponsors' agricultural-industrial centers, it is important to also evaluate their fulfillment of the goal of "normalization," or economic, social, and cultural adaptation to mainstream society, one of the few goals shared by the Am Olam, sponsors, and nonideological settlers. One main motive of the Am Olam in establishing colonies had been to solve the "Jewish problem" through the normalization of the Jewish occupational profile. Am Olam members believed that the roots of anti-Semitism lay in the concentration of Jews in unproductive occupations, particularly in trade. By engaging in farming, Jews would not only become "productive" but they would also alter their occupational profile so as to conform to most of the population—thus becoming "normal." In the Russian milieu, where almost all the population worked the land, to be a farmer was to be "normal."

Although many of the specific goals of the early colonists contrasted sharply with sponsor goals, the goal of normalization was shared by both parties. Sponsors, such as Hirsch, had focused on normalization, or Americanization, as the key to avoiding an outbreak of anti-Semitism in this country. Sponsors argued that by living in rural communities away from the major immigrant centers, the colonists would more readily shed their foreign ways and integrate with the American mainstream.

Later settlers differed in their goals from their predecessors and conformed more closely to sponsor goals—in part because these settlers were selected under sponsor-screening policies and because of the contrasts in premigration background with the earlier settlers. Many were aspiring farmers, lured by the opportunity to acquire a family farm, but they did not share the ideological goals of the Am Olam as far as either communalism or a return to agrarianism by the Jewish people was concerned. They hoped to establish themselves economically, to escape the city, and to live in a Jewish community with a Jewish cultural life while easing their way into American society. Although some were committed to farming as an occupation, they hoped to establish family farms, not communes. Others readily accepted factory work as the means to the fulfillment of their goals. The goals of these later settlers, though contrasting with the earlier group on many counts, can be linked to the Am Olam goal of "normalization"—although the two groups of settlers defined normalcy differently. Later settlers did not formally articulate this goal of normalization, but their emphasis on achieving American citizenship, their adaptation to American culture, and their embracing of the goals of economic advancement and education indicate a strong desire to participate in what they saw as the American way and for them represented normalization.

For the Am Olam settlers who remained in the colonies, the goal of normalization came to surpass the utopian, agrarian aims that they had brought from Europe. This occurred because in America the content of "normalization" changed to conform to the norm of their new society and drew closer to the goals of the later colonists. Thus as it became clear that the settlements would not be economically viable without industrial activity, the agrarians embraced the idea of bringing factory work, which was quickly becoming more dominant than agriculture in American economic life, into the colonies.[63] Similarly, as Am Olam stalwarts, such as Baily and Bayuk, came to recognize that the professions, rather than farming, were the route to successful integration with mainstream America, they encouraged their children to pursue professional training. As more traditionally religious settlers came to dominate the society, the idealist group realized that only by respecting the newcomers' religious beliefs and by participating in religious life would they be able to achieve the sense of community they desired. In any event, they discovered in America that religious practice and citizenship were not mutually exclusive— that secularism was not a prerequisite for normalization. Thus over time, the normalization desired by the early pioneers became like the integration sought by later settlers, who aimed for economic success for their families and aspired to property ownership.

It is not surprising that the goals of these immigrants would be revised as they became familiar with their new society, for the opportunities, assumptions, and values in America contrasted sharply with those under which the Am Olam had emerged in Russia. This reevaluation of goals has been noted among other immigrant groups. For example, in her study of East Central Europeans in Johnstown, Pennsylvania, Ewa Morawska observed how immigrants adapted their goals in accordance with the opportunities and restrictions of their environment, "alternately expanding and contracting their goals in response to situational exigencies."[64] Morawska found that immigrants used the parts of old attitudes that resonated with their new situation to formulate new goals. Similarly, the parts of Am Olam ideology that persisted—the desire to join mainstream society, as well as socialism among those who abandoned colonization to join the labor movement in New York and agrarianism among those who remained independent farmers—were the elements of the ideology that resonated in America. The parts of the ideology that did not fit the American milieu—the belief in a communal and purely agrarian network of colonies—did not persist.

Although unsuccessful in surviving as communal or agrarian colonies, the settlements established in Cumberland and Salem counties were highly successful in the underlying goal of normalization. In economic normalization, the settlements enabled Jews to enter agriculture, a field in which the Jewish presence continued to expand even after the dissolution of the colonies. In addition, the colonies provided a channel through which many entered the professions, industry, or commercial activity. As colony life disintegrated, the descendants of the colonists, by abandoning farming, began to conform to the norms of their new society—in which the farming sector was shrinking relative to industrial and professional occupations.

Socially, culturally, and politically, colonists found an opportunity in rural New Jersey to become participants in the mainstream of American life. Politically, in the colonies themselves, and later in Vineland and elsewhere, colonists and their descendants entered mainstream society by participating as citizens, voting and serving in political office, both locally and at the state level.[65] Socially and culturally, although a concentrated Jewish population in the area provided an opportunity for the development of a wide variety of specifically Jewish organizations and activities, the isolation of the communities from large immigrant centers forced colonists to interact more closely with native-born Americans. Colonists came into contact with native-born farmers and Vinelanders in school, business dealings, political activities, and professional organizations, as well as in social activities.[66] Thus in assessing the degree of success of the colonies, Arthur Goldhaft concluded, "In the big sense, wasn't it a success in that they somehow adjusted themselves and found a life in America and raised their children and put a lot of them through college, starting them in a creative life?"[67] In America, normalization ultimately required not a return to the land but entrance into mainstream society through the expanding urban middle class: "In America, by becoming a farmer after 1880, the Jew would not be normalizing his position; on the contrary, he would be making it abnormal."[68]

The colonies, then, did succeed in aiding the settlers to move into the American mainstream. The role of Jewish agricultural colonies in aiding the adaptation of settlers is one that has been explored by historian Judith Elkin with regard to the Argentine colonies. Elkin argues that although the settlements did not succeed in surviving as agricultural communities, they did accomplish the larger goal of "the establishment of a viable Jewish community in a new land of settlement."[69] She contends that the colonies played a key role in the normalization of the immigrants in their new country, serving as

> cultural decompression chambers where Jews underwent transmogrification from European *shtetl* to Argentine city. The very isolation that ultimately made life intolerable, in the short run provided the breathing space the immigrants needed in order to orient themselves linguistically, ecologically, and behaviorally to their new environment. The colonies naturalized the settlers and turned them into Argentines. . . . They became a halfway house where Jews paused before returning to the modern world, or sending their children out into it.[70]

Although the New Jersey colonies never achieved the scale of their Argentine counterparts, and cannot be credited with a large role in enabling the integration of the American-Jewish community as a whole, Elkin's argument applies well to the New Jersey experience. The colonies' failure to persist does not necessarily indicate the failure of the project, as Elkin argues: "The empty cocoon does not argue the failure of the butterfly."[71] The disintegration of the New Jersey colonies occurred not because Jews were incapable of farming but because they had successfully joined the American mainstream, which was flowing away from agriculture. A key goal of both sponsors and colonists— normalization—had been achieved.

**Notes
Glossary
Bibliography
Index**

Notes

Introduction

1. Simon Kuznets, "Immigration of Russian Jews to the United States: Background and Statistics," *Perspectives in American History,* vol. 9 (Harvard Univ.: Charles Warren Center for Studies in American History, 1975), 35–126; and "Economic Structure and the Life of the Jews," *The Jews: Their History, Culture, and Religion,* vol. 3 (Philadelphia: The Jewish Publication Society of America, 1960), 1597–1666.

2. At their peak in the 1920s, the Argentine colonies were home to more than 20,000 Jewish farm families and an additional 13,000 nonfarming Jewish artisans, merchants, and professionals. See Judith Elkin, "Goodnight Sweet Gaucho: A Revisionist View of the Jewish Agricultural Experiment in Argentina," *American Jewish Historical Quarterly* 67, no. 3 (Mar. 1978): 209. In 1920, 22 percent of Argentina's Jews resided in the colonies. See Robert Weisbrot, *The Jews of Argentina* (Philadelphia: Jewish Publication Society, 1979), 70. Because turnover was high, the percentage of Argentine Jews who *ever* lived in the colonies was considerably higher than the 22 percent figure.

3. Figures for 1908 are from the Jewish Agricultural and Industrial Aid Society, *Annual Report* (New York: Wm. O. Popper and Co., 1908).

4. For example, see Uri Herscher, *Jewish Agricultural Utopias in America, 1881–1910* (Detroit: Wayne State Univ. Press, 1981); and Joseph Brandes *Immigrants to Freedom: Jewish Communities in Rural New Jersey since 1882* (Philadelphia: Univ. of Pennsylvania Press, 1971).

5. For example, see Oscar Handlin, *The Uprooted* (Boston: Little, Brown and Co., 1951).

6. For example, see Ewa Morawska *For Bread with Butter* (Cambridge: Cambridge Univ. Press, 1985); Tamara Hareven *Family Time and Industrial Time* (Cambridge: Cambridge Univ. Press, 1982); and John Bodnar *The Transplanted* (Bloomington: Indiana Univ. Press, 1985).

7. See Samuel Baily, "The Adjustment of Italian Immigrants in Buenos Aires and New York, 1870–1914," *American Historical Review* 88, no. 2 (1980), 32–48.

8. Shaul Stampfer, "The Geographic Background of Eastern European Jewish Migration to the United States before World War I," in *Migration Across Time and Nations,* ed. Ira Glazier and Luigi DeRosa (New York: Holmes and Meier, 1986), 221.

9. Morton Winsberg, *Colonia Baron Hirsch* (Gainesville: Univ. of Florida Press, 1963).

10. Judith Elkin, *The Jews of the Latin American Republics* (Chapel Hill: Univ. of North Carolina Press, 1980), 238.

11. Eli M. Lederhendler, "Jewish Immigration to America and Revisionist Historiography: Decade of New Perspectives," *YIVO Annual of Jewish Social Science* 18 (1983), 395.

12. Several historians emphasize that variations in the configuration of the Jewish community resulted in different responses. Calvin Goldschieder and Alan Zuckerman make this argument by comparing eastern and western (as well as American and Israeli) Jewish communities in *The Transformation of the Jews* (Chicago: Univ. of Chicago Press, 1984). Within the Pale, Ezra Mendelsohn and Moshe Mishkinski both argue that the Bund developed out of the unique characteristics of the Northwest Pale. See Ezra Mendelsohn, *Class Struggle in the Pale* (New York: Cambridge Univ. Press, 1970); Ezra Mendelsohn, "The Russian Jewish Labor Movement and Others," in *Jewish Socialism and Jewish Labor Movements in the 19th Century,* ed. Moshe Mishkinski (Jerusalem: Israeli Histadrut, 1975); and Moshe Mishkinski, "Regional Factors in the Formation of the Jewish Labor Movement in Czarist Russia," *YIVO Annual of Jewish Social Science* 14 (1969). Robert Brym argues that regional origin and community characteristics greatly affected the affiliation of intellectual Jews with particular revolutionary movements in *The Jewish Intelligentsia and Russian Marxism* (New York: Schocken Books, 1978).

13. Kuznets, "Immigration of Russian Jews to the United States."

14. Correlations between premigration factors and the needs of the country of destination have been discovered in research on Italian migrations; see Herbert Klein, "The Integration of Italian Immigrants into the United States and Argentina: A Comparative Analysis," *American Historical Review* 88 (1983).

15. A sixth successful colony, Woodbine, became the largest of the South Jersey colonies. The Woodbine colony, founded in 1891, was established after the Am Olam, the organization of Russian Jews aiming to create colonies in the United States, had dissolved. Therefore the impetus for this colony came not from the settlers, as with the earlier New Jersey colonies. Rather, it was founded solely through the efforts of the Baron de Hirsch Fund. As a sponsor-led, rather than an immigrant-led, colony, it differed from those that are the subject of this study. Although Woodbine is considered during chap. 5 in the context of a discussion of sponsor policies, the Woodbine experience is a separate chapter in the colony story, and does not figure centrally in this study.

16. The concept of "culture as a tool kit" is presented by Ann Swidler in "Culture in Action: Symbols and Strategies," *American Sociological Review* (April, 1986). The emerging paradigm, described in Ewa Morawska's article, "The Sociology and Historiography of Immigration," in *Immigration Reconsidered,* ed. Virginia Yans–McLaughlin (Oxford: Oxford Univ. Press, 1990), is a basis for the theoretical conception of immigrant adaptation employed here.

1. The East European Background

1. Kate Herder, "Memories of Yesterday" (unpublished memoir, 1946).

2. Herbert Gutman, "Work, Culture, and Society in Industrializing America, 1815–1919," in *Work, Culture, and Society in Industrializing America* (New York: Vintage Books, 1966). On Italian migration, see Samuel Baily; John Briggs, *An Italian Passage: Immigrants to Three American Cities, 1890–1930* (New Haven: Yale Univ. Press, 1978); and Dino Cinel, *From Italy to San Francisco: The Immigrant Experience* (Stanford: Stanford Univ. Press, 1982).

3. Morawska, *For Bread with Butter,* 23.

4. For example, see Moses Rischin, *The Promised City* (Cambridge: Harvard Univ. Press, 1977); Irving Howe, *World of Our Fathers* (New York: Harcourt Brace Jovanovich, 1976).

5. David Weinberg, Jewish history lectures, Univ. of Pennsylvania, spring, 1988.

6. Irving Howe, "Introduction" and Jonathan Frankel, "The Crisis of 1881–2 as a Turning Point in Modern Jewish History," in *The Legacy of Jewish Migration,* ed. David Berger (New York: Brooklyn College Press, 1983), 1, 9.

7. Frankel, "The Crisis," 10.

8. Arthur Ruppin, *The Jews in the Modern World* (London: Macmillan and Co., 1934), 44.

9. Mark Wischnitzer, *To Dwell in Safety* (Philadelphia: Jewish Publication Society of America, 1948), 37.

10. Louis Greenberg, *The Jews in Russia: The Struggle for Emancipation* (New York: Schocken Books, 1976), 1: 8–9.

11. Salo Baron, *The Russian Jew under the Tsars and Soviets* (New York: Macmillan Publishing Co., 1964), 18–25.

12. Greenberg, 1, 76. Baron, 41.

13. Hans Rogger, *Jewish Policies and Right-Wing Politics in Imperial Russia* (Berkeley: Univ. of California Press, 1986), 186. Also see Baron, 17.

14. Ibid., 174, 24.

15. Baron, 95.

16. Greenberg, 1: 161–63.

17. Isaac Rubinow, *Economic Condition of the Jews in Russia* (1907; reprint, New York: Arno Press, 1975), 490–93.

18. Baron, 95.

19. Ibid., 83; Greenberg, 1: 165.

20. Kuznets, "Immigration of Russian Jews to the United States," 100. Also see Mishkinski, "Regional Factors"; Rubinow, 502.

21. Mendelsohn, *Class Struggle,* 17.

22. Rubinow, 522ff, 502, 555. Also see Arcadius Kahan, *Essays in Jewish Social and Economic History* (Chicago: Univ. of Chicago Press, 1982), 33.

23. Greenberg, 1: 33; Michael Stanislowski, "The Transformation of Traditional Authority in Russian Jewry: The First Stage," in Berger, 24.

24. Baron, 96; Rubinow, 572.

25. Baron, 108–9.

26. Stanislowski, 25–26.

27. Mordechai Spector, "A Meal for the Poor," in *A Treasury of Yiddish Stories,* ed. Howe and Greenberg (New York: Schocken Books, 1953). 254.

28. Steven Zipperstein, *The Jews of Odessa* (Stanford: Stanford Univ. Press, 1985), 22–23.

29. Greenberg, 1: 74.

30. Ibid., 77.

31. Ibid., 80.

32. Zipperstein, 40, 49–60, 87.

33. Greenberg, 1: 34.

34. Ibid., 80–83.

35. Ibid., 28.

36. Baron, 126.

37. Brym, 42.

38. Zipperstein, 130, 107.

39. Goldscheider and Zuckerman, 94, 62.

40. Patricia Herlihy, *Odessa: A History, 1794–1914* (Cambridge: Harvard Univ. Press, 1986), 126.

41. Zipperstein, 36–37.

42. Herlihy, 125.

43. Zipperstein, 39.

44. Raphael Mahler, "The Social and Political Aspects of the *Haskalah* in Galicia," in *Studies in Modern Jewish Social History,* ed. Fishman (1946; reprint, New York: Ktav Publishing Co., 1972).

45. Goldscheider and Zuckerman, 58–59, 62.

46. Baron, 40–41.
47. Greenberg, 1: 87.
48. Ibid., 95.
49. Ibid., 97; Baron, 41.
50. Zipperstein, 124. For causes of the pogrom, also see Herlihy.
51. Baron, 43.
52. Ibid. 44–45; Rogger, 33. Louis Greenberg discusses this debate among historians, *The Jews in Russia: The Struggle for Emancipation* (New York: Schocken Books, 1976), 2: 23–25. The reasons for the outburst of pogroms in the South are also discussed in Michael Aronson, "Geographical and Socioeconomic Factors in the 1881 Anti-Jewish Pogroms in Russia," *The Russian Review* 39, no. 1 (1980); and Stephen M. Berk, *Year of Crisis, Year of Hope* (Westport, Conn.: Greenwood Press, 1985).
53. Baron: 45–6. Also see Greenberg, 2: 26.
54. Greenberg, 2: 30–35, 41; Baron, 48.
55. Zipperstein, 125–28.
56. Yoav Peled, *Class and Ethnicity in the Pale* (New York: St. Martin's Press, 1989), 18.
57. Frankel, "The Crisis," 10.
58. Brym, 47, 49; Mendelsohn, *Class Struggle,* 29.
59. Brym, 49, 54. Also see Goldscheider and Zuckerman, 119; Mendelsohn, *Class Struggle,* 29.
60. Goldscheider and Zuckerman, 122. Also see Nora Levin, *While the Messiah Tarried* (New York: Schocken Books, 1977), 29; Baron, 138; Greenberg, vol. 1, 147.
61. Goldscheider and Zuckerman, 126.
62. Baron, 140–41.
63. Abraham Cahan, *The Education of Abraham Cahan* (Philadelphia: The Jewish Publication Society of America, 1969), 158, 183.
64. Sidney Baily, "Memoir," in Herscher, 148.
65. Katherine Sabsovich, *Adventures in Idealism* (New York, privately printed, 1922).
66. Levin, 60.
67. Both Mendelsohn and Brym focus on the key role of intellectuals in the Bund; Goldscheider and Zuckerman document the role of the intelligentsia in both the Bund and Zionism.
68. Brym, 66–72.
69. Mendelsohn, *Class Struggle,* 32; Goldscheider and Zuckerman, 123–24.
70. Goldscheider and Zuckerman, 123–24, quoting Deutsch.
71. Zipperstein, 114–28.
72. Moses Shulvass, *From East to West* (Detroit: Wayne State Univ. Press, 1971), 14–15.
73. Greenberg, vol. 2, 23.
74. Kuznets, "Immigration of Russian Jews," 87–88; Kahan, 33.
75. Rubinow, 495.
76. Kuznets, "Immigration of the Russian Jews," 100; Rubinow, 502.
77. Jacob Lestschinsky, "Jewish Migrations, 1840–1956," in *The Jews,* ed. Finkelstein (Philadelphia: The Jewish Publication Society of America, 1960), 1550.
78. Kuznets, "Immigration of the Russian Jews," 112.
79. Rubinow, 555; Kuznets, "Immigration of the Russian Jews," 106.
80. Brym, 6.
81. Ibid., 40–56.
82. Ibid., 66–68.
83. Mendelsohn, "The Russian Jewish Labor Movement"; Mendelsohn, *Class Struggle,* vii, x; Mishkinski, "Regional Factors."

84. Mishkinski, "Regional Factors," 47.

85. Mendelsohn, *Class Struggle,* x.

86. Rubinow, 491–95.

87. Ibid., 522, 557.

88. Mishkinski, "Regional Factors," 41–43.

89. Scott Miller, "The Am Olam Movement: Russian Jewish Immigration to the United States and the Idea of Productivization," paper presented before the Association for Jewish Studies (Dec. 1988).

90. Goldscheider and Zuckerman, 124.

91. Ibid., 123–24.

92. Brym, 68.

93. Greenberg, vol. 2, 172; also see Baron, 144.

94. Greenberg, vol. 2, 173.

95. Walter Laquer, *A History of Zionism* (New York: Schocken Books, 1976), 309.

96. Arthur Hertzberg, *The Zionist Idea* (New York: Atheneum, 1984), 250.

97. Brym, 66.

98. Ibid., 77, 56–57.

99. Greenberg, 2: 166–68; Goldscheider and Zuckerman, 134; Baron, 144.

100. Goldscheider and Zuckerman, 130–31, 112.

2. The Am Olam: Members, Philosophies, and Experiments

1. Abraham Menes, "The *Am Oylom* Movement," *YIVO Annual of Jewish Social Science* 4 (1949), 16.

2. Ibid., 11.

3. Zipperstein, chaps. 1 and 2.

4. Ibid., 130.

5. Menes, 11.

6. Miller, 3, 6. Also see Menes, 13.

7. On the BILU, see Laquer, 309. On Am Olam, see Menes, 10.

8. Baily, "Memoir," 148–49. On Bokal's background, 146–47.

9. Herder and Bokal are consistently identified in primary sources as the founders of Odessa Am Olam. Baily identifies himself as a cofounder, but he is not consistently recognized as such by others. Whether or not his role was as central as that of Herder and Bokal, Baily was an early member and heavily involved in the Odessa group.

10. Baily, quoted in Menes, 13.

11. Baily, "Memoir," 134–36. He also recounts his involvement in *maskilic* circles, 136–47.

12. Ibid., 143.

13. Ibid., 147. Woskoboynikoff was a founding member of Carmel colony, New Jersey. Freeman, Bokal, and Baily all joined Alliance colony.

14. Ezra Mendelsohn, "The Russian Roots of the American Jewish Labor Movement," *YIVO Annual of Jewish Social Science* 16 (1976), 152–55. Also see discussion in chap. 1.

15. Menes, 11–12.

16. Baily, "Memoir," 145–47. Miller discusses the Russian and western influences on the Am Olam.

17. Miller, 4.

18. Greenberg, 2: 167.

19. Miller, 5; see discussion of New Odessa below.

20. Sabsovich, 8.

21. Moses Freeman, *Fuftzig Yohr Geshichte fon Yidishen Leben in Philadelphia* (Philadelphia: Mid-City Press, 1929), 201.

22. Sabsovich, 15.

23. Baily, "Memoir," 151.

24. Cahan, 207.

25. Mendelsohn, "Russian Roots," 156.

26. Menes, 14. Also see Freeman, 200–201.

27. Freeman, 200.

28. Ben Ami, quoted in Menes, 16.

29. Freeman, 201.

30. Menes, 16.

31. Cahan, 204.

32. Baily, "Memoir," 148.

33. Freeman, 201–2.

34. Menes, 17–18.

35. Cahan, 204.

36. Menes, 18–19; Cahan, 222.

37. Menes, 19.

38. Ibid., 22.

39. Ibid., 18; Baily, "The First Fifty Years," 13.

40. Mendelsohn, "Russian Roots," 153.

41. Freeman, 202. Freeman is quoted in Mendelsohn, "Russian Roots," 154.

42. Alexander Harkavy, quoted in Mendelsohn, "Russian Roots," 150, 154.

43. Menes, 16. Also quoted in Greenberg, 2: 166.

44. Mendelsohn, "Russian Roots," 154.

45. Menes, 15.

46. George Price, "The Russian Jews in America" (1893); reprint, *Publications of the American Jewish Historical Society* 48, nos. 1 and 2 (1958), part 2, 80.

47. Menes, 25.

48. Cahan, 245.

49. Menes, 25.

50. Price, part 2, 83.

51. Sidney Baily's stay on the Shaker colony is mentioned by F. Beile in an interview, National Museum of American Jewish History, oral history for "Living on the Land" exhibit, Philadelphia. On Rubin, see Harris Rubin, *The Autobiography of Harris Rubin,* trans. Benson N. Schambelan. (Philadelphia: Bricklin Press, 1977), 96ff.

52. Cahan, 226.

53. Mendelsohn, "Russian Roots," 168.

54. A complete listing of the colonies is found in Pearl Bartelt, "American Jewish Agricultural Colonies," paper presented before the National Historic Communal Societies Association (1989), app.

55. Price, part 2, 80.

56. Menes, 17.

57. Jonathan Frankel, *Prophecy and Politics* (Cambridge: Cambridge Univ. Press, 1981), 67.

58. Quoted in Menes, 24.

59. Ibid., 23.

60. "Pioneers in the Land of Cotton," *The Jewish Tribune* (September 27, 1929); reprint, Gabriel Davidson, *Our Jewish Farmers* (New York: L. B. Fischer, 1943), 205. Also see Richard

Singer, "The American Jews in Agriculture: Past History and Present Condition" (Hebrew Union College Prize Essay, 1941), vol. 1, 330.

61. Price, part 2, 84.

62. Singer, 1: 335.

63. "Pioneers in the Land of Cotton," 205.

64. Ibid., 207–8. Also see Price, part 2, 85.

65. Menes, 24.

66. Singer, 1: 326.

67. Price, part 2, 83–84.

68. "Pioneers in the Land of Cotton," 206.

69. Quoted in Joel Geffen, "Jewish Agricultural Colonies as Reflected in the Russia Hebrew Press," *American Jewish Historical Quarterly* 60 (June 1971), 357.

70. A synopsis of the Sicily Island Constitution is presented in Singer, 1: 326–28.

71. "Pioneers in the Land of Cotton," 207.

72. Baron de Hirsch Fund papers, American Jewish Historical Society, Waltham, Mass. . Box 44.

73. Geffen, "Jewish Agricultural Colonies," 358; Singer, 1: 328.

74. "An Epic of the Prairies," *Detroit Jewish Chronicle* (Jan. 29, 1932); reprint in Davidson, *Our Jewish Farmers,* 213.

75. "An Epic of the Prairies," 214–15; Violet and Orlando Goering, "The Agricultural Communes of the Am Olam," *Communal Societies* 4 (Fall 1984), 79. For a detailed discussion of Heilprin, see chap. 4.

76. Baily, "Memoir," 156.

77. "An Epic of the Prairies," 215.

78. Goering, "The Agricultural Communes," 79.

79. Ibid. Also see "An Epic of the Prairies," 215.

80. Violet and Orlando Goering, "South Dakota's Jewish Farmers: The Am Olam," unpublished essay, on file at the American Jewish Archives, Cincinnati, 9.

81. "An Epic of the Prairies," 219.

82. Ibid., 220; Goering, "The Agricultural Communes," 79.

83. "An Epic of the Prairies," 217–18.

84. For a review of these hardships, see "Agricultural Colonies," *The Jewish Encyclopedia,* ed. Isidore Singer (New York: Funk and Wagnalls Co., 1901), 1: 257. Another account claims that the crop was destroyed by hail. See Goering, "The Agricultural Communes," 80.

85. "An Epic of the Prairies," 216.

86. Price, part 2, 86.

87. Goering, "South Dakota's Jewish Farmers," 9; Goering, "The Agricultural Communes," 80; "Agricultural Colonies," 257–58.

88. "An Epic of the Prairies," 220–21; Goering, "The Agricultural Communes," 80; Goering, "South Dakota's Jewish Farmers," 10.

89. Goering, "The Agricultural Communes," 80.

90. Menes, 25.

91. Ibid., 26.

92. Goering, "The Agricultural Communes," 80. Also see Menes, 25.

93. Menes, 26–27.

94. Ibid., 27. Also see Goering, "The Agricultural Communes," 81.

95. Menes, 28.

96. Goering, "The Agricultural Communes," 81; Goering, "South Dakota's Jewish Farmers," 12; Menes, 28.

97. Menes, 28.

98. Frankel, *Prophecy and Politics,* 67.

99. Menes, 28.

100. Herman Rosenthal, "A History of the Communitarian Settlement Known as 'New Odessa'," trans. Gary P. Zola. In *The American Jewish Farmer,* ed. Abraham Peck (published for American Jewish Archives exhibit, 1986), 14.

101. Menes, 28.

102. Michael Heilprin, letter dated November 1883. Baron de Hirsch Fund papers, box 45. This letter is also reprinted in Gustav Pollak, *Michael Heilprin and His Sons* (New York: Dodd, Mead, and Co., 1912), 207–12.

103. Gabriel Davidson and Edwin Goodwin, "A Unique Agricultural Colony," *The Reflex* (May 1928); reprint, Davidson, *Our Jewish Farmers,* 228–30. On William Frey, also see Menes, 30; Rosenthal, 15; Cahan, 247; and Price, part 2, 91.

104. Davidson and Goodwin, 230; Price, part 2, 91; Rosenthal, 14.

105. Rosenthal, 14.

106. Davidson and Goodwin, 230.

107. Colonist letter, quoted in Menes, 31.

108. Price, part 2, p. 91. The railroad contract is also referred to in Heilprin's letter of November 1883, reproduced in Pollak, 207–12. Also see Menes, 30; Davidson, "A Unique Agricultural Colony," 231; letter from Rabbi Wechsler, quoted in Geffen, "Jewish Agricultural Colonies," 375.

109. Records of Land Purchases and Incorporations, Douglas County, Oregon, 1883–84.

110. Menes, 29.

111. Davidson and Goodwin, 230.

112. "A Wedding among the Communistic Jews in Oregon," *The Overland Monthly* 6, no. 39 (Dec. 1885), 608.

113. New Odessa Community, Articles of Incorporation, (December 31, 1883); Records of Land Purchases and Incorporations, Douglas County, Oregon.

114. Menes, 31.

115. "A Wedding," 608.

116. Ibid., 611.

117. Rosenthal, 15.

118. Cahan, 247–48.

119. Colonist letter, quoted in Menes, 29–31.

120. Rosenthal, 15–16; Wechsler is quoted in Menes, 32; and in Geffen, "Jewish Agricultural Colonies," 375.

121. See Wechsler in Geffen, "Jewish Agricultural Colonies," 375. Frey's comments are found in Mendelsohn, "Russian Roots," 169.

122. Rosenthal, 15.

123. Davidson and Goodwin, 233.

124. Rosenthal, 16.

125. Robert Rosenbluth, letter to George Abdill (historian of New Odessa), 1965, notes on research on New Odessa, Douglas County Historical Society, Roseburg, Oregon.

126. Cahan, 341–42.

127. Rosenthal, 16.

128. Cahan, 341–43.

129. Cahan, 343.

130. On the demise of New Odessa, see Davidson and Goodwin, 233; Rosenthal, 16; Menes, 33.

131. Because Kate Herder's work contains the memories of a small child, it must be regarded with caution. The fact that Herder wrote her memoirs some sixty years after the settlement of the Arkansas colony compounds this problem. However, the memoir is useful for Herder's general descriptions of the area and the colony. As a child, Herder was unconcerned with the organization and governance of the colony, and provides no information about these issues.

132. "An Arkansas Colonization Episode," *Jewish Tribune* (July 12, 1929); reprint, Davidson, *Our Jewish Farmers,* 209. Also see I. Singer, ed., 1: 321.

133. "An Arkansas Colonization Episode," 210.

134. Herder, 6–9.

135. "An Arkansas Colonization Episode," 208–13.

136. Ibid., 213.

137. Singer, vol. 1, 321. Singer says that the colony was abandoned in 1884; Herder's account says that her family was there for nine months (Herder, 6). "An Arkansas Colonization Episode" indicates that the colony was abandoned by early fall 1883, which would give it a life span of only six or seven months.

138. Baily, "Memoir," 152.

139. "Agricultural Colonies," 259.

140. Lipman Goldman Feld, "New Light on the Lost Jewish Colony of Beersheba, Kansas, 1882–1886," *American Jewish Historical Quarterly* 60, no. 2 (Dec. 1970), 159–68.

141. Feld, 162.

142. Charles K. Davis, unpublished diary, American Jewish Archives, Cincinnati, (July 26, 1882).

143. Feld, 163.

144. Davis, July 31, 1882; August 1, 1882.

145. Ibid., August 6, 1882; Feld, 164.

146. Feld, 164–65.

147. Ibid., 168, 165.

148. I. Singer, ed., 1: 466.

149. Ibid., 466–68; Feld, 165–66.

150. Feld, 166–67. Feld determined occupation from tax records, which recorded only the primary occupation. It is possible that many of those working in other fields might still have practiced small-scale farming.

151. Feld, 168.

152. "The Jewish Covered Wagon," *Jewish Criterion* (Jan. 29, 1932); reprint, Davidson, *Our Jewish Farmers,* 221.

153. "Agricultural Colonies," 259.

154. "The Jewish Covered Wagon," 222; "Agricultural Colonies," 259.

155. "The Jewish Covered Wagon," 222–25.

156. Ibid., 224–25.

157. Ibid.

3. Colony Sponsors

1. The western colonies and their relationships with their sponsors are discussed in chap. 2. The Woodbine, New Jersey, colony is discussed in chap. 5.

2. Moritz Ellinger, "The Report of Moritz Ellinger" (New York: Hebrew Emigrant Aid Society of the United States, 1882), 32–33.

3. Abraham Mendelssohn, "Why I Have Raised You as a Christian: A Letter to His Daughter" (July 1820); reprint, *The Jew in the Modern World,* ed. Mendes-Flohr and Reinharz

(New York: Oxford Univ. Press, 1980), 223. On the debate over citizenship in Germany and attitudes toward Judaism, see Ismar Schorsch, *Jewish Reactions to German Anti-Semitism, 1870–1914* (New York: Columbia Univ. Press, 1972), 2–12.

4. Schorsch, 12.

5. Ibid., 25, 36, 20–21.

6. Steven Ascheim, *Brothers and Strangers: The East European Jews in Germany and German-Jewish Consciousness, 1800–1923* (Madison: Univ. of Wisconsin, 1982), 5.

7. Ibid., 33.

8. On German-Jewish aid, see Ascheim, 33–35; Jack Wertheimer, *Unwelcome Strangers: East European Jews in Imperial Germany* (Oxford: Oxford Univ. Press, 1987), 20. Despite these pressures, the community did offer considerable support to those who did settle in Germany; see Wertheimer, 172–74, and Zosa Szajkowski, "How the Mass Migration to America Began," *Jewish Social Studies* 4, no. 4 (Oct. 1942), 305. On the German government's attitude, see Ascheim, 35–36; and Wertheimer, 25.

9. Wertheimer. On stereotypes of Jews in Germany, 29–30. On the rationale for German policy, 25. On the range of German policies, 50–60.

10. Elias Tcherikower, "Jewish Immigrants to the United States," *YIVO Annual of Jewish Social Science* 6 (1951); reprint, *Studies in Modern Jewish History,* ed. Joshua Fishman (New York: Ktav Publishing House, 1972), 180–87. Also see Howard Morley Sachar, *The Course of Modern Jewish History* (New York: Dell Publishing Co., 1958), 308–9.

11. David Weinberg, " 'Heureux comme Dieu en France': East European Jewish Immigrants in Paris, 1881–1914," *Studies in Contemporary Jewry* 1 (1984), 31–32.

12. S. M. Dubnow, *History of the Jews in Russia and Poland,* trans. I. Friedlaender. (New York: Ktav Publishing House, 1975), 2: 415.

13. Weinberg, 33.

14. Ibid. Also see Nancy Green, *The Pletzl of Paris* (New York: Holmes and Meier, 1986), 44.

15. Szajkowski: 293–95.

16. Green, 55.

17. Ibid., 56.

18. Szajkowski, 295.

19. Ibid. 296–97; on the sponsorship of the two Am Olam groups, see Frankel, *Prophecy and Politics,* 67.

20. Sacher, 308; Szajkowski, 298.

21. Szajkowski, 299.

22. Sacher, 308; also see Szajkowski, 301–2.

23. Szajkowski, 302–4.

24. Lloyd Gartner, *The Jewish Immigrant in England, 1870–1914* (London: George Allan, 1960), 53.

25. Szajkowski, 304.

26. Gartner, 43.

27. Szajkowski, 304–5.

28. Ellinger, 16.

29. Pittsburgh Platform, adopted 1885; reprint, Nathan Glazer, *American Judaism* (Chicago: Univ. of Chicago Press, 1972), 187.

30. Steven Birmingham, *'Our Crowd': The Great Jewish Families of New York* (New York: Harper and Row, 1967), 147–48.

31. Berk, 155.

32. Quoted in Myron Berman, *The Attitude of American Jewry Towards East European Jewish Immigration* (New York: Arno Press, 1980), 31–32; Price, part 1, 38.

33. Quoted in Gilbert Osofsky, "The Hebrew Emigrant Aid Society of the United States," *Publications of the American Jewish Historical Society* 49, no.3 (1960), 183.

34. Berk, 155; Birmingham, 160ff.

35. Birmingham, 318.

36. Berman, 33.

37. Ibid., 35.

38. Ellinger, 9.

39. Osofsky, 174.

40. Ibid., 175. Isaacs opposed the plan because he thought the crisis would be temporary; Schiff, like his Viennese counterparts, felt that a solely Jewish organization was "smacking of sectarianism."

41. Ibid., 176–77; 174.

42. Ellinger. Osofsky argues that these claims were greatly exaggerated, 177.

43. Ibid., 8.

44. Ibid., 20.

45. Ibid., 19–21.

46. Berman, 39.

47. Ellinger, 17.

48. Ibid., 20.

49. Ibid., 10.

50. Report quoted in Price, part I, 39.

51. Papers of the Association for the Protection of Jewish Immigrants, American Jewish Archives, Cincinnati.

52. Berk, 174.

53. Osofsky, 175.

54. Ellinger, 20.

55. Ibid., 5.

56. Osofsky, 177; Frankel, *Prophecy and Politics,* 67.

57. Osofsky, 179.

58. Miller, 10–11.

59. Quoted in Miller, 12–13. Michael Heilprin is discussed in greater detail in chap. 4.

60. Ellinger, 12.

61. Ibid., 5.

62. Price, part 2, 79.

63. Michael Heilprin, "An Appeal to the Jews," (Nov. 1883); reprint, Pollak, 207–12.

64. Osofsky, 180.

65. Price, part 2, 79.

66. Osofsky, 179.

67. Ibid., 180.

68. Ibid., 182–84; also see Berman, 50–65; and Szajkowski, 301–4.

69. For accounts of local aid societies sponsoring Am Olam colonies, see chap. 2. Other, non-Am Olam projects were sponsored by local committees, such as a Michigan colony sponsored by the Minneapolis Jewish community and a Virginia colony sponsored by the Baltimore Jewish community.

70. These colonies are discussed in chap. 2. Heilprin's involvement in Carmel is discussed in chap. 4. On Heilprin's MAAS activities, also see Pollak, chap. 14.

71. Kuznets, "Immigration of Russian Jews," 39.

72. For a list of the Baron de Hirsch Fund trustees, see Samuel Joseph, *History of the Baron de Hirsch Fund: The Americanization of the Jewish Immigrant* (Fairfield: Augustus M. Kelley, 1978), app. E, 286.

73. Birmingham, 173. The Lewisohn family was also wealthy before migration, 234.

74. Ibid. On Loeb, 67; on the Straus family, 82; on the Seligman family, 52, 90ff.

75. Ibid., 150.

76. Ibid.

77. On Hirsch's family background, see Kurt Grunwald, *Turkenhirsch: A Study of Baron de Hirsch, Entrepreneur and Philanthropist* (Israel Program for Scientific Translations, 1966), 1–7.

78. Baron Maurice de Hirsch, "My Views on Philanthropy," *North American Review,* no. 416 (July 1891); reprint, Joseph, app. A, 275.

79. Grunwald, chap. 6.

80. Joseph, 11.

81. Samuel J. Lee, *Moses of the New World* (New York: Thomas Yoseloff, 1970), 12.

82. Joseph, 13.

83. Baron de Hirsch Fund, "Deed of Trust"; reprint, Joseph, app. B, 278. Disputes about these aims and the outcome in fund policies are discussed in chap. 5.

84. Ibid., chap. 8.

85. Baron de Hirsch Fund, "Provisional Plan of Organization," American Jewish Historical Society, Waltham, Mass. Examples of this anticharity policy in action can be found in chap. 5.

86. Michael Katz, *The Undeserving Poor* (New York: Pantheon Books, 1989), 9; *In the Shadow of the Poorhouse* (New York: Basic Books, 1986), 16–18.

87. Michael Katz, *Poverty and Policy in American History* (New York: Academic Press, 1983), 3.

88. Michael Katz, *The Undeserving Poor,* 14.

89. Michael Katz, *In the Shadow;* David Rothman, *The Discovery of the Asylum* (Boston: Little, Brown and Co., 1971).

90. Michael Katz mentions this as one of four motives; see *In the Shadow,* x–xi. The social control motive is emphasized in Frances Fox Piven and Richard Cloward, *Regulating the Poor* (New York: Random House, 1971).

91. Rothman, *The Discovery,* 5.

92. Ibid., 164–65.

93. Michael Katz, *Poverty and Policy,* 91.

94. David Rothman, *On Their Own* (Reading, Mass.: Addison-Wesley Publishing Co., 1972), 4.

95. Ibid., 9.

96. Robert Hunter, *Poverty* (New York: The Macmillan Co., 1972), 331.

97. Paul Boyer, *Urban Masses and Moral Order in America* (Cambridge: Harvard Univ. Press, 1978), 167.

98. Hunter, 63, 69.

99. James Patterson, *America's Struggle Against Poverty, 1900–1985* (Cambridge: Harvard Univ. Press, 1986), 23.

100. Mary F. Berry and John W. Blassingame, *Long Memory: The Black Experience in America* (Oxford: Oxford Univ. Press, 1982), 273–74.

101. Michael Heilprin, letter (Jan. 1888), reprinted in Pollak, 216.

102. Letter from Jewish Colonization Association to Baron de Hirsch Fund (May 17, 1894), Baron de Hirsch Fund papers, box 52.

103. Letter from Isaacs (Baron de Hirsch Fund) to Jewish Colonization Association (Nov. 22, 1898), Baron de Hirsch Fund papers, box 50.

104. Letter to Baron de Hirsch (Aug. 15, 1889), Baron de Hirsch Fund papers, box 35.

105. Baron de Hirsch Fund, "Plan of Organization." Classes are discussed by Joseph, chaps. 6 and 8.

106. On the HEAS plan, see Ellinger and Osofsky. Also see Goldman letter to JCA on the need to clean out the ghetto (Oct. 6, 1896), American Jewish Archives, Cincinnati. The idea of denying aid to families refusing to relocate is suggested in Goldman's letter. On the United Hebrew Charities, see Peter Romanofsky, "'To Rid Ourselves of the Burden . . .': New York Jewish Charities and the Origins of the Industrial Removal Office, 1890–1901," *American Jewish Historical Quarterly* 64, no. 4 (June 1975), 336.

107. Philadelphia Committee Records, Baron de Hirsch Fund papers, box 8.

108. Romanofsky, 340ff.; Joseph, 184–205.

109. Gary Dean Best, "Jacob Schiff's Galveston Movement: An Experiment in Immigrant Deflection, 1907–1914," *American Jewish Archives* 30, no.1 (1978), 46ff.; Bernard Merinbach, *Galveston: Ellis Island of the West* (Albany: SUNY Press, 1983). Also see Joseph, 205–10. Sponsoring organizations had long sought to avoid the perception that they were encouraging immigration; see Alliance Israélite Universelle papers, Cincinnati; and Baron de Hirsch Fund papers, box 37a.

110. The early difficulties of the New Jersey colonies are discussed in chap. 4.

111. There was a strong affinity for farming in the Hirsch family. Hirsch's grandfather, Jacob, was the first Jew in Bavaria allowed to buy real estate and farm, and, in his will, bequeathed money to promote agriculture among Jews. Hirsch's uncle, Joel Jacob, was "devoted to agriculture," as was his father, Joseph, who left the Munich banking house to Maurice's brother Emil so that he could become a gentleman farmer. See Grunwald, 3–7.

112. Fund activities, including loan policies, are discussed in chaps. 4, 5, and 6.

4. The First Years in Jersey: Settlers and Sponsors, 1882–1890

1. Most memoirs written by the Alliance colonists refer to 43 families, although several official sources, including the 1911 Report of the Immigration Commission, Philip Goldstein's dissertation, "Social Aspects of the Jewish Colonies of South Jersey," and several contemporaneous newspaper reports, cited in Joel Geffen's "Jewish Agricultural Colonies as Reported in the Pages of the Russian Hebrew Press," all refer to 25 families. The descendants of the Alliance families almost uniformly claim that the 43 families made the voyage from Russia (or from Hamburg) to New York and then to Alliance together. This claim is disproved by examination of the ship records, which clearly show that the "original 43 families" arrived singly or in small groups throughout late 1881 and early 1882. Thus it seems unlikely that the 43 families arrived in Alliance together. Rather, the popular identification of the 43 "original families" in Alliance colony histories and at later reunions seems to derive from the list of settlers who arrived during the first few months and who remained in the settlement for at least a few years.

2. Brandes, 55.

3. The tent provision was approved in U.S. House Resolution 230.

4. I. Harry Levin, "History of Alliance, New Jersey, First Jewish Agricultural Settlement in the U.S.," *The Vineland Historical Magazine* 54 (1978), 5; see also Brandes; and Uri Herscher, *Jewish Agricultural Utopias in America, 1880–1910* (Detroit: Wayne State Univ. Press, 1981), 74ff.

5. Report from July 2, 1882, quoted in *Ha-Melitz* 18, no. 34 (Aug. 31, 1882), 679–82; reprint and translation in Geffen, "Jewish Agricultural Colonies," 365.

6. Geffen, "Jewish Agricultural Colonies," 364–65.

7. United States Immigration Commission, "Recent Immigrants in Agriculture." In *Immigrants in Industries* part 24, vol. 2 (Washington: Government Printing Office, 1911), 90.

8. Geffen, "Jewish Agricultural Colonies," 366.

9. On the Goldhaft family, see Arthur Goldhaft, *The Golden Egg* (New York: Horizon Press, 1957), 43. On the Bayuk family, see Bluma Bayuk Rappaport Purmell, *A Farmer's Daughter* (Hayvenhurst, 1981). Details on Moses Bayuk also came from an interview with his daughter,

Bluma Bayuk Rappaport Purmell (Oct. 16, 1988). See also Richard Brotman, "First Chapter in a New Book" (video, 1982), interview with I. Harry Levin (grandson of Moses Bayuk).

10. For identities of Am Olam members, National Museum of American Jewish History, interview with Bea Harrison for "Living on the Land"; and Baily, "Memoir." The United States Census was used to determine whether settlers remained in Alliance until 1900, United States census, Salem County, N.J., 1900.

11. Hamburg Ship Records, Church of Jesus Christ of Latter-day Saints, Family History Center. The Coltuns and Bokals were on the *Viola,* which left Hamburg for New York, via London, on Apr. 15, 1882. The Levins, Levinsons, Mennies, and Strausnicks were on the *Gemma,* which left Hamburg for New York, via London, on Mar. 1, 1882. Esther Levin was Leah Levinson's daughter from a previous marriage.

12. As no comprehensive membership list of the organization survives, identification of Am Olam members can be made only through descendants or references to individuals in personal memoirs. Because descendants were not located for all the colonists and because many descendants do not have complete information, it is highly likely that some Am Olam colonists have been missed. In addition, the only lists of founding Alliance colonists include those who remained in the settlement for at least a few years. It is very likely that there were additional Am Olam members who joined the colony for only a brief period.

13. Cahan, 246.

14. Baily, "Memoir," 146.

15. Freeman.

16. George Seldes, "Anarchist Colony of My Father, George Seldes," *Free Worker's Voice* (Mar. 1976).

17. Baily, "Memoir," 157. A David Steinberg continued to live in Alliance, but it is not clear whether he was the same person.

18. Hamburg Ship Records.

19. Sidney Baily, "The First Fifty Years," *Yoval: A Symposium upon the First Fifty Years of the Jewish Farming Colonies of Alliance, Norma, and Brotmanville, New Jersey* (Aug. 1932), 12.

20. Geffen, "Jewish Agricultural Colonies," 364–65.

21. Goldhaft, 35.

22. Baily, "Memoirs," 148; and "The First Fifty Years," 18. National Museum of American Jewish History, interview with F. Biele.

23. Goldhaft, 44.

24. Purmell interview, Oct. 16, 1988.

25. Martin Douglas, "Chronological Summary of Annotated Cards Toward the History of the Jewish Agricultural Colonies in South Jersey" (Ph.D. diss., Jewish Theological Seminary, New York, 1960), 40.

26. Baily, "Memoir," 152. The differences between the two synagogues are discussed further in chap. 5.

27. "Recent Immigrants in Agriculture," 90.

28. Ibid.

29. Goldhaft, 34, 43.

30. Ellen Eisenberg, interviews, conducted 1988–89.

31. I. Harry Levin, 4.

32. Herscher, 33.

33. See chap. 3 for a complete discussion of sponsor goals and beliefs.

34. Geffen, "Jewish Agricultural Colonies," 364–66.

35. Brandes, 56; and Geffen, "Jewish Agricultural Colonies," 364–66.

36. Geffen, "Jewish Agricultural Colonies," 367.

37. Moses Bayuk, "Report to the Alliance Israélite Universelle" (in German), 1885, American Jewish Archives, Cincinnati; also see letter to Isaacs of AIU from Henry S. Henry (Feb. 18, 1884), AIU files, American Jewish Archives.

38. Leonard Robinson, "Agricultural Activities of the Jews in America," *American Jewish Yearbook* (1912).

39. Brandes, 57–58.

40. Bayuk, report to the AIU.

41. Ibid.

42. Ibid.

43. Henry S. Henry letter to Isaacs (Feb. 18, 1884), AIU files.

44. Henry S. Henry letter to M. Bayuk and Others, Colony Alliance (Dec. 31, 1884), in possession of Mrs. I. Harry Levin, Alliance, N.J.

45. Herscher, 75.

46. See minutes of Baron de Hirsch Fund and Jewish Agricultural and Industrial Aid Societies for records of incentives to industrialists, American Jewish Historical Society, Waltham, Mass. Specific examples of such incentives follow below and in chap. 5.

47. Moses Klein, *Migdal Sofim* (Philadelphia, 1889).

48. Brandes, 67.

49. Douglas, 5.

50. Dropsie letter to AIU (June 7, 1882), AIU files.

51. AIU correspondence, AIU files.

52. *South Jerseyman* (Feb. 6, 20, and 27, 1883). Also see *Jewish Record* (Feb. 23, 1883), quoted in Douglas, 5.

53. Reported in *Ha-Melitz* 20, no. 76 (Oct. 28, 1884), 1226–28; reprint and tran., Geffen, "Jewish Agricultural Colonies," 371.

54. Douglas, 30; Brandes, 82. Unfortunately, the records of these interviews do not survive.

55. Michael Heilprin, "Jewish Colonies in America," appendix to Benjamin F. Peixotto, *What Shall We Do with Our Immigrants* (New York: YMHA, 1887).

56. Hebrew Emigrant Aid Society of Philadelphia records, Balch Institute for Ethnic Studies, Philadelphia. The established aid organizations later acknowledged this misunderstanding; see Jewish Agricultural and Industrial Aid Society, Annual Report, 1902, 9; Douglas, 47–48.

57. Committee of Alliance, letter to Baron de Hirsch, (July 24, 1894), Baron de Hirsch Fund papers, box 44.

58. Kahan, 123.

59. Rubinow, 572–73.

60. Kahan, 124.

61. Brandes, 60; Davidson, *Our Jewish Farmers,* 251; Philip Goldstein, "Social Aspects of the Jewish Colonies of South Jersey" (Ph.D. diss., Univ. of Pennsylvania, 1921), 16.

62. Bureau of Statistics of New Jersey, "The Jewish Colonies of New Jersey" (1901), New Jersey Archives, Trenton, N.J.

63. Venezky Family History, unpublished.

64. "Recent Immigrants in Agriculture," 95; Goldstein, 16.

65. Davidson, 251.

66. Moses Klein, 53. Also see R. Singer, 290.

67. Moses Klein, 53.

68. "Recent Immigrants in Agriculture," 95–96.

69. Brandes, 61–62.

70. Joseph, 7.

71. On the life of Michael Heilprin, see Joseph, 7ff; Goldstein, 16; Brandes, 30; and Pollak.

72. Pollak, 206–7; Brandes, 31.

73. Heilprin, "Jewish Colonies in America."

74. Ibid. Also see Goering, "The Agricultural Communes," 79.

75. Joseph, 7.

76. Carmel colonists' letter to Alliance Israélite Universelle, (July 13, 1885), AIU files. "Recent Immigrants in Agriculture," 96.

77. Ibid., 96–97.

78. Goldstein, 17.

79. Louis Mournier, "An Elopement," *Vineland Historical Magazine* (Jan.–Apr. 1965).

80. Herder.

81. Moses Klein, 57.

82. Hamburg Ship Records, the *Bohemia;* also see Charles Waskoff, "The Carmel Story," unpublished memoir; and Herder.

83. Deed for this sale is in the possession of Faith Klein, great-granddaughter of Moses Herder.

84. Douglas, 58–59.

85. Industrial Co-operation in Combination with Consumer Patrons, By-Laws, American Jewish Historical Society.

86. Waskoff, 8.

87. Ibid., 9.

88. Industrial Co-operation in Combination with Consumer Patrons, By-Laws.

89. Waskoff, 11.

90. Ellen Eisenberg, interview with Faith Klein, great-granddaughter of Moses Herder (Sept. 16, 1989).

91. Ibid.

92. Waskoff, 11.

93. Goldhaft, 50–51.

94. Brandes, 63–64, 226.

95. Ellen Eisenberg; this view was expressed in virtually every descendant interview.

96. Joseph, 117.

97. See Herscher, 19; also see Joseph. This failure to distinguish between immigrants is a product of the tendency of historians of American-Jewish immigration to view the background of the East European Jews as uniform. See the discussion of this tendency in the Introduction.

98. Rosenhayn is not included in the discussion of 1882–85 because the lasting settlement there did not emerge from the colonization in this period.

99. Determination of the regional and occupational background of the colonists required the use of a variety of sources. For those settlers arriving after 1900, citizenship papers provided information on background factors, such as age, regional origin, and date of immigration, as well as supplying information on postmigration occupation and residence. The 1900 federal census also provided information on age, postmigration occupation, household size, residence, and date of migration. However, neither the census nor the earlier citizenship records provided information on regional origin or premigration occupation. For this information, the ship passenger lists for the port of Hamburg, compiled by the Church of Jesus Christ of Latter-day Saints were indispensable. These records provided crucial background information for many of the earliest settlers. Only when exact or near-exact matches could be found was the information from the passenger lists utilized. Names and ages were compared with census listings and the list of "original settlers" provided in *Yoval: A Symposium upon the First Fifty Years of the Jewish Farming Colonies of Alliance,*

Norma, and Brotmanville, New Jersey, (published for the 50th anniversary of the founding of Alliance, Aug. 1932). Exact matches consisted of identical names (both first and last) and ages for all members of the family. Near-exact matches, in which the spelling of names varied slightly and ages differed by only one or two years, were also accepted. Because several family members were needed to determine a match, these passenger lists were used only to identify couples and families, and not for persons traveling alone, unless an independent source confirmed that a person had been on a particular boat or arrived on a particular date. For those who did not pass through Hamburg, or for whom reliable matches could not be found, it was necessary to rely on information gleaned from surveys and interviews of descendants, and from written memoirs. Because information held by descendants two or three generations removed from the immigrants can be unreliable, occupational and regional data were used in the analysis only where two independent sources provided the same information.

The difficulty of obtaining data on premigration origins, and the standard for acceptance used in this study, limited the samples. Figures for regional origin in the 1882 to 1885 period, for example, come from the known origins of 57 heads of household out of the total of 140 heads of household known to have arrived in the colonies in this period.

After the turn of the century, naturalization forms were standardized and included information on birthplace. However, because many later colonists settled in the colonies after living in the United States for a number of years, they often completed naturalization before arriving in New Jersey. This limited sample sizes for later periods.

100. Robinson, 63.

101. Moses Klein, 41; Charles Bernheimer, *The Russian Jew in the United States* (Philadelphia: John C. Winston Co., 1905), 379.

102. Kuznets, "Immigration of Russian Jews," 119.

103. Price, part I, 33.

104. Rubinow, 492.

105. Mendelsohn, "The Russian Roots," 152–53. See chap. 2 for more discussion of this point.

106. Menes, 17. In my sample, of the 26 colonists from the South Pale arriving between 1882 and 1885 for whom a more specific place of origin was given, 17 were from Odessa or Kiev. The number from these cities is imprecise because in many cases only a region was given, with no city. In addition, it is probable that many immigrants from small neighboring towns gave the name of the nearby city, rather than their exact town of origin.

107. Bayuk, report to the AIU. Bayuk mentions in his letter that most of the colonists at Alliance were tradesmen. Rubinow reports that in the 1897 census, 35.5 percent of Jews from the South Pale were merchants, while only 23.8 percent and 27.4 percent of Lithuanian and White Russian Jews were merchants, 502.

108. The sources for previous occupation are varied and include Hamburg Ship Records, colonist memoirs, records of sponsoring organizations, and interviews/surveys of descendants.

109. Kuznets, "Immigration of Russian Jews," 101–2. Note that occupational profiles in Kuznets are for the post-1899 period. Comparable statistics for the earlier period are not available, as Jews were not then distinguished from their non-Jewish countrymen in immigration statistics.

110. Price, 98; Moses Klein, 53.

111. Singer, 326.

112. Kuznets, "Immigration of Russian Jews," 101–2. Again, using the post-1899 statistics, Kuznets reports 2.3 percent of the immigrants were employed in agriculture.

113. See chap. 1 for discussion of regional differences within the Pale. On the figures for agricultural occupation, see "Agricultural Colonies."

114. Robinson, 59.

115. Dubnow, 2: 417–18.

116. Dropsie letter to AIU (June 1882), AIU file.

117. Joseph, 117; Rubinow, 510.

118. Mendelsohn, "The Russian Roots."

119. Ellen Eisenberg, interviews; National Museum of American Jewish History interviews. Several interview subjects cited this as their reason for moving to the colonies, among them, the Greenblatt family.

5. The Middle Years: Settlers and Sponsors, 1890–1910

1. Moses Klein, 47, 53, 57.

2. United States federal census, Salem County, N.J., 1900. Because Alliance was not an incorporated township, it is not listed separately on the census. Therefore, it is not always possible to positively determine whether a particular family was a part of the colony. A Baron de Hirsch Fund census for 1901 confirms these figures, reporting that there were 840 persons in the colony, among 145 households. Baron de Hirsch Fund papers, box 44.

3. United States federal census, Cumberland County, N.J., 1900. It is difficult to separate Carmel and Rosenhayn on the census, as parts of both were included in Deerfield Township, Cumberland County.

4. *Vineland Evening Journal* (Sept. 22, 1891), quoted in Douglas, 75.

5. John Higham, *Strangers in the Land* (New York: Atheneum, 1985), 71.

6. *Jewish Exponent* (Feb. 15, 1895), cited in Douglas, 78. The temperance issue in the Vineland area is discussed in Brandes, 185–86.

7. Alliance Committee letter to Baron de Hirsch (1894), Baron de Hirsch Fund papers, box 44.

8. Ibid.

9. Arthur Reichow, "Report" (1897), Baron de Hirsch Fund papers, box 44.

10. Seldes (Alliance settler) letter to Adolphus Solomons (Baron de Hirsch Fund), Baron de Hirsch Fund papers, box 44. Seldes also recommended the establishment of a food bank where food could be canned or refrigerated until prices rose.

11. Alliance Colony Board of Trade, description, Baron de Hirsch Fund papers, box 44.

12. Hirsch letter to Myer Isaacs and Jacob Schiff (1889), Baron de Hirsch Fund papers, box 35.

13. A. S. Solomons interview, *New York Times* (1891), Baron de Hirsch Fund papers, box 35.

14. Ibid.

15. Baron de Hirsch Fund, provisional plan of organization, Baron de Hirsch Fund papers.

16. Directory of New York charities (1906), Baron de Hirsch Fund papers, box 38.

17. Baron de Hirsch Fund, report (1906); and Philadelphia Committee, reports (1890s). Both from Baron de Hirsch Fund papers, boxes 8 and 38.

18. Philadelphia and New York Committees, correspondence (1889), Baron de Hirsch Fund papers, box 35.

19. Ibid.

20. Hirsch letters to New York Committee (July 6, 1889) and to Jacob Schiff (Dec. 23, 1891), Baron de Hirsch Fund papers, box 35.

21. Baron de Hirsch Fund, Deed of Trust; reprint in Joseph, 278; Baron de Hirsch Fund, Articles of Incorporation, Jewish Agricultural and Industrial Aid Society (JAIAS) minutes (Feb. 12, 1900), Baron de Hirsch Fund papers.

22. Isaacs letter to Jacob Schiff (Oct. 1889), Baron de Hirsch Fund papers, box 35.

23. Robinson, 69.

24. Joseph, 48.

25. Goldstein, 22; Brandes, 115; Robinson, 87–88.

26. Brandes: 113–14. Also see Joseph, 48.

27. Joseph, 50; Brandes, 116. Naturalization records from Cape May County show that, of those Woodbine settlers for whom a home town is listed, 41 percent were of South Pale origin.

28. Joseph, 32.

29. Isaacs letter to Jewish Colonization Association (1898), Baron de Hirsch Fund papers, box 50.

30. Brandes, 114–15.

31. Notice to Woodbine farmers from Woodbine Land and Improvement Co. (Sept. 20, 1892), National Museum of American Jewish History exhibit, "Living on the Land."

32. A description of this dispute from Sabsovich's point of view is found in Sabsovich, 90–98. The telegram from Woodbine to the Baron de Hirsch Fund (Apr. 1893) was part of the National Museum of American Jewish History exhibit. The dispute is also discussed in Brandes, 122.

33. Woodbine Land and Improvement Co., notice (Sept. 10, 1893), National Museum of American Jewish History, exhibit.

34. Joseph, 55.

35. Ibid., 56.

36. Ibid.

37. Sabsovich, 92–93.

38. Herscher, 95–98; Joseph, 53–54.

39. Sabsovich, 93.

40. Ibid., 95.

41. Dropsie letter (1889), Baron de Hirsch Fund papers, box 35. This concern is discussed in Brandes, 118–19.

42. Goldman letter to the Jewish Colonization Association (Oct. 6, 1896), American Jewish Archives.

43. Isaacs letter to the Jewish Colonization Association (Nov. 22, 1898), Baron de Hirsch Fund papers, box 50. JAIAS minutes (Feb. 18, 1900), Baron de Hirsch Fund papers.

44. Isaacs letter to the Jewish Colonization Association (Nov. 22, 1898).

45. Hackenburg letters to Loeb (May 24, 1901; Mar. 21, 1902), Baron de Hirsch Fund papers, box 8.

46. Isaacs letter to the Jewish Colonization Association (Nov. 22, 1898).

47. JAIAS, "Annual Report" (1910), 11. JAIAS minutes, 1902 and 1903, show discussion of several limited ventures as well as the Special Executive Committee of the JAIAS discussion of a large-scale program (Apr. 17, 1902), Baron de Hirsch Fund papers.

48. JAIAS, minutes of the Special Executive Committee (Apr. 17, 1902), Baron de Hirsch Fund papers.

49. Ibid.

50. Ibid.

51. JAIAS, minutes of the board of directors (June 1, 1904; July 26, 1904; Nov. 7, 1906; Oct. 10, 1906), Baron de Hirsch Fund papers.

52. Reichow report to Goldman (June 8, 1897), Baron de Hirsch Fund papers, box 44. Additional examples of this correspondence are also found in box 38.

53. Goldman letter to the Jewish Colonization Association (Oct. 6, 1896), American Jewish Archives.

54. Ibid.

55. Reichow report to Goldman (June 8, 1897).

56. The JCA was the European version of the Baron de Hirsch Fund. Both were financed by Hirsch. The JCA was the principal sponsor of the Argentine colonization.

57. List of the mortgages taken over by the fund, Baron de Hirsch Fund papers, box 44.

58. Reichow letter to Goldman (Mar. 5, 1898), Baron de Hirsch Fund papers, box 44. This amount included $3,000 for Brotman's factory.

59. JAIAS, minutes (Oct. 8, 1903), Baron de Hirsch Fund papers, box 66.

60. Ibid.

61. JAIAS, "Annual Report" (1905), 7. See also JAIAS, "Annual Report" (1906), 13.

62. Bureau of Statistics of New Jersey, 3–5, 9.

63. On Baily, see F. Biele interview, National Museum of American Jewish History. On Crystal, see interview with Crystal descendants, National Museum of American Jewish History.

64. Moses Klein, 38, 48–49.

65. Ibid., 53, 58.

66. 1901 Alliance census, Baron de Hirsch Fund papers, box 44.

67. Bureau of Statistics of New Jersey, 3–5, 9.

68. Interview with F. Biele, National Museum of American Jewish History.

69. Brandes, 65–66.

70. Ellen Eisenberg, interview with Judge Stanley Brotman, grandson of Abraham Brotman (Camden, N.J., Feb. 1989).

71. Hebrew Emigrant Aid Society of Philadelphia records, Balch Institute for Ethnic Studies, Philadelphia.

72. Ellen Eisenberg, interview with Judge Brotman.

73. Reichow report to Goldman (June 8, 1897).

74. The population figure was determined using a map created for the reunion celebrated in Alliance, Norma, and Brotmanville in 1982 by the Alliance Colony Foundation. Because Brotmanville was not a separate township, it is impossible to determine its exact population using official sources. Information on the Levinsohns from Molly Kravitz, unpublished memoir, 10.

75. Woskoff, 9. Also see Gerson Katz, "History of Carmel," Vineland Historical Society.

76. Losada Carlisle, "Carmel at the Turn of the Century" (1971).

77. Reichow report (Jan. 1899), Baron de Hirsch Fund papers, box 38.

78. Reichow letter to Solomons (Mar. 28, 1898), Baron de Hirsch Fund papers, box 44.

79. Reichow letter and reports (1898–1900), Baron de Hirsch Fund papers, boxes 38 and 44.

80. Solomons report (Apr. 1900), Baron de Hirsch Fund papers, box 44.

81. Brandes, 112.

82. Solomons report (Apr. 1900).

83. New Jersey Bureau of Statistics.

84. JAIAS, "Annual Report" (1902), 8, 9.

85. Ibid., 2.

86. Ibid., 7, 8.

87. Reichow letter to Eppinger (February 10, 1898), Baron de Hirsch Fund papers, box 44.

88. Seldes investigation, Baron de Hirsch Fund papers, box 44.

89. Spirt investigation, Baron de Hirsch Fund papers, box 45.

90. Schlossberg investigation, Baron de Hirsch Fund papers, box 45.

91. Records of foreclosures, recorded in JAIAS minutes, Baron de Hirsch Fund papers, boxes 66 and 67.

92. Luberoff case, Baron de Hirsch Fund papers, box 44.

93. Real Estate investment records, Baron de Hirsch Fund papers, box 15.

94. JAIAS, "Annual Report" (1902), 5.

95. Hirsch letter to Schiff (Sept. 16, 1891), Baron de Hirsch Fund papers, box 35.

96. Philadelphia and New York committees, letter to Hirsch (Aug. 15, 1889), Baron de Hirsch Fund papers, box 35.

97. JAIAS, minutes of the board of directors meetings (Dec. 4, 1907, Apr. 1, 1908), Baron de Hirsch Fund papers. The outcome of the JAIAS denial of aid was discussed by Barney Stavin (formerly Stavitsky), one of the sons placed in an orphanage, in an interview (Philadelphia, Feb. 1989).

98. Correspondence with Steiner, Baron de Hirsch Fund papers, box 60.

99. Brandes, 79.

100. Hackenburg letters to Sabsovich and Solomons (Feb. 1, 1901), Baron de Hirsch Fund papers, box 8. Also see Brandes, 80. Praise of the canning factory can be found throughout the JAIAS minutes for the 1901–12 period.

101. Carmel colonists' letter to Fels (1892), Baron de Hirsch Fund papers, box 45.

102. Solomons report (Apr. 22, 1900).

103. JAIAS, "Annual Report" (1902), 11.

104. Ibid., 11–13.

105. JAIAS minutes, Baron de Hirsch Fund papers, box 66. For library aid, see Mar. 4, 1904; for the Carmel doctor, see Nov. 11, 1904; for Chautauqua aid, see Feb. 13, 1910; for Rosenhayn doctor, see Jan. 4, 1905; for discontinuation of music lessons, see Oct. 5, 1909; for Carmel synagogue, see Mar. 6, 1907. Refusals can be found throughout the JAIAS minutes. One example is the refusal to finance a new synagogue in Carmel (July 26, 1904).

106. Figures for 1900 are from the U.S. census. Figures for 1909 are from "Recent Immigrants in Agriculture," 92ff, 113–14.

107. Herman Eisenberg, "The Golden Age," in *Yoval*, 21. Such accounts also can be found in the National Museum of American Jewish History interviews; Ellen Eisenberg, interviews.

108. Herman Eisenberg refers to Krassenstein's *heder*. The relationship between JAIAS and the Jewish Chautauqua Society is revealed in JAIAS minutes (Feb. 13, 1910), Baron de Hirsch Fund papers, box 67.

109. Goldstein, 51–52.

110. Brandes, 227. Also see Herman Eisenberg, 22, 25; and National Museum of American Jewish History interviews with Levin, Krassenstein, and Harrison.

111. "Recent Immigrants in Agriculture," 115.

112. Herman Eisenberg, 24.

113. "Recent Immigrants in Agriculture," 114.

114. JAIAS, "Annual Report" (1905), 10.

115. Ibid., 9. On industry, 16–17; on agriculture, 9–10.

116. Ibid., (1906), 9. See also the report for 1912, 38–39.

117. Brandes, 63, 162.

118. "Recent Immigrants in Agriculture," 107–8.

119. Incorporation of Workingmen's Cooperative Business and Loan Co. (Mar. 23, 1909), Salem County records of deeds.

120. Rubin, 129.

121. Ibid., 128.

122. Waskoff, attachment on "The Incident of Coxey's Army."

123. Ibid., 13.

124. Elizabeth Rudnick Levin, "Pioneer Women of the Colonies," in *Yoval*, 32–33.

125. Rudnick Levin, 30–31.

126. The 1900 federal census indicates that many women worked at least part of the year in the garment industry (either in factories or doing home work), but there is no indication of women employed in agricultural labor. Women who worked on their family farms would not be listed as agricultural laborers on the census, so it is not possible to determine from the census the extent of this practice, the types of jobs performed by women on family farms, or whether this work changed over time.

127. JAIAS, "Annual Report" (1910), 32.

128. "Recent Immigrants in Agriculture," quoted in JAIAS, "Annual Report" (1912), 44–45.

129. In 1900, according to the U.S. census, 40.96 percent of families were agricultural; the 1911 "Recent Immigrants in Agriculture" report showed that in 1909, 45.96 percent of the families were agricultural. All 1900 figures in the discussion that follows are from the U.S. census; all 1909 figures are from the 1911 "Recent Immigrants in Agriculture" report.

130. Geraldine Schneeberg, "Religious and Ethnic Identity in an American Jewish Family, 1882–1987," unpublished paper.

131. Serata interview, National Museum of American Jewish History.

132. Brandes, 67.

133. For example, Gilbert Brotman uses this term in his interview, Richard Brotman, "First Chapter in a New Book."

134. "Recent Immigrants in Agriculture," 100.

135. Levin interview, National Museum of American Jewish History.

136. Goldhaft, 70. Also see Baily, "Memoir."

137. Kravitz.

138. Ellen Eisenberg, interview with Jay Greenblatt (Mar. 1989). Also see Jacob Kotinsky, "The Autobiography of an Immigrant," *Saturday Evening Post* (Apr. 12, 1902 and Apr. 19, 1902).

139. Joseph Greenblatt interview for R. Brotman, "First Chapter in a New Book."

140. JAIAS, "Annual Report" (1905), 10.

141. Kotinsky.

142. Moses Klein, 76.

143. Brandes, 215; Goldstein mentions two Hebrew schools, one modern and one traditional, 51; Baily talks about the Hebrew school and library established at Eben ha'Ezer, "The First Fifty Years," in *Yoval,* 18.

144. Ellen Eisenberg, descendant surveys. It is important to note that many descendants claim that the two synagogues developed because of the distance between some of the colonists' houses and the one synagogue. However, two of the Tiphereth Israel founders, Salunsky and Perski, lived as close to Eben ha'Ezer as to Tiphereth Israel, so it seems unlikely that convenience was the only issue.

145. Brandes, 301.

146. Bayuk's daughter, Bluma Bayuk Rappaport Purmell, discussed Bayuk's return to religion in later life. Ellen Eisenberg, interview with Purmell.

147. Kravitz, 18.

148. Herman Eisenberg, 26; Kravitz, 18.

149. For a discussion of the conflict over *heder* education, see Zvi Halevy, *Jewish Schools under Czarism and Communism* (New York: Springer Publishing Co., 1978).

6. Dissolution of the Colonies

1. JAIAS, "Annual Report" (1912), 36ff. Also see Herman Eisenberg, 21; and "Recent Immigrants in Agriculture."

2. For 1900 figures, see United States federal census, Salem and Cumberland counties, N.J. For 1909 figures, see "Recent Immigrants in Agriculture."

3. JAIAS, "Annual Report" (1902), 11.

4. Deeds for these organizations are on display at the Alliance Colony Museum, Alliance, N.J.

5. Discussion of community activities in this period can be found in "Recent Immigrants in Agriculture," 114–17; and Goldstein, 53–54.

6. Herman Eisenberg: 24–25.

7. Goldstein, 29.

8. Ibid., 30, 38.

9. Ibid., 37. Discussion of the difficult farming conditions can be found throughout the JAIAS reports. For example, see JAIAS, "Annual Reports" (1910–12).

10. Goldstein, 35, 37.

11. "Recent Immigrants in Agriculture," 118.

12. Goldstein, 58.

13. Elizabeth Frazer, "Our Foreign Farmers," *Saturday Evening Post* (Oct. 13, 1923).

14. Ibid. Goldstein also tells of the farm labor problem, 37.

15. Ibid. On Baily's earlier attitudes see Baily, "Memoir," 149; and "The First Fifty Years," 12.

16. "Recent Immigrants in Agriculture," 118; Goldstein, 59.

17. Goldstein, 38.

18. "Recent Immigrants in Agriculture," 114.

19. Bea Harrison interview for National Museum of American Jewish History.

20. A. L. Schalit, "The Jews and Jewish Immigration in the United States" (1910), MS in Baron de Hirsch Fund papers, box 78.

21. Bea Harrison interview for National Museum of American Jewish History.

22. Jack Helig and Moey Lihn interviews, National Museum of American Jewish History.

23. See discussion of JAIAS policies, chap. 5. Also see Brandes, 280.

24. JAIAS, "Annual Report" (1905), 17; (1906), 13.

25. JAIAS, minutes of the board of directors (Mar. 6, 1907; Oct. 8, 1907; and Oct. 5, 1909), Baron de Hirsch Fund papers.

26. Ibid., Oct. 12, 1908; Jan. 12, 1909.

27. JAIAS, "Annual Report" (1905), 17.

28. Brandes, 155ff.

29. *Salem Standard and Jerseyman* (Oct. 15, 1913), Salem, N.J.

30. Ibid. On court case, see Apr. 29, 1914; and *Salem Sunbeam* (Oct. 10, 1913; May 1, 1914). Records of court cases resulting from the riots are found in the Salem County pleas and sessions minutes for *State v. Morris Eisenberg; State v. Aaron Ruvinsky;* and *State v. Nathan Borish, Aaron Ruvinsky, John Levin, Samuel Glassman, Samuel Borish, John Lihn, Isaac Bleznak, Harry Rosenblitz, and Benjamin Halpert,* all on May 1, 1914.

31. Brandes, 165–68.

32. Brandes, 158–59, 167.

33. Goldstein, 42. Similarly, a 1915 report by Jacob Levin of the Woodbine Land and Improvement Co. indicated that two of the four factories in Carmel were vacant, Baron de Hirsch Fund papers, box 45.

34. Ibid.; Brandes, 158ff.

35. Kravitz, 29–30.

36. Benjamin letter to the Norma Improvement Association (Mar. 2, 1928), Baron de Hirsch Fund papers, box 45.

37. Ibid.

38. Brandes, 290; I. Harry Levin, 9.

39. Ellen Eisenberg, interviews with Jacob Greenblatt (Mar. 1, 1989) and Tevis Goldhaft (July 25, 1989). Also see Kravitz, 30, on the Greenblatt family; and Brandes, 290.

40. Gerson Katz. On Bluma Bayuk, Ellen Eisenberg, interview with Bluma Bayuk Rappaport Purmell.

41. Brandes, 323ff.

42. Davidson, 128–29.

43. Ibid., 130–32. By 1941, 324 families, including about 2,500 refugees, had been settled on farms.

44. Ibid., 138; Brandes, 327.

45. Davidson, 128.

46. Goldhaft, 232–33.

47. Brandes, 299–300.

48. Ibid., 299–301.

49. Ibid., 319–22, 328.

50. Gerson Katz.

51. Herman Eisenberg, 27.

52. Goldhaft, 231.

53. Elkin, "Goodnight, Sweet Gaucho," 208.

54. Goldhaft, 231–32; The idea that most of the settlers were not fit for farming was expressed by a number of informants, Ellen Eisenberg, interviews. Also see interviews conducted for the "Living on the Land" exhibit.

55. Joseph, 120–21. Also see Davidson, chap. 6.

56. Davidson, 150. Davidson's analysis of Jewish farming in America emphasizes the success of settling individual farmers, while giving scant attention to the colonies.

57. See chap. 2.

58. Seldes.

59. Ellen Eisenberg, interview with Faith Klein. Goldhaft makes similar comments about his father, 37.

60. Only one of Bayuk's children remained in Alliance; the remainder moved to Philadelphia and other cities, see Purmell. On Baily, see Frazer.

61. Frazer.

62. For discussion of sponsor goals see chaps. 3, 4, and 5.

63. See chap. 4. For example, see Moses Bayuk, "Report to the Alliance Israélite Universelle," 1885.

64. Morawska, *For Bread with Butter*, 298.

65. Brandes, 261–62.

66. Many former residents recalled in interviews a high level of interaction with non-Jews. For example, see Molly Greenblatt Kravitz interview in R. Brotman, "First Chapter in a New Book." The significance of political activity in the community is discussed in Brandes, 260ff.; and Baily, "First Fifty Years," 17, 19.

67. Goldhaft, 232.

68. Herscher, 113. Elkin makes the same argument with regard to the Argentine colonies in "Goodnight, Sweet Gaucho."

69. Elkin, "Goodnight, Sweet Gaucho," 209.

70. Ibid., 222–23.

71. Ibid., 223.

Glossary

AIU: Alliance Israélite Universelle

Am Olam: The Russian-Jewish movement advocating the establishment of agricultural colonies in the United States in the early 1880s.

BILU: An acronym for the Hebrew *Bet Yaakov Lechu ve Nelcha* (House of Jacob, come and let us go). One of the early Zionist groups active in eastern Europe. BILU activists worked to establish cooperative agricultural settlements in Palestine.

Bund: Jewish socialist labor movement established in the 1890s in Russia.

Chevrah Kadisha: Burial society

Haskalah: Jewish enlightenment movement emphasizing secular studies and the entrance of Jews into productive occupations.

HEAS: Hebrew Emigrant Aid Society.

heder(im): Traditional Jewish school(s) for boys.

Hovevei Zion: Lovers of Zion, early Zionist organization in Russia.

JAIAS: Jewish Agricultural and Industrial Aid Society, subsidiary of the Baron de Hirsch Fund, founded in 1900.

JCA: Jewish Colonization Association, European-based aid organization founded by Baron de Hirsch.

kahal: Traditional Jewish community organization in eastern Europe.

kibbutz: Collective farm settlement in Palestine/Israel.

maskilim: Advocates of the Haskalah.

maskilic: Adjective form of Haskalah.

melamed: Teacher in a *heder.*

Mizrachi: A religious strand of Zionism.

Narod: Russian populist movement. Also *narodnichestvo, narodnik.*

ostjude(n): Derogatory term used by Jews of the United States and western Europe to describe East European Jewry.

Pale (of Settlement): The area to which Jews were confined in Tsarist Russia, running from the Ukraine in the south, to Lithuania in the north, and including Russian Poland.

Poalei Zion: Labor Zionism.

pogrom: Anti-Jewish riot.

yeshivah: Traditional Jewish secondary school for boys.

Yishuv: The Jewish settlement in Palestine before Israeli indpendence.

Bibliography

Primary Sources

A. Memoirs, Interviews

Baily, Sidney. "Memoir." In *Jewish Agricultural Utopias in America, 1880–1910* by Uri Herscher, 133–58. Detroit: Wayne State Univ. Press, 1981.

———. "The First Fifty Years." In *Yoval*. Privately published for the 50th anniversary of the colonies, 1932: 12–15.

Brotman, Richard. "First Chapter in a New Book." Video, 1982. Includes interviews with Judge I. Harry Levin, Morris Greenblatt, Molly Greenblatt Kravitz, Lillian Greenblatt Braun, Jay Greenblatt, Jake Helig, Benny Stavitsky, Barney (Stavitsky) Stavin, Gilbert Brotman, Judge Stanley Brotman.

———. Raw video footage for "First Chapter in a New Book."

Cahan, Abraham. *The Education of Abraham Cahan*. Philadelphia: Jewish Publication Society of America, 1969.

Davis, Charles K. Unpublished diary. American Jewish Archives, Cincinnati.

Eisenberg, Ellen. Interviews with Bluma Bayuk Rappaport Purmell, Oct. 16, 1988; Judge Stanley Brotman, Feb. 21, 1989; Barney (Stavitsky) Staven, Feb. 27, 1989; Doris (Coltun) and Sanford Rosenman, Feb. 28, 1989; Jay Greenblatt, Mar. 1, 1989; Dorothy (Venezky) Street, Mar. 26, 1989; Dorothy Levin, Mar. 31, 1989; Geraldine (Konnowitch) Schneeberg, Apr. 4, 1989; Tevis Goldhaft, July 25, 1989; Morris Krassenstein, Sept. 15, 1989; Faith (Herder) Klein, Sept. 16, 1989; June (Herder) Stark, July 7, 1989; Ben Luberoff, June 21, 1989; Sylvan Goldfein, July 4, 1989; Mildred Magen, July 10, 1989; Gertrude (Rosinsky) Spielberg, July 24, 1989.

———. Descendant surveys (1987–89).

Freeman, Moses. *Fuftzig Yohr Geshichte fon Yidishen Leben in Philadelphia*. Philadelphia: Mid-City Press, 1929.

Heilprin, Michael. "Jewish Colonies in America." In *What Shall We Do with Our Immigrants?* by Benjamin F. Peixotto. New York: YMHA, 1887.

Herder, Kate. "Memories of Yesterday." Unpublished memoir, 1946.

Klein, Doris Lihn. "The Lihn Family." Unpublished family history.
Kotinsky, Jacob. "The Autobiography of an Immigrant." *Saturday Evening Post,* Apr. 12, 1902 and Apr. 19, 1902.
Kravitz, Mollie. Unpublished memoir.
National Museum of American Jewish History, interviews for "Living on the Land Exhibit." Includes interviews with Rose Helig Applebaum, Dr. Flora Biele, Stavitsky family, Shea and Pearl Crystal, Tevis Goldhaft, Molly Kravitz, Gilbert Greenblatt, Bea Harrison, Jack Helig, Ted Krause, Morris Krassenstein, Judge I. Harry Levin, Moey Lihn, Rose Lindenbaum, Mildred Megan, Bluma Bayuk Rappaport Purmell, Gertrude Serata.
Purmell, Bluma Bayuk Rappaport. *A Farmer's Daughter.* Hayvenhurst, 1981.
Rubin, Harris. *The Autobiography of Harris Rubin.* Translated by Benson N. Schambelan. Philadelphia: Bricklin Press, 1977.
Sabsovich, Katherine. *Adventures in Idealism.* New York: privately printed, 1922.
Venezky family history. Unpublished.
Waskoff, Charles. "The Carmel Story." Unpublished memoir.

B. Government Documents

Bureau of Statistics of New Jersey. "The Jewish Colonies of New Jersey." 1901. New Jersey Archives, Trenton, N.J.
Cape May, Cumberland, and Salem counties, New Jersey, court records. Records used include naturalization records and records of court cases involving colonists.
Douglas County, Oregon. Records of land purchases and incorporations, 1883–85.
United States Immigration Commission. "Recent Immigrants in Agriculture." In *Immigrants in Industries.* Part 24, vol. 2. Washington, D.C.: Government Printing Office, 1911, 89–123.
United States Census Bureau. Federal census, Salem and Cumberland counties, New Jersey. 1900.

C. Organizational Records

Alliance Israélite Universelle papers. American Jewish Archives, Cincinnati.
Association for the Protection of Jewish Immigrants papers. American Jewish Archives, Cincinnati.
Baron de Hirsch Fund papers. American Jewish Historical Society, Waltham, Mass. (Includes the records of the Jewish Agricultural and Industrial Aid Society.)
Ellinger, Moritz. "The Report of Moritz Ellinger." New York: Hebrew Emigrant Aid Society of the United States, 1882.
Hamburg Ship Records. Church of Jesus Christ of Latter-day Saints, Family History Center.
Hebrew Emigrant Aid Society of Philadelphia records. Balsch Institute for Ethnic Studies, Philadelphia.
Henry S. Henry letter to M. Bayuk and Others, Colony Alliance (Dec. 31, 1984). In possession of Mrs. I. Harry Levin, Alliance, N.J.

Jewish Agricultural and Industrial Aid Society, Annual Reports. New York: Wm. O. Popper and Co., 1900–1906, 1910–12.

D. Contemporaneous Eyewitness Reports

Frazer, Elizabeth. "Our Foreign Farmers." *Saturday Evening Post,* Oct. 13, 1923, 23.
Goldstein, Philip. "Social Aspects of the Jewish Colonies of South Jersey." Ph.D. diss., Univ. of Pennsylvania, 1921.
Klein, Moses. *Migdal Sofim* (The Watchtower). Philadelphia, 1889.
Price, George. "The Russian Jews in America." 1893. Reprint. *Publications of the American Jewish Historical Society* 48, nos. 1 and 2 (1958): 28–133.
Rosenthal, Herman. "A History of the Communitarian Settlement Known as 'New Odessa'." Translated by Gary P. Zola. In *The American Jewish Farmer,* edited by Abraham Peck. Published for American Jewish Archives exhibit (1986): 13–17.
"A Wedding among the Communistic Jews in Oregon." *Overland Monthly* 6, no. 39 (Dec. 1885): 606–11.

Secondary Sources

Adler, Cyrus. *Jacob H. Schiff.* 1921. Reprint, Antin Press, 1947.
"Agricultural Colonies." In *The Jewish Encyclopedia,* Vol. 1, edited by Isadore Singer, 254–66. New York: Funk and Wagnalls, 1901.
"An Arkansas Colony Episode." *The Jewish Tribune,* July 12, 1929. Reprint in Davidson, *Our Jewish Farmers.*
Aronson, Michael. "Geographical and Socioeconomic Factors in the 1881 Anti-Jewish Pogroms in Russia." *The Russian Review* 39, no. 1 (1980): 18–31.
Ascheim, Steven. *Brothers and Strangers: The East European Jews in Germany and German-Jewish Consciousness, 1800–1923.* Madison: Univ. of Wisconsin, 1982.
Baily, Samuel. "The Adjustment of Italian Immigrants in Buenos Aires and New York, 1870–1914." *American Historical Review* 88 (1983): 281–305.
Baron, Salo. *The Russian Jew under the Tsars and Soviets.* New York: Macmillan Publishing Co., 1964.
Bartelt, Pearl. "American Jewish Agricultural Colonies." Paper presented before the National Historic Communal Societies Association. Oct. 1989.
Berger, David, ed. *The Legacy of Jewish Migration.* New York: Brooklyn College Press, 1983.
Berk, Stephen. *Year of Crisis, Year of Hope.* Westport Conn.: Greenwood Press, 1985.
Berman, Myron. *The Attitude of American Jewry Towards East European Jewish Immigration.* New York: Arno Press, 1980.
Bernheimer, Charles. *The Russian Jew in the United States.* Philadelphia: John C. Winston Co., 1905.
Best, Gary Dean. "Jacob Schiff's Galveston Movement: An Experiment in Immigrant Deflection, 1907–1914." *American Jewish Archives* 30, no. 1 (1978): 43–79.
Birmingham, Steven. *'Our Crowd', The Great Jewish Families of New York.* New York: Harper and Row, 1967.

Bodnar, John. *The Transplanted.* Bloomington: Indiana Univ. Press, 1985.

Boyer, Paul. *Urban Masses and Moral Order in America.* Cambridge Mass.: Harvard Univ. Press, 1978.

Brandes, Joseph. *Immigrants to Freedom: Jewish Communities in Rural New Jersey since 1882.* Philadelphia: Univ. of Pennsylvania Press, 1971.

Briggs, John. *An Italian Passage: Immigrants to Three American Cities, 1890–1930.* New Haven: Yale Univ. Press, 1978.

Brym, Robert. *The Jewish Intelligentsia and Russian Marxism.* New York: Schocken Books, 1978.

Carlisle, Losada. "Carmel at the Turn of the Century." 1971.

Cinel, Dino. *From Italy to San Francisco: The Immigrant Experience.* Stanford: Stanford Univ. Press, 1982.

Davidson, Gabriel. *Our Jewish Farmers.* New York: L. B. Fischer, 1943.

Davidson, Gabriel and Edward Goodwin. "A Unique Agricultural Colony." *The Reflex,* May 1928. Reprint in Davidson, *Our Jewish Farmers.*

Douglas, Martin. "Chronological Summary of Annotated Cards Toward the History of the Jewish Agricultural Colonies in South Jersey." Ph.D. diss., Jewish Theological Seminary, New York, 1960.

Dubnow, S. M. *History of the Jews in Russia and Poland.* Translated by I. Friedlaender. New York: Ktav Publishing House, 1975.

Dubrovsky, Gertrude. "In Search of America: Lexington, Kentucky and Farmingdale, New Jersey." *Midstream* (1988): 29–33.

———. "The Rural Experience in Farmingdale, New Jersey." In *New Jersey's Ethnic Heritage,* edited by Paul A. Stellhorn, 36–57. Trenton: New Jersey Historical Commission, 1978.

Elkin, Judith. "Goodnight, Sweet Gaucho: A Revisionist View of the Jewish Agricultural Experiment in Argentina." *American Jewish Historical Quarterly* 67, no. 3 (Mar. 1978): 208–23.

———. *Jews of the Latin American Republics.* Chapel Hill: Univ. of North Carolina Press, 1980.

"An Epic of the Prairies." *Detroit Jewish Chronicle,* Jan. 29, 1932. Reprint in Davidson, *Our Jewish Farmers.*

Feld, Lipman Goldman. "New Light on the Lost Jewish Colony of Beersheba, Kansas, 1882–1886." *American Jewish Historical Quarterly* 60, no.2 (1970): 159–68.

Frankel, Jonathan. "The Crisis of 1881–2 as a Turning Point in Modern Jewish History." In *The Legacy of Jewish Migration,* edited by David Berger, 9–22. New York: Brooklyn College Press, 1983.

———. *Prophecy and Politics.* Cambridge: Cambridge Univ. Press, 1981.

Gartner, Lloyd. *The Jewish Immigrant in England, 1870–1914.* London: George Allan, 1960.

Geffen, Joel. "America in the First European Hebrew Daily Newspaper: *Ha-Yom.*" *American Jewish Historical Quarterly* 51, no. 3 (1962): 149–67.

———. "Jewish Agricultural Colonies as Reflected in the Russian Hebrew Press." *American Jewish Historical Quarterly* 60 (1971): 355–82.

———. "Whither: To Palestine or to America in the Pages of the Russian Hebrew Press." *American Jewish Historical Quarterly* 59, no. 2 (1969): 179–200.

Glazer, Nathan. *American Judaism.* Chicago: Univ. of Chicago Press, 1972.

Glazier, Ira, and Luigi DeRosa, eds. *Migration Across Time and Nations.* New York: Holmes and Meier, 1986.

Goering, Violet, and Orlando Goering. "The Agricultural Communes of the Am Olam." *Communal Societies* 4 (1984): 74–86.

———. "South Dakota's Jewish Farmers: The Am Olam." Unpublished essay. On file at the American Jewish Archives, Cincinnati.

Goldberg, Robert. "Shooting in the Dark: Recovering the Jewish Farmers of an American Zion." *Historical Methods* 16, no. 4 (1983): 155–56.

Goldhaft, Arthur. *The Golden Egg.* New York: Horizon Press, 1957.

Goldscheider, Calvin, and Alan Zuckerman. *The Transformation of the Jews.* Chicago: The Univ. of Chicago Press, 1984.

Green, Nancy. *The Pletzl of Paris.* New York: Holmes and Meier, 1986.

Greenberg, Louis. *The Jews in Russia: The Struggle for Emancipation.* 2 Vols. New York: Schocken Books, 1976.

Grunwald, Kurt. *Turkenhirsch: A Study of Baron de Hirsch, Entrepreneur and Philanthropist.* Israel Program for Scientific Translations, 1966.

Gutman, Herbert. *Work, Culture, and Society in Industrializing America.* New York: Vintage Books, 1966.

Halevy, Zvi. *Jewish Schools under Czarism and Communism.* New York: Springer Publishing Co., 1978.

Handlin, Oscar. *The Uprooted.* Boston: Little, Brown and Co., 1951.

Hareven, Tamara. *Family Time & Industrial Time.* Cambridge: Cambridge Univ. Press, 1982.

Herlihy, Patricia. *Odessa: A History, 1794–1914.* Cambridge Mass.: Harvard Univ. Press, 1986.

Herscher, Uri. *Jewish Agricultural Utopias in America, 1880–1910.* Detroit: Wayne State Univ. Press, 1981.

Hertzberg, Arthur, ed. *The Zionist Idea.* New York: Temple Books, 1984.

Higham, John. *Strangers in the Land.* New York: Atheneum, 1985.

Howe, Irving. *World of Our Fathers.* New York: Harcourt Brace Jovanovich, 1976.

Hunter, Robert. *Poverty.* Reprint. New York: The Macmillan Co., 1972.

"The Jewish Covered Wagon." *Jewish Criterion* Jan. 29, 1932. Reprint in Davidson, *Our Jewish Farmers.*

Joseph, Samuel. *History of the Baron de Hirsch Fund: The Americanization of the Jewish Immigrant.* Fairfield N.J.: Augustus M. Kelley, 1978.

Kahan, Arcadius. *Essays in Jewish Social and Economic History.* Chicago: Univ. of Chicago Press, 1982.

Katz, Gerson. "History of Carmel." Vineland Historical Society. File on Carmel colony.

Katz, Michael. *In the Shadow of the Poorhouse.* New York: Basic Books, 1986.

———. *Poverty and Policy in American History.* New York: Academic Press, 1983.

———. *The Undeserving Poor.* New York: Pantheon Books, 1989.

Klein, Herbert. "The Integration of Italian Immigrants into the United States and Argentina: A Comparative Analysis." *American Historical Review* 88 (Apr. 1983): 306–46.

Kuznets, Simon. "Economic Structure and the Life of the Jews." In *The Jews: Their History, Culture and Religion,* vol. 3, edited by Louis Finkelstein, 1597–666. Philadelphia: The Jewish Publication Society of America, 1960.

———. "Immigration of Russian Jews to the United States: Background and Structure." In *Perspectives in American History* 9, edited by Fleming and Bailyn, 35–124. Cambridge Mass.: Charles Warren Center for Studies in American History, 1975.

Laquer, Walter. *A History of Zionism.* New York: Schocken Books, 1976.

Lederhendler, Eli. "Jewish Immigration to America and Revisionist Historiography: Decade of New Perspectives." *YIVO Annual of Jewish Social Science* 18 (1983): 391–410.

Lee, Samuel J. *Moses of the New World.* New York: Thomas Yoseloff, 1970.

Lestschinsky, Jacob. "Jewish Migrations, 1840–1956." In *The Jews,* vol. 2, edited by Louis Finkelstein, 1536–98. Philadelphia: Jewish Publication Society of America, 1960.

Levin, I. Harry. "History of Alliance, New Jersey, First Jewish Agricultural Settlement in the U.S." *Vineland Historical Magazine* 54 (1978): 1–14.

Levin, Nora. *While the Messiah Tarried.* New York: Schocken Books, 1977.

Mahler, Raphael. "The Social and Political Aspects of the Haskalah in Galicia." In *Studies in Modern Jewish Social History,* edited by Joshua Fishman, 58–79. Reprint. New York: Ktav Publishing Co., 1972.

Manners, Ande. *Poor Cousins.* New York: Coward, McCann, and Geoghegan, Inc., 1972.

Mendelsohn, Ezra. *Class Struggle in the Pale.* New York: Cambridge Univ. Press, 1970.

———. "The Russian Jewish Labor Movement and Others." In *Jewish Socialism and Jewish Labor Movements in the 19th Century,* edited by Moshe Mishkinski, 239–50. Jerusalem: Israeli Histadrut, 1975.

———. "The Russian Roots of the American Jewish Labor Movement." *YIVO Annual of Jewish Social Science* 16 (1976): 150–77.

Menes, Abraham. "The Am Oylom Movement." *YIVO Annual of Jewish Social Science* 4 (1949): 9–33.

Merinbach, Bernard. *Galveston: Ellis Island of the West.* Albany: SUNY Press, 1983.

Miller, Scott. "The Am Olam Movement: Russian Jewish Immigration to the United States and the Idea of Productivization." Paper presented before the Association for Jewish Studies, Dec. 1988.

Mishkinski, Moshe. "Regional Factors in the Formation of the Jewish Labor Movement in Czarist Russia." *YIVO Annual of Jewish Social Science* 14 (1969): 27–52.

Morawska, Ewa. *For Bread with Butter.* Cambridge: Cambridge Univ. Press, 1985.

———. "A Replica of the 'Old Country' Relationship in the Ethnic Niche: Eastern European Jews and Gentiles in Small-Town Western Pennsylvania, 1880s–1930s." *American Jewish History* 77, no. 1 (1987): 27–86.

———. "The Sociology and Historiography of Immigration." In *Immigration Reconsidered,* edited by Virginia Yans-McLaughlin, 187–240. Oxford: Oxford Univ. Press, 1990.

Mounier, Louis. "An Elopement." *Vineland Historical Magazine* (1965).

———. "Trials and Hardships of Immigrants." *Vineland Historical Magazine* 19 (1934): 17–21.

Osofsky, Gilbert. "The Hebrew Emigrant Aid Society of the United States." *Publications of the American Jewish Historical Society* 49, no. 3 (1960): 178–87.

Patterson, James. *America's Struggle Against Poverty, 1900–1985*. Cambridge Mass.: Harvard Univ. Press, 1986.

Peled, Yoav. *Class and Ethnicity in the Pale*. New York: St. Martin's Press, 1989.

"Pioneers in the Land of Cotton." *Jewish Tribune,* Sept. 27, 1929. Reprint in Davidson, *Our Jewish Farmers.*

Piven, Frances Fox, and Richard Cloward. *Regulating the Poor.* New York: Random House, 1971.

Pollak, Gustav. *Michael Heilprin and His Sons.* New York: Dodd, Mead, and Co., 1912.

Rischin, Moses. *The Promised City.* Cambridge Mass.: Harvard Univ. Press, 1977.

Robinson, Leonard. "Agricultural Activities of the Jews in America." *American Jewish Yearbook,* 1912, 21–115.

Rogger, Hans. *Jewish Policies and Right-Wing Politics in Imperial Russia*. Berkeley: Univ. of California Press, 1986.

Romanofsky, Peter. "'To Rid Ourselves of the Burden . . .': New York Jewish Charities and the Origins of the Industrial Removal Office, 1890–1901." *American Jewish Historical Quarterly* 64, no. 4 (1975): 331–43.

Rothman, David. *The Discovery of the Asylum.* Boston: Little, Brown and Co., 1971.

———. *On Their Own.* Reading, Mass.: Addison-Wesley Publishing Co., 1972.

Rubinow, Isaac. *Economic Condition of the Jews in Russia.* 1907. Reprint. New York: Arno Press, 1975.

Ruppin, Arthur. *The Jews in the Modern World.* London: Macmillan and Co., 1934.

Sachar, Howard Morley. *The Course of Modern Jewish History.* New York: Dell Publishing Co., 1958.

Sarna, Jonathan. "The Myth of No Return: Jewish Return Migration to Eastern Europe, 1881–1914." *American Jewish Historical Quarterly* 71 (1981): 256–68.

Schalit, A. L. "The Jews and Jewish Immigration in the United States." (1910). Manuscript. Baron de Hirsch Fund papers. American Jewish Historical Society, Waltham, Mass. Box 78.

Schneeberg, Geraldine. "Religious and Ethnic Identity in an American-Jewish Family, 1882–1987." Unpublished student paper (1987).

Schorsch, Ismar. *Jewish Reactions to German Anti-Semitism, 1870–1914.* New York: Columbia Univ. Press, 1972.

Seldes, George. "Anarchist Colony of My Father, George Seldes" (in Yiddish). *Free Worker's Voice,* 1976, 40–45.

Seldes, Marian. *The Bright Lights: A Theater Life.* Boston: Houghton Mifflin Co., 1978.

Shulvass, Moses. *From East to West.* Detroit: Wayne State Univ. Press, 1971.

Singer, Richard. "The American Jews in Agriculture: Past History and Present Condition." Hebrew Union College Prize Essay, 1941.

Stampfer, Shaul. "The Geographic Background of Eastern European Jewish Migration to the United States before World War I." In *Migration Across Time and Nations,* edited by Ira Glazier and Luigi de Rosa, 220–30. New York: Holmes and Maier, 1986.

Stanislowski, Michael. "The Transformation of Traditional Authority in Russian Jewry:

The First Stage." In *The Legacy of Jewish Migration,* edited by David Berger, 23–30. (New York: Brooklyn College Press, 1983).

Swidler, Ann. "Culture in Action: Symbols and Strategies." *American Sociological Review* (Apr. 1986): 273–86.

Szajkowski, Zosa. "How the Mass Migration to America Began." *Jewish Social Studies* 4, no. 4 (1942): 291–310.

Taylor, Philip. *The Distant Magnet.* New York: Harper and Row, 1971.

Tcherikower, Elias. "Jewish Immigrants to the United States." *YIVO Annual of Jewish Social Science* 6 (1951). Reprinted in *Studies in Modern Jewish History,* edited by Joshua Fishman, 180–99. (New York: Ktav Publishing House, 1972.

Weinberg, David. " *'Heureux comme Dieu en France':* East European Jewish Immigrants in Paris, 1881–1914." *Studies in Contemporary Jewry* 1 (1984): 26–54.

Weisbrot, Robert. *The Jews of Argentina.* Philadelphia: Jewish Publication Society of America, 1979.

Wertheimer, Jack. *Unwelcome Strangers: East European Jews in Imperial Germany.* Oxford: Oxford Univ. Press, 1987.

Winsberg, Morton. *Colonia Baron Hirsch.* Gainesville: Univ. of Florida Press, 1963.

Wischnitzer, Mark. *To Dwell in Safety.* Philadelphia: Jewish Publication Society of America, 1948.

Yoval: A Symposium upon the First Fifty Years of the Jewish Farming Colonies of Alliance, Norma, and Brotmanville, New Jersey. Published privately for the 50th anniversary celebration, 1932.

Zipperstein, Steven. *The Jews of Odessa.* Stanford: Stanford Univ. Press, 1985.

Index

Abraham, Abraham, 78

Adler, Cyrus, 103, 141

Agrarianism, 22, 30, 34

Alliance Colony: Am Olam members in, 91–98, 104, 106; attrition and decline of, 161, 171; Chevrah Kadisha, 97, 157; communal period, 91–92, 97–99; economic development and transformation of, 97–102, 113–14, 125–28, 130, 136–39, 141, 149, 152, 162; industry in, 100–101, 104, 120, 135–36, 139, 152, 167; initial settlement of, 90–93; population of, xviii, 124, 138–39, 147, 160–61; relations with sponsors, 75, 98–105, 113, 125–26, 136–37; religious life in, 96–97, 148, 156–57; settlers, 35, 57, 92–93, 98, 102, 115, 153; social and cultural life in, 148–49, 153, 161

Alliance Israélite Universelle, 37, 45, 62, 64–67, 70, 74–75, 79, 90, 100–102, 104, 108, 117

Alliance Land Trust, 99, 104, 119, 123, 125, 136, 143

Am Olam: establishment of colonies, 2, 25–26, 43–54, 57–61, 90, 116–17, 173; formation and ideology, 21–24, 26–35, 175–76; migration to the United States, 1, 24, 35–37; relations with sponsors, 61–62, 66, 75, 87–89. *See also* Alliance Colony; Arkansas Colony; Balta Am Olam; Bethlehem Judea Colony; Carmel Colony; Kiev

Am Olam; Kremenchug Am Olam; New Odessa Colony; Odessa Am Olam; Vilna Am Olam

Argentina, xviii, xx, 127, 130, 176–77

Arkansas Colony, 39, 41, 52–53, 56, 58–59, 109

Autoemancipation, 2–4, 14–24, 26. *See also* Migration; Revolutionism; Territorialism

Baily, Esther, 41, 94–96, 139, 150

Baily, Sidney, 15, 27–32, 34, 36, 41, 54, 94–97, 138–39, 157, 163–64, 173, 175

Balta Am Olam, 31, 33–36, 41, 94

Baron de Hirsch Fund: colony support, 103, 123, 137, 139, 141–42, 145–49, 158–59, 161–62, 165–66; cultural activities, 145–48; goals and policies, 73–74, 78, 80–81, 84–87, 99, 124, 126–29, 135, 143–45; industrial support, 123–24, 126–28, 135–36, 140–41, 144, 152–53; refugee aid, 117, 169; selection of settlers, 73, 88, 130–33, 142–44, 152; training and Americanization projects, 124, 127, 133

Bayuk, Moses, 92, 96, 100, 116–17, 148, 157, 168, 173, 175

Beersheba Colony (Kans.), 54–56, 58, 62, 75

Benjamin, Eugene, 167–68

Bethlehem Judea Colony, 43–45, 47–48, 58–59, 77, 91–92, 94

Utopianism and Communitarianism
Lyman Tower Sargent and Gregory Claeys, Series Editors

This series offers historical and contemporary analyses of utopian literature, communal studies, utopian social theory, broad themes such as the treatment of women in these traditions, and new editions of fictional works of lasting value for both a general and scholarly audience.